White Knuckles and Wishful Thinking

George Manter DuWors, MSW, BCD has worked in virtually every phase of chemical dependency and mental health treatment, including in- and outpatient, employee assistance, drinking drivers, and private practice. He received his BA in 1969 and his Masters of Social Work in 1977, both from the University of Washington. An enthusiastic trainer and speaker, George maintains a full-time addictions practice in Everett, WA. He has presented "Learning From Relapse" workshops across the United States and Canada, and in the United Kingdom. He may be reached at gduwors@gte.net or a website to be linked to the page for this book at http://www.hhpub.com.

About the Cover
The first sketch of the cover illustration was drawn at the author's request and faxed to him in the Winter of 1992. The blurred transmission triggered the author's memory of another "Thinker" sketch. That charcoal was done as a spoof, with his father's physiognomy, for the elder DuWors' 39th birthday. That would make it 1953, when the author was 5. Thirty-nine years later, it returned as an "idea" for the cover of this book. And the artist friend who drew the original caricature had long since died of alcoholism.

PS: The author has seen full-size "Thinkers" in Los Angeles, Santa Barbara, and in Paris. But the most striking one was the miniature presiding over Rodin's elaborate "The Gates of Hell."

George Manter DuWors, MSW, BCD

White Knuckles and Wishful Thinking —

Learning From the Moment of Relapse in Alcoholism and Other Addictions

Illustrations
Sylvane Despretz, Woodland Hills, CA, and Paris, France

Cover Art
Don Wissusik, Newberg, OR

Hogrefe & Huber Publishers
Seattle • Toronto • Göttingen • Bern

Library of Congress Cataloging-in-Publication Data

DuWors, George Manter, 1948-
    White knuckles and wishful thinking : learning from the moment of relapse in alcoholism and other addictions / George Manter DuWors. — 2nd rev. & expanded ed.
    p. cm.
    Includes bibliographical references and index.
    ISBN 0-88937-224-1
    1. Alcoholism — Relapse — Prevention. 2. Alcoholics — Rehabilitation. I. Title
RC565 .D79 1999
616.86'106 -- dc21

99-45881

Canadian Cataloguing in Publication Data

DuWors, George Manter, 1948-
    White knuckles and wishful thinking : learning from the moment of relapse in alcoholism and other addictions / George Manter DuWors.
2nd rev. & expanded ed.
Includes bibliographic references.
ISBN 0-88937-224-1
1. Alcoholism counseling. 2. Alcoholism — Psychological aspects.
3. Alcoholism — Treatment. 4. Compulsive behavior — Treatment. I. Title
HV5275.D88 1999   362.292'86   C99-932048-3

USA:	P.O. Box 2487, Kirkland, WA 98083-2487
	Phone (425) 820-1500, Fax (425) 823-8324
CANADA:	12 Bruce Park Avenue, Toronto, Ontario M4P 2S3
	Phone (416) 482-6339
SWITZERLAND:	Länggass-Strasse 76, CH-3000 Bern 9
	Phone +41 31 300-4500, Fax +41 31 300 4590
GERMANY:	Rohnsweg 25, D-37085 Göttingen
	Phone +49 551 496090, Fax +49 551 4960988

Printed and bound in the USA

ISBN 0-88937-224-1

Dedication

For Joseph and Christina DuWors, grandsons Joshua and Ethan, and for Michael Shannon DuWors and John David DuWors.

Table of contents

4
The Links of the White-Knuckle Relapse [1]

16
Linking The Links:

Introduction to Second Edition

This book builds upon a single, relentless fact about the disease of addiction and the phenomenon of relapse. The fact is that those who relapse have an overwhelming tendency to be saying just one of two things at the moment of actually deciding to pick up the first drink/drug. Those two relapse thoughts ar "One won't hurt" and "F--- it." Yes, there are variations. Yes, there are exceptions, the kind that truly "prove the rule."

The book asks the same questions, over and over, that the author has been asking for over twenty years. What does it mean? What does it mean that so many different people, different backgrounds, different addictions, different stages of the disease, all say the same two hackneyed things at the critical moment of picking up the first drink/drug of relapse? And if we can understand what it means, how can we use our understanding to help the relapser not have to do that again.

The reader will find out in the first chapter how we are going to look at real behavior, not in isolation from the real world. Rather, we look at it as living reactions, the way both client and helper must deal with it. We will look at both relapse behavior and at recovery behavior through the same lens. This model for looking at real behavior is part of what binds the chapters and topics together.

There are four main topics. Relapse itself, what happens at that moment and what leads up to it, is the first. The second one is denial, three chapters' worth. The third is acceptance, another three chapters. Finally, the material on acceptance transitions into several chapters on coping, what it is and how to do it.

Every chapter has one point of reference, one question it must answer. How does this material, these facts, observations and inferences, relate to an abstinent alcoholic/addict either saying or not saying those fatal words again? How can we help? What can the addict/alcoholic do for him or herself?

The reader will learn soon enough that this is the book of an in-the-trenches practitioner, not a lab man or a theoretician. Like most of his readers, the author is a somewhat intimidated consumer of what "hard science" thinks it knows. The research always seems to be one step ahead of us and one step behind the real people we try to help. But scientific information will be processed in the text right along with the real behavior of our clients.

The reader will also learn soon enough that the author has a primary source for observing recovery that does occur, people who have learned to do something other than relapsing. That source is Alcoholics Anonymous and other Twelve Step Programs. It includes anonymous flesh-and-blood people, as well as documented concepts and experience that continue to be tested in the laboratory of real life. Both recovery and relapse are observed from the vantage point of a professional helper, using the tools and model for understanding described in Chapters 1 and 2.

A word about what this book is not. It is not a book on how to prevent relapse that is triggered by "cues," reminders of the pleasure of use. That work is as valid as it is valuable and someone else is doing it. The book is not about withdrawal craving, which is the province of medical people, and it is not about the craving triggered by actual ingestion. Nor is this book an attempt to be the last or only word on relapse prevention.

If anything, the author has picked one crucial piece of the relapse puzzle and tried to connect it to as many other pieces as he could. This includes hard science reports, outcome research, clinical theories, and human experience. There is nothing here to refute other abstinence-based approaches to helping alcoholic/addicts not relapse again. Hopefully, there are solid pieces and lucid connections that will strengthen the work of others, not replace it. Part of that strength will come from how the material here interconnects with itself.

Who is the book for? Three groups: the first is my fellow soldiers in the trenches of alcoholism treatment, as embattled by politics and economics as we are by the disease we would defeat. It is my hope to share what I think I have learned and also that the shared tools and understanding may help you to help others.

The second group is those hearty and idealistic souls who are in training to join the fray, students of chemical dependency programs and your instructors. For you, there is a set of direct and literal "review questions" for each chapter. There is also a set of "Chemical Dependency Student Exercises," for each chapter. The exercises are designed to create an experience that helps you connect with the material and be able to use it. This is not a comprehensive or scholarly enough book to be a text for a full-term course on alcohol studies. However, as an economical ancillary text, it addresses generic issues of relapse, denial, acceptance, and coping in a hands-on way that is instructor and student friendly.

The third group for whom this book is written is those patients of chemical dependency treatment whose counselors see fit to recommend it. There is a set of recovery exercises at the end of each chapter for you, too. However, this is not a self-help book meant to be completed in isolation. The issues raised and the questions asked are tough-minded and may be disturbing. They are meant to be processed with the support of a counselor and/or sponsor.

Why write a book for three different groups? First because we are not all *that* different. Today's patient is tomorrow's student and the day-after-tomorrow's counselor or therapist. Need I mention that today's counselor may be tomorrow's patient? In addition, as I used this material in the trenches at work, and then on the road with my fellow professional, I found there was little difference in what I said or did with different groups.

Having three different audiences does raise the issue of point of view for the book. In the text, the author refers to himself only in the third person. With one huge, clearly marked exception, "I" means anyone, a philosophical Everyman, not to be confused with the regal "we." The recurring exception to this is when the author has the audacity to write from the subjective point of view of the relapsing alcoholic. These passages are set off in a different, italic font and are intented. They try to capture what is universal in the experience of addiction and relapse, and reflect on no one individual the author has ever worked with. In fact the case illustrations, unless otherwise marked, are fictitious.

By the time you read this, the author will hopefully have a website up and running. It can be found through the publisher, which will have a link from their page (www.hhpub.com) for this book back to my current website. Let me know what you think and what results you get with the exercises.

George DuWors
Everett, WA, March, 2000

1

Reaction Chains:
Physical *and* Mental

The Case of the Broken Shoelace

My shoelace breaks when I am late and in a hurry, and I immediately perceive what has happened. This would appear to form the first "link" in the "chain" of my reaction. At first, it seems that each "link" triggers the next in a sequence, often too fast to observe or experience. I appear to simultaneously interpret the broken lace and to have feelings about it. And my memory seems to go into scanning mode, spitting out "associations" to this type of experience — broken shoelaces, broken gadgets, being late and under pressure. My mood and physiological state just before the lace broke also affect my reaction — were *they* the first links? For instance, broken shoelaces seem much more exasperating when we are hungry. The associations and feelings also affect mood and physiological state, while feelings trigger associations and associations trigger more feelings. Links fold into links in a way that can be maddeningly sequential, simultaneous, and circular, like the mirrors in a funhouse. Or like a seemingly infinite sequence of chickens hatching out of eggs that are being hatched out of chickens that are ... welcome to the study of human behavior!

Some of these thoughts, feelings or memories about broken shoelaces may be intolerable to me. New (links of) "defenses"

Human Behavior as "Chain Reaction"

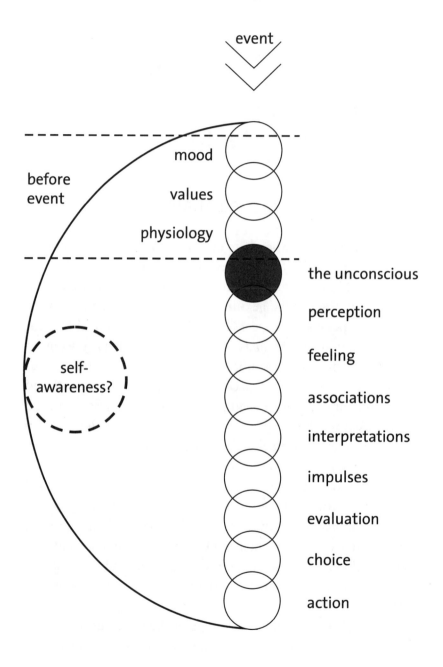

activate to shift my attention away from the unacceptable, whatever it was, without my even knowing what has just happened! Whatever I *am* able to be aware of constitutes "the problem" as I see it. As my perception of the problem develops, I cast about for alternative responses. Each possibility triggers its own load of feeling and association links. Some of my options are blocked out of hand, also being unacceptable to my unconscious. I am literally unable to *think* of them. Choices are held up against the powerful links of what I want versus what I feel I deserve, pulling me between desire and self-worth.

If my self-image (link) includes "Alcoholic-in-Recovery," I will act one way. If my self-image is "(grimly-perfectly) NORMAL," I may act another. If I am alcoholic and take that first drink, my neurochemistry sets off the familiar chain reaction of lost control — it is utterly indifferent to my self-image or my saying I will have "just one." No "self-fulfilling prophecy" here! I may well have no awareness (link) of this, or of the possibility that my neurochemistry was generating a "craving" before the shoelace even broke. By definition, I am not aware of unconscious links in my emotional reaction especially when they control whatever choice I make. Finally, my reaction is completed and others would say I have acted or reacted. I say "damn!" and start looking for a new lace.

To increase understanding of the above section, complete Recovery Exercise #1 at the end of the chapter.

A Model, Not a Theory

So much is going on in the most trivial of human reactions, and none of it can happen without a living brain. Sometimes that brain is only a vehicle or instrument, so we can treat it as a "given." Like the water in a pond, it does not "cause" the ripples that begin when you toss in a pebble, yet no ripples happen if the pond is empty. At other times, the condition of the pond must be taken into consideration. A saltwater fish may react a bit differently if you throw him in a freshwater pond.

This descriptive example of "links" in a "chain" of reaction to a broken shoelace uses a model, not a theory. It is merely a guide for looking at real human behavior without losing sight of the fact that "the mental" and "the physical" are never actually separated. Except in our heads! Most of the major theories of human behavior identify links that may well be important for understanding the reaction of any given person on any given day. *No* theory accounts for all possible links for any human being in every situation.

☞ In this book, we (reader and author) try to explore and understand real addictive behavior in live situations. Make your own observation and experience the yardstick of all that follows. Yes, we will refer to theoretical concepts and even research. The text abounds with comparisons, analogies and deductions. But we will be making particular use of the observations of the one person who can observe an experience from within, the person having the experience. We will use structured tools for looking at experience, for creating it, entering into it and, hopefully, for modifying it. We are concerned with the links of addictive reaction at any given moment and with how they change over time.

We take our focus somewhat relentlessly from one particular addictive action, the moment of taking the first drink/drug of relapse. In fact, we will be almost obsessed with two seemingly universal links in the relapser's mind at that moment, the thoughts "One won't hurt" and/or "F--- it." Why? Because this is the moment the entire field of chemical dependency strives to prevent. Whether you read this book for your own recovery, for that of others, or both, this is precisely the moment that troubles and challenges *you.*

☞ Is it such a leap to think that understanding the reaction we are trying to prevent might make us more effective? What do these links mean in themselves? If different people mean different things, why do we all say pretty much the same words at the critical moment, or simple variations such as "This time will be different" or "I can handle it now"? What other links are operating and how did they come to be? What happened to links that had been sustaining recovery? Where did they go and how and when did they "leave?"

A book like this cannot answer all of these questions, but it can share the author's understanding to date. It can share tools for continuing to chip away at them, encouraging the reader to keep asking these same questions. In reality, the questions themselves are tools, tools to help all of us continually develop our awareness and understanding of the moment of relapse.

To increase understanding of the above section, complete Recovery Exercise #2 at the end of the chapter.

Schools of Thought

Most theories of human behavior are defined by the reaction links which the theory emphasizes. A psychoanalyst emphasizes the unconscious links of transference reactions from childhood. Behaviorists emphasize external contingencies in the present. Gestalt therapists elicit here-and-now emotional links, while Cognitive therapists pinpoint the mental logic present in the most passionate of emotion. Biochemists explore neurotransmitters and their micropathways, while Sociologists variously advocate the macro role of culture and society, or the micro role of family. All schools, theories, disciplines, and therapies, tend to value their specialty at the expense of links stressed and studied by other schools. This appears to be due to two of the most powerful links in all human reaction, "Rice Bowl" and "Ego."

Virtually all of the schools fight over the corpus delicti of the near-dead alcoholic/addict. The alcoholic, society, and the would- be helper are consumers of theories claiming to explain addictive behavior. As consumers of these theories, we must "take what we can use and leave the rest." Somehow, we must recognize the bias in the most sincere and well-researched theory. Above all, we constantly seek ways to recognize accessible links of addictive reactions, and to "break" them when we can.

The links emphasized in this book are primarily "psychosocial" because that is where the author earns *his* rice. The spiritual links of recovery do not appear to become effective until a psychological event called "acceptance" occurs. Acceptance must join other links already present in the person, such as the will-to-survive, a conscience, and values. The biochemical links as such are outside the author's expertise as a therapist. Yet all students of the disease must grapple with such links, in theory and in the flesh. That grappling has continued for this consumer since the first edition, and some of it is shared below and throughout this book.

Distillation of Purely Biochemical Theory

What is the (purely) biochemical theory of alcoholism? When you stumble through the terminology, it seems to come down to this:

Alcoholics are born with a different neurochemical reaction to alcohol. This gives them excessive pleasure when they drink and causes them excessive pain when they stop, so they drink to an extent that baffles a person who does not have that reaction.

The purest form of this theory would have us believe that the alcoholic brain is born a different "pond." Throw the pebble of the first drink in there and you won't just get ripples. And this is offered as the entire explanation for the entire disease, for all of its reactions and behavior.

Put another way, alcoholics "love" what alcohol does inside them! And the "love" is triggered by mixing alcohol into a predisposed biochemical system. The rest is just Mother Nature doing her thing to one of her critters, making no sense at all to the critters who don't have the same neurochemistry.

Putting Biochemistry in Perspective — *Without* Getting Rid of it!

The physical reality of addiction, of craving and loss control, seems well established by observation and by research. With a few major exceptions, the field pretty much accepts that the brain of a diagnosable alcoholic/addict *is* different. Most, including this author, accept the reality of "predisposing" links for some alcoholic/addicts. Evidence for genetic factors grows and the quest for the "holy Grail" of genetic markers gains ever more credence and funding.

But one question haunts this picture of why alcoholics drink and then drink again — Where was the person?

> *If alcohol did something special for me, how did I interpret that? What did it mean to me? Was I offered no glimpse of the garden path down which biochemistry might be leading? Did I have to hear a lecture on genetics or neurotransmitters to realize this stuff had an effect? When I quit drinking, three days later? What stopped me from putting two and two together — blackouts and drinking, fighting and drinking? Being sick and drinking, personality change and divorce and termination and drinking?*

Some would seem to portray the alcoholic/addict as physiological robot without awareness or choice. But the author has worked with Vietnam Vets, alcoholics who avoided hard drugs in Vietnam. Why? - "Because I know me, I would get hooked." He has worked with "party animals" who avoided cocaine "because I knew I would love it too much." He knew a physician who had one experience as a young man with medically prescribed pain-killers. This future doctor loved it. And because he loved it so much, he avoided all such drugs *and* gave up alcohol for life.

The Vietnam veterans above, in mortal combat and surrounded by horror, were able to live with the alcohol monkey. But they would not take on the heroin gorilla. The party animals could tolerate the drinking lifestyle but wanted no part of the cocaine trip. The physician read his feelings and chose a path that avoided them. These people may be a minority. But more than half the adult children of alcoholics out there do *not* become alcoholic, many by abstinence or close to it. In Goodwin's landmark adoptions study [1], seventy-five percent of the adopted-out children of alcoholic parents did *not* become alcoholic. And the rate of non-addiction was even higher among those raised by their alcoholic parents! Many codependents describe loathing the same apparent loss of inhibition (control?) that seems to appeal to most drinkers in the early stages. Just biochemistry?

Alcoholics have been both dying and recovering for centuries. Each alcoholic who begins to recover has the last drink when the biochemical addiction is presumably the worst it has ever been. This is the meaning of "progression." If physiological addiction alone controls behavior, how are people able to quit at all, let alone at the point where the disease is worse than it has ever been? Biochemistry? And why do some people have one arrest for drunk driving and never drink again, while others must collect a colorful resume of jail and mental hospitals, with a few stops in the gutter in between? Just biochemistry?

It is certainly not that the biochemical enthusiasts are all wrong. (The author has not taken a drink himself since reading a monograph in 1976 by Dr. James Milam, which later evolved into his excellent book, *Under the Influence* [2].) What can make them troublesome is the same thing that can make some behavior modifiers dangerous, failure to recognize the reality of the person. (Some behavior modifiers also deny the reality of the organism! They assume all bodies are created equal, that organic differences play no part in what an organism learns.)

A person has alcoholism or does not. A person faces the addiction, including the biochemistry, or does not. And a person does what it takes to recover, or does not.

We have learned so much from animals in the laboratory of the organic scientist and of the behavior modifier. But rats and white mice cannot step back and observe their own lethal behavior. Their very neurochemistry does not permit them to recognize what they are doing. As a result, they cannot "understand" what is controlling them or even that they are being controlled. There is not even anecdotal evidence of "alcoholic mice" switching to another "lab" down the hall, run by recovering mice who have learned to protect themselves from their own "conditioning," and/or "biochemistry." Mice and rats cannot "wake up," any more than they can tell the story of how it happened. But people can and people do, an empirical fact that can be neither researched nor rationalized away.

The original wisdom of Alcoholics Anonymous lies in two potentially contradictory insights. One, acknowledging the biology of the disease. Two, laying responsibility for the work of recovery in the hands of the person who has it. And even AA never claimed to address all of the deadly links in the relapse reactions of all potential members, links both physical and mental.

What is a Hang-up?

A "hang-up" is a problem reaction to similar recurring situations. For example, the inability to say what I really want to a friend or spouse. What makes it a "hang-up" is that I tend to react the same way most of the time, "automatically." The situation triggers the links so quickly and powerfully that choice seems impossible. I have to just watch myself "do it again." I walk away feeling badly about myself. And I keep doing the same thing even though I vow not to, futilely pitting my willpower against this knee-jerk response. I may know what situation triggers my hang-up or I may only know that I am very unhappy, that my life does not work in some way.

Alcoholism is a mixed reaction. Physiological craving can be triggered by psychological stress and/or mental association (memory). Whether I act on my physical craving may depend on psychological beliefs, some of which may be unconscious. The whole process is tangled up with mental/physical chicken-and-egg questions, an omelet the field has become comfortable calling "bio-psycho-social." Whether we use this term, or the old language of AA "obsession of the mind coupled with an allergy of the body," [3] the overall sense remains much the same. And the addictive Humpty-Dumpty will likely always need help from all the King's men, both medical and mental. At the same time, the King's men will get nowhere unless Humpty does his part.

How to Permanently Alter an "Automatic" Reaction

Theoretically, there are three levels at which an automatic reaction may be altered for good. In many cases, temporary relief (ie., talking, distraction, physical exercise) may be necessary in the meantime. In others, long-term maintenance strategies may be necessary. Certain positive links (ie., memory, awareness, commitment) may tend to fade without a "boost." Likewise, certain negative links (stress, resentment, etc.) may require on-going "preventive maintenance." The three levels of intervention are presented below for conceptual clarity. The reader is cautioned that much of the acceptance for on-going recovery is based on precisely this: that there is no permanent "cure," that old reactions tend to rebuild their old links over time. This fact often seems as hard for therapists to accept as for their clients.

Still, the first and simplest level for permanent alteration of an automatic reaction is awareness, especially where it has been absent. "Awareness" is that special capacity of the human mind to step back and see itself its own triggers and reactions. Traditionally, this has been referred to as the "I" observing the "me." It is as if the "I" were a freestanding link able to step outside its own "chain" and observe the other links. This is what makes choice possible, and this is where human neurology leaves animal neurology behind.

Let's say the author has been mindlessly watching television when he notices himself reacting, a tug or a longing perhaps. He realizes the TV ad is promising eternal love (or just hot sex) if he buys "Smellyface" aftershave. Awareness just chuckles, "Nice try, fellahs." It is the sacred mission of the American advertising business to trigger such craving and their success is legendary. Witness the excitement, restlessness, and demanding cries of the author's three-year-old grandson when he sees a big yellow "M." It is the sacred task of awareness (= "spirituality?") to help us see our triggers for what they are.

But sometimes awareness does not evaporate the impulse or craving. Something more is needed, so awareness calls up a heavier gun called "willpower," which should probably be called "won't power." We all need it at times and it often works, at least temporarily. Yet the collision between impulse and "No-you-don't-power" almost always generates one side-effect. Tension, the collision of opposing energies at a muscular level.

The deepest way to alter a specific reaction is to alter its most powerful links, to reduce or eliminate them. If a link is physiological, a physiological intervention (such as an anti-craving or antidepressant drug) may do the trick. If the link is emotional, it may require a combination of up to three processes. One, bringing to awareness (from the unconscious.) Two, releasing of pent-up emotional charge from a previous experience. And, three, bringing adult thinking to bear on beliefs and/or vows formed under duress in childhood. This, of course, assumes the problem stems from an already existing link. Self psychology points out that many problem reactions result from *missing* links. The task is to build them.

In addition, most of us already carry links or reactions that oppose the automatic or compulsive one we wish to change, starting with the (link of) our desire to change! It may work to strengthen links (attitudes, behavior) that counter the problem links. At the same time, it may help to weaken the links that surround and support the target. In this way, increasing "acceptance" links and decreasing "denial" links may help "break" automatic impulses to drink, *without* altering the physiological links of addictive neurochemistry. One AA wisdom advises, "If you don't want to slip, stay out of slippery places." In other words, use your awareness and desire (links) to avoid cravings triggered by situational (memory, stress) links.

"Solution-focused brief therapy" [4] focuses on developing positive links through a progressive awareness of when they already occur. "Motivational enhancement," [5] appears to work in similar fashion. Both approaches avoid a fruitless power struggle within the alcoholic/addict and between patient and counselor. The AA tool (link) of "one day at a time" counters links of imagination (life as an endless, intolerable desert) and emotion (overwhelmed, hopeless.) How? By self-talk.

Literally, by telling myself to "just take it one day at a time,"
I insert a positive link into a distressing chain, one that was
dragging me toward relapse.

Links over Time and the Process of Relapse

A little reflection and observation reveals that we may react to similar situations in very different ways on different days. So what is going on?

Evidently, the "links" in our reactions do not sit still over time. They may cycle in some predictable way, i.e., hunger, sleep, sexual drive. They may increase in some cumulative way, i.e., stress, frustration, resentment. And positive links may diminish or degrade over time, i.e., motivation, acceptance, hope. And any of these changes may radically alter how we react to the same "trigger."

As mentioned above, hunger is a link that may well alter the patience of our reactions to frustration. Obviously, it varies with stomach content and blood sugar. The AA relapse prevention tool, "HALT (Don't get **H**ungry, **A**ngry, **L**onely, or **T**ired)," warns the alcoholic/addict of four such variable links. Two are physical and two are mental, but each increases the likelihood of an alcoholic/addict reacting by relapsing, especially in early abstinence. The effectiveness of this relapse prevention tool for the individual depends on several other personal links. These might include awareness, actual previous relapse experience, and trust in the person who gave the advice. Not to mention the strength of the belief it really *is* the first drink/drug.

The "relapse process" can be seen as the subtle, progressive change in links that determine how the alcoholic/addict will react. In each chapter of this book we look at links that appear to be involved. These links tend to strengthen either relapse reactions ("One won't hurt" or "F--- it") or recovery reactions (coping, asking for help, acceptance). First, let the author introduce a tool designed to surface and identify specific links of *any* human reaction.

To increase understanding of the above section, complete Recovery Exercises #3 and #4 at the end of the chapter.

The Tool: Reliving the Reaction

To identify and to modify one of our ingrained reactions is an ambitious task, since it usually feels as automatic as a knee triggered by a rubber hammer. We are up against the powers of habit and of the unconscious mind, not to mention the sheer quantity of experience and conditioning over time. In most cases of addiction, we are also up against inalterable neurochemical links, regardless of how they came to be. The reaction itself may "fire" in a split second, yet it may consist of twenty or more links. How do we overcome this disadvantage?

First of all, the helper must clarify for the client just what we are trying to do. The person must be involved in the process, and then we look together for ways to turn the time advantage around. Principal among these is "reliving" the reaction [6]. Your "hang-up" was triggered day before yesterday? — great, let's take a look at it. Your mind carries a tape of the event as it happened, of the experience itself as you lived it. We need you reliving that experience, playing your "tape" out loud, present tense and unedited.

It is similar to the process by which every absent-minded person learns to find lost keys or checkbooks: let the memory tape replay until you get an "aha." In more dramatic terms, reliving the reaction strives to recapture how things went wrong internally, like that "black box" from a downed airliner.

A split-second decision or a five-minute reaction can be slowed down and rewound. It can be played again and again (by person or tape recorder) for an entire session, as many times over as many months or years as it takes to clarify critical links and begin to weaken them. Every time you "screw up" is an opportunity to work with your problem reaction again. Expanded time and almost unlimited opportunities for repetition, join with undistracted adult thinking. If you then add the support and skill of the helper and all the tools of recovery, this levels the field to allow us to tackle what had seemed like a hopeless, overwhelming task.

There are other tools for exploring and modifying reaction links as they appear. Use of intellectual memory and discussion are often necessary before reliving the reaction is even possible. But real people reliving real reactions is the primary source of whatever understanding comes through in the pages of this book. It all began with the courageous work by thousands of relapse victims who were willing to look at what made them do what they did.

References

[1] Levin, Jerome David. *Introduction to Alcoholism Counseling, A Bio-Psycho-Social Approach.* Washington, DC, London: Taylor and Francis, 1995.

[2] Milam, James R., and Ketchum, Katherine. *Under the Influence, A Guide to the Myths and Realities of Alcoholism.* New York, London: Bantam Books, 1983.

[3] Anonymous. *Alcoholics Anonymous.* New York: Alcoholics Anonymous World Services, Inc., 1955.

[4] Berg, Insoo Kim and Miller, Scott D. *Working With The Problem Drinker.* New York, London: W.W. Norton, 1992.

[5] Miller, William R., Zweben, Allen, DiClemente, C.C., Rychtarik, Roberto G., (Editor: Matteson, Margaret E.,). *Motivational Enhancement Therapy Manual. (NIAAA PROJECT MATCH Monograph Series, Volume 2).*

[6] Meisler, Jules. *Effective Psychotherapy for Patient and Therapist.* New York, London: Praeger Publishing, 1991.

Recovery Exercises

1. Think of a relatively minor frustration or irritation — broken shoelace, missing a stoplight. Make a list of the four "links" in "HALT." ("Don't get **H**ungry, **A**ngry, **L**onely, **T**ired.") Write and/or share how your reaction changes if one of those links is affecting you. Try spelling out how your reaction might change if two, three, or all four are true for you.

2. Have you ever been abstinent and started to drink/use again? How many times? Did you ever say "One won't hurt?" as you started to drink/use again? How many times? Did you ever say "F--- it" as you started to drink/use again? How many times? Looking back, what other (situations, feelings, thoughts, moods, physical conditions) links seemed to be affecting your reaction at those moments. Answer this question for up to three of your most recent relapses, more if you wish. Any patterns?

3. Try describing to a group or one objective person what was going on when you relapsed. Tell them what links you think were effecting you at the time. Ask if they notice any links you were not aware of. See what you think.

4. Read Chapters 2 and 3 of the Big Book of Alcoholics Anonymous. Underline everything you can find about how an alcoholic thinks about taking the first drink, at the moment of taking it. How is it different from what you have read so far in this book? How is it similar?

2

The Moment of Relapse —
Using the "Lost Keys" Approach

In the first chapter we looked at human behavior as chain reactions consisting of links. Now we want to work directly with a reaction and its mental links. Somehow, they must be brought into the awareness of both helper and the person with the reaction. This chapter describes a technique to bring out any reaction, including the two that are the focus of the book. That is, the woefully recurring moment when abstinent alcoholic/addicts say "One won't hurt" and/or "F--- it," taking the first "dose" of whatever they are addicted to.

The author used to say there was only one thing he knew for sure about addiction. Namely, if you don't take the first drink (dose) you can't get drunk (loaded.) He now adds a second thing, that he may not know *who* in the room may relapse or to what. But he has no doubt that they *will* be saying "One won't hurt" or "F--- it," or a handful of recognizable variations. This chapter presents one reliable way to demonstrate this fact about addiction for yourself and others.

Into the Moment

The first step is to stop thinking so hard, to simply picture ourselves in the actual moment of relapse. We then have a chance to let our memory tape itself replay, the way it was recorded, all senses tracking.

In a group, we start by identifying a volunteer who has relapsed, hopefully someone who thought they were quitting for good. It is nice but not necessary for them to have gone to a self-help group and/or some kind of treatment. The author prefers a volunteer who stayed sober at least ninety days. But the least we need is some kind of decision, however feeble, to remain abstinent. The length of time abstinent is far less of a concern when helping one person look at their own experience with no group present.

The volunteer for this illustration has been picked and asked to wait briefly down the hall.

The therapist (T) explains to the group:

"I want to tell you something about relapse, then show you. The idea is for you to check it out against your own experience. Don't take my word for it — it is not a theory out of a book. (Pause.) The simple fact is that, at the moment of relapse, we are almost always saying one of two things. "F--- it" or "One won't hurt," or obvious variations.

"The way we learned this is by asking people to share their actual thoughts and feelings leading up to the first drink or drug or bet or twinkie, etc. In a minute, we will invite our volunteer back to do just that. This is the key, the fact being tested by both our volunteer and by your own experience. If this is really a fact, "Jane" will tell us she was thinking either "F--- it" or "One won't hurt" at the moment of her relapse.

"We will get these thoughts by asking her to role-play herself the day of relapse. And in the role-play, we will interview the self she was *that* day. This is a group exercise. Feel free to ask questions about what she is thinking and feeling this day (of relapse.) Also, listen to your own feelings and watch for memories or for answers you would give as we go through the "interview." We will not be finished until the group has shared with our volunteer."

Fictitious Jane (J) Doe is in her late twenties, a self-described "party animal." She had been treated in an Intensive Outpatient

Program after her second drunk driving charge. Inviting the volunteer back in, the therapist (T) explains:

"The whole group has a chance to learn something about relapse from your experience. Thank you for your willingness to look at it with us.

"What I am asking you to do is simply be yourself the day of your last relapse. I will ask questions as if I am there that day. What I need you to do is answer me as honestly as possible, in the present tense, like today really is that day. Don't be surprised if I have to remind you a couple times. It may seem strange at first, but it is just a tool to help you better remember your own experience. The group (G) will ask any questions that occur to them and they will also share their experiences after you do.

"Let's see if we can get you back there and into the role, starting when you first wake up that day. The group can help by asking questions like, "What day of the week is it (if you recall?)"

J "Saturday."

T "Where are you living?"

J "An apartment on the west side."

T "Group?"

G "Do you have a job?"

J "Yes."

G "Do you like it?"

J "No."

G "How long have you been doing it?"

J "Since I got outta detox. Three months."

T "Do you live alone?"

J "Yes."

T "Boyfriend?"

J "No. Not since detox."

T Have you had sex since detox?" (Judgment call, whether to be this direct.)

J "Nah."

T "Lonely?"

J "I don't think about it."

G "Are you going to any AA meetings?"

J "Not for a while."

T "Any reason?"

J "Boring. Same thing night after night."

G "Are you taking antabuse?"

J "No, that's a crutch."

T "So. It's Saturday morning. You wake up in your apartment alone. How do you feel?"

J "Just sort of normal. Maybe a little restless."

T "When you get up in the morning, do you know you are going to drink today?"

J "No."

Author note: You will seldom here anyone say "yes" to that question. It seems more common in cocaine addiction to know in advance. For learning purposes, the key is to relive the moment of actual decision.

At this point, especially in an individual session with a recent relapse, other questions might also be asked. Dreams? Any recent cravings? Even nightmares or fantasies, if the helper works with these things. It is usually a good idea to check for any physical conditions, too.

T "How do you feel overall?"

J "Okay, I guess?"

T "What is the biggest problem you've got?"

J "Boring job. No future."

G "Any plans to do anything about that?"

J "Like what?"

T "Good question. But let's stay with the relapse itself for now." (Therapist makes mental note of issue.)

T "Do you have plans for the day?"

J "Wash my hair — clean the apartment — watch TV. Same old stuff."

T "Any recovery activities? For example, reading a meditation, some recovery literature, calling someone?"

J "Nah. I'm not into that stuff."

T "So when does it first occur to you to drink?"

J "I didn't think about it. I just did it."

T "Try to stay in present tense, like this is the day. What we are looking for is when you first start some physical action to get a drink in your hand."

J "Are you an alcoholic?"

(Judgment call, whether to answer.)

T "What makes you ask?"

J "If you were, you would just understand."

T "That's possible. But maybe if you help me understand you will learn something, too, as well as the whole group. Will you at least try to see where this goes?"

J "Okay."

T "So. What do you physically do to get a drink?"

J "I go to the Rendezvous."

T "When do you decide to do that?"

J "I don't really. I mean, I'm restless after I got my chores done. Bored. Nothing to do. So I just get in the car and start driving. Listening to oldies on the radio."

G "When do you first think about the Rendezvous?"

J "Well, I keep driving around, thinking where I can go or what I can do. I just come up with nothing. Then I realize I am on the old street."

T "You're suddenly aware of being on the street where you used to party? How do you feel?"

J "Kind of surprised and excited."

T "Do you know what you are going to do?"

J "Pretty much."

T "What are you thinking about?"

J "This guy named Jerry that used to hang out there. Saw him at a meeting once and he liked me, but I hear he is drinking again.

Think I might just see if I can find him. Maybe dance or have some fun for once."

T "Are you going to drink?"

J "I feel like it but I'm not thinking that yet."

T "Any thoughts against going?"

J "Oh yeah, like maybe this isn't such a good idea. I don't need to screw up now. Just starting to get it together."

T "Do you think of AA or of calling anyone?"

J "Not that I recall."

T "How are you feeling as you park your car and go in?"

J "Free. Excited."

T "Are you going to drink?"

J "I'm starting to look forward to some music and dancing and maybe......," she trails off.

T "Anything telling you not to?"

J "Yeah, 'you-know-you-shouldn't, you-know-you-shouldn't ... a little voice."

T "What do you say to the little voice?"

She blushes and asks, "Do you want to know what I really said?"

T "Not if it's too embarrassing. But it might help everyone here if you could share your exact thought."

After a little hesitation, she blurts out, "F--- it!"

The whole group bursts out laughing, as they often do.

The volunteer looks sheepish, and "T" explains to her what the group had been told. "T" immediately surveys the group for a show of hands. How many said "F--- it?" "One won't hurt?" And who wants to share their experience?

After the group has shared, T asks the volunteer to be the first to express what she has noticed about her relapse.

"I was lonely and wanted a man!" she says. "I never knew that could get me drunk! I thought I just drank because I wanted to." Her eyes are wide with realization. She has just connected the links of her other feelings and desires to the mental/action link of

"F--- it." In a real patient this sort of connection can save a life. At the very least, it spells out a recovery task.

The group members can share their own lonely, bored relapses. Members may discuss dealing with passivity and unrewarding work, the meaning of "boredom" with AA and how to overcome it. Not to mention the whole gigantic issue of creating a healthy social/sex life. The therapist's job is to reinforce the connection between what the person experiences and what he or she chooses to do about it.

In a group that will meet again, debriefing can focus on "F--- it" or "One won't hurt." It usually depends on whichever thought came out in that particular demonstration. A volunteer may be identified for next group and, if it is a relapse group as such, everyone's relapses may be explored. The counselor may use this tool or the full "Relapse Postmortem" described in the chapter of that name.

Hopefully, there will be time to work on the issues identified in each particular relapse and these will be the basis for the individual recovery plan. If time does not permit so much role-playing, the "Learning From Relapse" (LFR) Workbook (Chapter 6) can be used. Everyone can complete and process it together, or new members can complete and process it as they join the group.

Predictable Resistance

This fictitious example shows what can happen when an addict/ alcoholic "relives" a moment of relapse. The reader may repeat it to your own satisfaction, until you are as confident and comfortable as the author that "One won't hurt" and "F--- it" are inseparable from the moment of relapse.

Resistance to the exercise can take the common form "You're not an alcoholic." The same patient is equally capable of complaining, "If you are, you've forgotten where you came from." Or,

"Okay, but how much *training* have you had?"

Resistance to reliving the moment of apparent decision can likewise take several forms. Clinging to past tense, remembering intellectually instead of genuinely reliving, hearing the question as "why?", or claiming no memory of the event at all. Interpreting the resistance will likely be less helpful than an authentic learning-together attitude. If there is anything that triggers shame for an addict/alcoholic, it is looking at the sober self in the act of "deciding" to drink/drug again.

In actual experience, the tool almost never fails to produce "One won't hurt" or "F--- it." The author has *never* been embarrassed by the "prediction" in front of an audience. This makes "One won't hurt/F--- it" both quantifiable and predictable, an empirical fact right near the heart of addiction and relapse. And every time we hear it is an opportunity to learn more about it.

To increase understanding of the above section, complete Recovery Exercises #1 and #2 at the end of the chapter.

Different Tools, Same Job

The above exercise, while consistently effective, is not always necessary or possible. A helper comfortable with the consistency of "One won't hurt" and "F--- it" will likely find shortcuts, the most direct one being to be very direct. Ask whoever had the relapse (including self), "Which was it — "Just one" or ""F--- it?" *Exercise:* You can also ask a group to each picture themselves at a personal moment of relapse. Have them write down and then share what they said at that moment. Dividing your whiteboard in half, put the variations of "One" on one side and the variations of "F--- it" on the other. The author often has a third column for possible exceptions or variations, especially doing the exercise with professional helpers not in recovery. After all, we are dealing with real human behavior and the English language. It is enough for your demonstration if the obvious majority falls into the white-knuckle ("F--- it") or wishful ("One won't hurt") group. It turns out that most adults have at least one bad habit, addiction, compulsion, or vice, something they know perfectly well is not good for them. And most have tried to quit their self-destructive behavior at least once. When these alleged "normies" start their minor vices again, guess what they are all saying?!

Recovery Exercises

1. With your group, count up how many total relapses you have had. How many times did it start with "F--- it" and how many with "One won't hurt." Do any of you have distinct patterns of saying one rather than the other. For the most recent relapse of each person in the group, what is the breakdown between wishful and white-knuckle relapses. What does this say about what you may need to focus on in group? How will you help each other with this?

2. As an individual, talk to 3 (5, 10) people with varying lengths of sobriety before they relapsed. Tell them you are doing treatment homework and would like to know what they were saying at the moment they picked up the first drink/drug. Do you see any patterns? If some refuse to answer, what is your guess about what they said as they relapsed? Can you say why you suspect this?

3

Exploring Links of the Wishful Relapse (One Won't Hurt)

Why Look?

"One won't hurt."
"I can handle it now."
"This time will be different."
"I can't do drug A, but drug B never got me in trouble."
"I'll just get high once, then get back in recovery."
"No one will know."
"I deserve it."
"It must be OK. The doctor prescribed it!"
To summarize: "I control my use of the substance and it is, therefore, both safe and morally okay to use it."

This thought, assumed or explicit, relentlessly accompanies the act of taking the first drink/drug of relapse. The more we relive that moment [1] with clients and/or with ourselves, the more we here these words or their "white knuckle" counterpart, "F--- it." It is no coincidence at all that, "One won't hurt" also appears in virtually every other addictive/compulsive problem; food, gambling, smoking, workaholism, spending, even codependency ("We'll just be friends!"). Other than some very important exceptions, the field has been surprisingly slow to study this mental phenomenon. And this seems particularly strange when you realize how consistently it accompanies the behavioral event we are all trying to prevent, the first drink/drug.

Exception 1: To give them credit, the cognitive therapists (Beck, 1993) recognize the "permission giving belief" [2] at the moment of relapse. And their attack on other addictive beliefs seems to more directly "corrupt the alibi system" [3] of alcoholic/addicts than any other treatment system. But they seem to have little interest in the wishful thought itself, beyond countering it with a "rational response." Cognitive therapy seems to be theoretically disinclined to ask "Where did that thought come from? What else does it tell us about the person having it, and about the process leading up to the fateful moment?"

Exception 2: Excellent work is also happening in examining physical craving and environmental triggers. Those who focus on craving tend to be preoccupied with the physical links, external "triggers" and/or internal brain responses. They seem not to be as concerned with what the relevant thoughts are. The rationale would seem to be: if an anti-craving drug or technique prevents relapse, it prevents "One won't hurt." And this is true, as far as it goes. But the opposite is also true, as far as it goes: when understanding "One won't hurt" prevents relapse, it must somehow effect craving. In other words, craving can effect thought and thought can apparently effect craving. And it seems likely that, the more we can merge our understanding of what goes on in both the mind and body of the relapse victim, the more lives we may save. This chapter and this book focus primarily on the psychological links of relapse reactions. But the author occasionally joins in speculation on how they connect and interact with more physical ones. The clinical reader is reminded to view the author as a fellow consumer of the hard science about which he is speculating. The recovering reader is encouraged to use one yardstick for all you read — your own experience.

Exception 3: Alcoholics Anonymous [4] has been concerned with the fatal thought, "One won't hurt," from the very beginning. "What sort of thinking dominates an alcoholic who repeats time after time the desperate experiment of the first drink?" (p. 35). An answer is given a page later. The famous whiskey-and-milk story all comes down to the moment when an abstinent alcoholic says "... an ounce of whiskey in my milk ... couldn't hurt me" (p. 36). The relapser here is saying *one* (ounce) *won't hurt.* The Big Book remarks: "We call this plain insanity." And it emphatically concludes "... this kind of thinking has been characteristic of every single one of us" (p. 37). There are two other relapse stories in that chapter, each making powerful points about the chronicity of the disease and the power of relapse thinking. Each of these relapse examples also falls into the "One won't hurt" trap. In the chapter on "Working with others," the founders of AA make very specific suggestions about what to discuss with a prospective member. Right along with sharing his or her own drinking experience, it urges the twelve-stepper to "Show him (sic) the mental twist that leads to the first drink of a spree" (p. 91). It is the object of *this* book to show that twist in as many lights as possible, with as many ways to untangle it as the author has learned to date.

The treatment field's puzzling lack of interest in "One won't hurt" as a concrete problem in itself seems to grow from several sources:

- Personal experience: We think we already know all there is to know about it (because we are recovering and we don't do that anymore.)
- Theoretical bias: We don't believe thinking has much to do with behavior. We see the person as the victim of biological programming or of external conditioning. Thoughts and feelings are just background noise, the whirr and click of other machinery grinding our patient toward his or her fate.
- Clinical fatigue: The stereotyped thinking is so boring and its rebuttal so obvious that we lose interest in its signifi-

cance. The author has himself fallen prey to this subtle burnout at times.

To increase understanding of the above section, complete Recovery Exercises #1 and #2 at the end of the chapter.

One Won't Hurt — Moment of Decision

W.I. Thomas, the "dean of American sociology," postulated [5]:

"Situations which men define as real will be real in their consequences."

An alcoholic lives out this principle when saying "One won't hurt" or any of its variations. (I "define" myself as a normal drinker and my drinking as harmless.) The first real result of this self-definition is: I drink! The subsequent real consequences of that are nauseatingly real and predictable — loss of control and a world of "hurt."

AA counters the cheery belief, "One won't hurt," with the counter belief, "It's the first one!" The program then offers the advice, "Don't take it!" (One day at a time, no matter what.) The majority of treatment programs attempt to benignly brainwash clients with the AA doctrine, using lecture, intervention, autobiography, and confrontation to persuade the alcoholic/addict that one does hurt and why. Sometimes this approach is successful and much of the time it is not.

If we are going to increase our batting average at preventing the wishful relapse, we need to increase our effectiveness at preventing this mental event, "One won't hurt." If we are to prevent this fatal belief from returning, we need to understand both what it is and how it redevelops. "One won't hurt" seduces patients who have graduated from the best programs in the country. Once we begin to understand what it is about, it appears that it may never be completely preventable. But our mission will always be to reduce the number of times "One won't hurt" speaks again, hurts and destroys again.

Part of what limits our understanding may be that we look at this belief only as a true/false statement. Inductive logic notes that the first drink hurt 975 times out of the last 1,000. A person with reason unclouded by other factors (links) concludes, "Yep, that first one sure does hurt, probably will next time, this time, any time."

If inductive logic alone does not seem to help, let us start with the deductive variety. Because one simple, logical thing is clear when anyone drops out of recovery with the swan song "One won't hurt." The alcoholic/addict does not *at that moment* believe the professional authority or the personal experience of others. We all *told* them it is the first drink/drug. Apparently, neither professional credentials nor personal recovery were permanently convincing.

What follows in this chapter are a number of ways for understanding and working with "One won't hurt" when it occurs. Some of the reaction links identified overlap and connect, occurring every time the thought does. Others happen only in some instances of relapse by "One won't hurt." Each section attempts to isolate at least one link in the "chain" between abstinence and relapse, between thought and first drink/drug. The order of presentation is admittedly somewhat arbitrary. Common sense tells us to concentrate on links most likely to get this person drunk or loaded today. These are often, but not always, the first to appear when an alcoholic/addict relives a relapse. The helper will, of course, most commonly get a chance to work with the thought itself only after it has already led to action. That is, until we begin routinely looking and asking for relapse thinking with people who are still trying to abstain. The recovering reader, of course, has the opportunity to study and challenge the thought every time it whispers in your ear.

To increase understanding of the above section, complete Recovery Exercises #3 and #4 at the end of the chapter.

Starting with the Obvious: Two Observations and an Exercise

☞ The first, pitifully obvious thing about this belief is: *it is not true!*
If I am alcoholic/addict, "one" will hurt — sooner or later, it
will *always* hurt. In other words, our wishful relapser is believing
and acting on a falsehood. The facts are "black" and the alcoholic/
addict is proclaiming them to be "white." But that is not what
☞ makes it pitiful. The second obvious thing, almost too obvious
and pitiful to mention, is that no mind-altering substance has yet
entered the mind and the mind has already altered! Our "dry"
drunk or "clean" addict has already left reality — his or her feet
are firmly planted in midair. Talk about "powerless!" Talk about a
"break" with reality! The break has already occurred and the drug
has yet to enter the bloodstream. Schizophrenics and bipolars have
psychotic breaks and neurotics have nervous breakdowns. This is
alcoholic breakdown. Talk about the "psycho" in our "bio-psycho-
social" disease! We are faced with a psychological event that strips
the person of all other defenses against drinking.

> *I mean, if a drink or a line won't hurt me, what do I need
> defenses for anyway?*

Many people in the field still need to realize the full significance of this crucial fact, helpers and relapsers alike, whether in
personal recovery or not They need to feel it, taste it, touch and be
touched by it. Hearts and minds, values and beliefs, theories and
experience, none will help if they do not include this simple, painful truth: the abstinent alcoholic/addict, believing "One won't hurt"
and picking up the first drink/drug of relapse, does not yet have
alcohol or drugs in the brain. Yet that brain is being controlled by
this delusion...yes, controlled, overrun, corrupted, swallowed up,
disconnected, possessed, invaded, dissociated, driven, and, above
all, rendered "powerless."

Three exercises in this book are designed to make this point from different angles. The "Addiction Conviction Scale," at the end of this chapter, graphs the deterioration of the belief and acceptance "I cannot have so much as one." The "Jekyll-Hyde" exercise, in the chapter of that name, attempts to startle the relapser into the awareness of relapse as a *sober* decision. And the following, called "Exhaustion of the Obvious," tries to bring home the significance of precisely what most fail to notice about the moment of relapse.

Exhaustion of the Obvious:

1. With any group interested in relapse, identify the fact that "one won't hurt" is one of the two inevitable relapse thoughts. You can just tell them, or use the whiteboard to get their collective relapse thoughts. (Make two columns, one for the wishful thoughts and another for the white-knuckle thoughts.) Then have them complete this list-generating task.

2. "If we know an addict/alcoholic is picking up the first drink/drug of relapse and thinking, 'One won't hurt,' what else does that tell us about them at that moment? What is obvious, obvious about the words themselves or the person saying them in that situation? And what else might be reasonably guessed about the person, based only on their words and behavior in that situation? Brainstorm as a group and don't be afraid to be repetitive, simple-minded, or even a bit academic." (If someone in the group has read this book, ask them to keep what they know to themselves. In processing, ask them what impact it had for them originally.)

3. Your group's list will hopefully include many of the following:

- Person does not believe they have disease — they are wrong!
- Person does not believe they will lose control.
- Person "in denial," by definition.
- Prediction is not true, judgment is impaired.

- Person has forgotten reason for quitting (suffering).
- Person wants more than "just one".
- Person is unaware of own desire, how strong it is. This would seem to mean they are dissociating and/or suppressing.
- Person *may* be medicating pain that has been suppressed.
- Person feels need to justify. Why say anything?
- Fear, guilt and/or anxiety are likely covered by the justification.
- Person wants to drink/drug, far more than they are admitting to self, or experiencing.
- Person is believing what they desire to be true — wishful thinking!

4. What most groups will leave out is the reality of experiencing all this *before* taking that first drink/drug. The brain saying "One won't hurt" has a B.A.L of zero, zero nannograms of THC and/or metabolites of any other drug. If your group omits this obvious fact from their list, watch their reactions when you point it out. Look into as many eyes as you can find with the significance of this truth and their omission burning in your own. And then get them talking, sharing what it means to *them* to see all that happens in the mind of an addict/alcoholic before the drug enters the brain. Even if someone includes the fact on their list, ask how many others thought of it themselves.

5. Emphasizing the "break with reality," the mental problem is the next step. Connecting it to the "insanity" of the "whiskey-and-milk" story in the Big Book is just one way to do it. The author has been known to elaborate on the word "insanity" by reminding a group where their diagnosis is found, that their insurance claims are not coded from a book of internal medicine. Even holding up a big red *Diagnostic and Statistic Manual of the American Psychiatric Association* [6], he will remind them "Substance Dependence" shares the same pages as "Schizophrenia" and "Bipolar" disorders. And this is true even if the craving for alcohol/drugs is

genetically programmed, and even if the thought itself of "just one" is caused by biochemical craving. Whatever the "drive" itself is for drugs, it works on and through the mind. This is what makes it a *mental illness.*

Alcoholic/addicts seem to appreciate the chance to process about this aspect of their relapse experience. Painful as it may be, this may be their best opportunity to deepen and soften their acceptance, to face what has really been going on. If you are reading this book in recovery you may find this section particularly disturbing. Now may be a good time to talk to someone about what it triggers. Write about it. Pray about it, if you pray. Whatever you do, see the truth, but do not judge yourself for what you may never have been able to see before. Painful as it may be, if you can see the truth more clearly, be grateful that you *can.* Let your self-esteem grow with the courage it takes to face a painful reality. And if all else fails, there is one reliable safety valve ... the human being who wrote this book *could* be wrong!

Regardless of the fallibility of the author, it seems necessary and healthy for anyone in recovery to continuously monitor their level of acceptance:

> *Do I truly accept today that "it's the first drink/drug?" Does my acceptance go to the "unconscious" bone? Will it hold up under fire, real life? I need to share and explore my "mental reservations," to understand AA and treatment as places to be protected from these subtle processes. Above all, I need a healthy fear of this giddy thought, "One won't hurt," a fear strong enough to galvanize me into self-protective action, if and when it returns.*

This is apparently what happened in 1935 [7] in Akron, Ohio, with Bill W. Bill recognized his own relapse thinking as a deadly symptom and got on the phone, looking for another alcoholic to talk to. This led directly to his first meeting with his eventual AA cofounder, "Dr. Bob."

☞   At the very least, this protective action should consist of telling someone else the relapse thinking has returned, someone who recognizes the voice of the serpent when it slips back in the garden. At best, the recovering person will recognize an opportunity for growth:

> *What makes the wish for a drink/drug appealing on this particular day? Is something bugging me? What mood or feeling will the drug alter? Is there something I would avoid or escape by return trip to fantasyland? Maybe I can't put my finger on anything specific, but what can I do to prevent this mental recurrence from completing itself in physical relapse? Am I willing to take up tools I have been taught for this task? Alternatively, am I willing to work on my personal blocks to picking them up?*

To increase understanding of the above section, complete Recovery Exercises #5 and #6 at the end of the chapter.

Denial of Denial

"One won't hurt" is an innocuous and abbreviated statement, which is one source of its sedative-hypnotic power. It is an "automatic thought," one that comforts and reassures the old behavior. It does not motivate the thinker for change by causing depression or anx-
☞   iety, as neurotic thoughts so often do. One way to process it, an exercise or group discussion in itself, is to ask those who have fallen prey to the belief to spell out all that it really implies, to "translate" it. The most complete translation the author himself has come up with is:

> *"I can make a decision, stone cold sober, to consume one drink/drug and let it enter my bloodstream. After it has reached my brain, I will then comply with the decision made by my mind prior to putting alcohol in it." In short, my brain with alcohol in*

☞ *it will remember and obey the orders of my brain without al-*
cohol in it. (Mr. Hyde will do exactly what Dr. Jekyll said!)
    More briefly still, "I can and will choose to terminate my
intake of alcohol/drugs at any point after intake begins." Or
just, "I can take the first drink/drug without losing control."
Briefest of all, "I am not an alcoholic or addict."

Approached this way, we see again that the relapser does not,
at this life-and-death moment, believe they have the disease. It
often amazes the author how many people who fell for "One won't
hurt" claim to have "known" for years they were addicted. One
response to such "denial of denial" can go:

"Tell me again — what did you say to yourself as you took that
first one."

"Oh, I thought I could have just one."

"And what is your definition of an alcoholic/addict?"

"Well, someone who cannot handle it, loses control, gets in
trouble, if they drink."

"Even one?"

"Yeah."

"Okay. At the precise moment you were saying "One won't hurt,"
did you believe you were alcoholic, by your own definition?"

Silence. The person will often look visibly shaken.

"Gee, I never thought of it that way," may be the response.

It does not hurt a bit to let the person (including the person
reading this) sit there with what they are seeing and feeling. By all
means, let them think about it, and feel about it, and think some
more. And give them a chance to talk about their denial of their
denial, what it means to them to now see their previous lack of
sight. What we all need to keep in mind is that "One won't hurt" is
the voice of denial. As such, it is one of the primary psychological
symptoms of the very disease that it hides. It is the means by which
the word of denial becomes the flesh of relapse.

To increase understanding of the above section, complete Recov-
ery Exercise #7 at the end of the chapter.

Experience, a Missing Link

There is more to this denial than mere belief in one statement over its opposite.

How is it we come to "know" we have a chronic problem? By experience over time of the pain caused by that problem. Let's say I get tennis elbow every time I play for five years. I know before I step on the court I have a chronic condition, and I know what I do to aggravate it. So what stops me from knowing I have chronic addictive disease at the moment I say "One won't hurt?" or "I can handle it now." Forgetting! More precisely, a focused inability to look at, consider, or feel my own experience. The Big Book [4] spelled it out (p. 24) both poignantly and clinically over sixty years ago:

> *"We are unable, at certain times, to bring into our consciousness with sufficient force the memory of the suffering and humiliation of even a week or a month ago."*

This mysterious inability is vividly portrayed as being "without defense" against the first drink/drug. And this description of the problem is in no way contradicted by a further observation of the author's. The defenses are working all right, but what they are defending is *not* sobriety! Rather, they create a tunnel vision that walls out the very facts which might have dampened the desire to drink/drug. That is how "they" defend my right and ability to drink "just one".

"What about all the other times you said 'One won't hurt' and tried it?"

"I always lost control."

"What made you think it would be different this time?"

"I didn't think about the past." Of course, some actually say "This time will be different," implicitly recognizing what has happened before, explicitly discounting the voice of all those experiences!

What blocks out the voice of experience, the painful associations, the memories? We use the term "euphoric recall" without

much attention to what "euphoria" means, and with little recognition that this person does have a voice of experience within. The problem is that they seem unable to hear it. Witness the change in many people after their second or third (or tenth) serious relapse. The spontaneous memories of long-ago drinking or drugging events, the realization of what those memories mean: "My God, I was addicted even then!"

If we are going to understand anything, we must understand that the memories have been present in this person through all the years, including the dry periods between relapses! Somehow they were stored behind the haze of alcohol/drugs and/or the stone wall of denial. Like family and friends, they were waiting to be heard.

Buried memories are like a photo album of the disease-in-action which the person is initially unable to open. Whatever keeps those memories locked up, it was not biochemistry or they would be there still. The force that imprisons those experiences goes by the names of "denial," "suppression," "repression," etc. It campaigns with the slogan, "One won't hurt" and it's other name is "wishful thinking." In order to have its way again, it must bury the facts of the person's own experience, making it impossible to learn.

Note: it seems logical to translate the "wish" of "wishful thinking" into the word "craving." A wish that has that much power would seem worthy of such a label. In this sense, Dr. Alex Stalcup [8] is correct when he equates treatment of chemical dependency with "craving management." Neither the helper nor the person "craving" may ever know how much of any given "wish" to drink/drug is physical or mental.

> *The good news is that this is not what matters most if I am not to die of addiction. What matters is that I see the power of this force operating in my mind before relapse, that I realize the power of the wishful process to undermine my recovery.*

This seems more important than theories of what causes it. And yet one exception to this may already be occurring: if anti-craving drugs restore enough functioning to build hope, the hope might then lead to renewed work at personal recovery.

To increase understanding of the above section, complete Recovery Exercise #4 at the end of the chapter.

Desire, Another "Missing Link"

My past is not all that I deny with "One won't hurt."

My words imply that "one" is all that I want, thus denying the desire that holds my memory and judgment in its grip!

Zoe Sinclair[1], recovering counselor, spoke for many a relapser when he said, "As many times as I said I was going to have only one drink, that was never all I wanted."

"One won't hurt" would be literally true, after all, if I only have one. I will come to no major grief, no matter who I am. But how many do I really want, inside my being, at the precise moment I declare the harmlessness of a single drink? How many drinks will it take to dampen the coals of my desire for alcohol? Just one?

It may be true I am so emotionally disconnected that I feel no "craving." It may also be true that I experience an increasing frenzy to drink/drug after I pour some "gas" on the coals.

But no serious student of the disease of addiction will look inside an addict/alcoholic at this moment and find a puny desire to match the verbal camouflage.

Even if biochemistry is the source of the desire, why not just admit it? Does a person dying of thirst pretend to want "just one?"

As clear and obvious as the desire may seem to the outside observer, it seems just as clear how sincerely unaware the relapse victim may be. We can blame "society" or even its voice/link in

---

[1] Quoted by permission.

everyone's head, the "superego." Various defenses driven by societal shame keep the person from seeing they are about to act "shamefully" again. As plausible as this explanation may be, many alcoholic/addicts would counter that the real source of their block is the desire itself. Craving! If I can pretend it will only be one, I am free to start. If I admit I actually want twenty or thirty, I might have to consider both the consequences and the alternatives. And that could spoil the whole party!

Dr. Alex Stalcup gives a list of different types of craving in his workshops and Dr. Beck generates a similar list in his book, *The Cognitive Therapy of Substance Abuse* [9]. What strikes the author is the absence from both lists of this form of "subliminal" craving. Like those ultra-rapid messages on a movie screen, they move us to act without our awareness, robbing us of the choice we might have had. They are probably the closest thing to a theory of causation that this author and would-be helper has for the "wishful relapse."

To increase understanding of the above section, complete Recovery Exercise #8 at the end of the chapter.

A Decision in the Dark

Make no mistake — the mind and the brain that pronounce "One won't hurt" are making a decision. But what kind of decision? Any decision is only as good as the information on which it is based. We have already seen that this decision lacks a genuine realization of what it means to be addicted. It lacks access to the data banks of past experience, and it is blinded to here-and-now awareness of the most immediate desire of the person/organism, for the drug! It is a blind decision, channeled by "defense mechanisms" which seem both machine-like and mysteriously willful at the same time.

The "Big Book" of Alcoholics Anonymous [4] scorns the value of "self-knowledge" (p. 39) in recovery from alcoholism, but the

program urges calling a fellow drinker when tempted. Would AA have ever been founded if Bill Wilson had not been aware of his own desire to drink that day he first called Doctor Bob? The challenge to the treatment profession has always been to find ways to help alcoholic/addicts develop the sort of self-awareness that Bill apparently had that day. The kind that enables them to work their programs more effectively. We cannot make decisions for people, but we can help them to get in touch with the facts of their own experience. Cut off from personal reality, healthy personal choices are not even possible.

The Big Book calls alcohol itself, "cunning, powerful and baffling." Judging by the context, this seems to be a way of describing what it feels like to have had a "wishful relapse." Dr. Alan Marlatt [10] uses the concept of "seemingly irrelevant decisions" to describe the same progressive sequence. The image is one of decisions made under the control of something other than reason or reality. In fact, they are painfully "relevant" and have a visible direction. As relevant as a moth "wandering" toward a flame, or a lemming joining his tribe for a mad dash to the sea.

A "decision?"

Yes.

A free choice?

No.

The Affirmation

Denial is disbelief.

I do not believe I am an alcoholic, foodaholic, that I have cancer, or that I have severed my spinal cord and will never walk again. But denial is the flip side of affirmation, meaning I do believe I am a "social drinker," free of disease, able to walk again.

> *The belief "one won't hurt" denies the loss of control that defines addiction. It affirms my freedom to drink alcohol without guilt or anxiety. Result: no anxiety or guilt or awareness or understanding to block my impulse.*
>
> *What makes the human mind affirm what is not true? The desire for something else to be real. I believe she still loves me as she walks off with her head on his shoulder, because I want to believe it. In clinical work this is referred to as "delusion" or "denial;" in everyday life it's "wishful thinking."*

We will never understand anyone's denial, our own or another's, without looking for this "link." What is it the person wants or needs so desperately, so badly that their mind rejects real facts and sees only what it wishes were true?

To increase understanding of the above section, complete Recovery Exercises #8 and #10 at the end of the chapter.

One Drink of What?

The relapsing alcoholic/addict is not wishing for "just one" orange juice:

> *I am not selling myself that I can "handle" a glass of milk. What I wish for is the effect of a liquid drug, alcohol. And what is that effect? Alcohol travels to the gut and brain and changes my "gut feeling!" It travels to the mood centers and changes my mood. Do I need a PhD or an MD to understand that someone who wants a drug that will change feeling wants to feel differently? More precisely, I do not like or tolerate the feeling that I wish to alter, so much that I am emotionally incapable (now) of paying attention to it, of experiencing it. So much so, that thoughts of alcohol are beginning to sound friendly again, especially with the candy-coated assurance "One won't hurt."*

☞ An emotional problem is a feeling you don't like or a feeling that makes you *do* something you wish you hadn't. Regardless of hereditary and biochemical factors, all alcoholic/addicts have an emotional problem at some point:

> *The problem is that I do not like the way I feel and have found a powerful way to change the feeling. It is theoretically possible I had no identifiable emotional problem prior to drinking or drugging. It is also possible that I have been corrupted by an exceptional effect of alcohol/drugs on my feelings, an effect that occurs due to a unique biochemistry. Alcohol may seem to give a power to alcoholics that it does not provide for non-alcoholics. But power corrupts, and the power to alter (my experience of) my universe may be the most corrupting of them all.*

Perhaps, "normies" don't find that power in alcohol or drugs because their biochemistry doesn't interact with the drug in the same way. No matter, recovery from alcoholism still requires each alcoholic/addict to relinquish that power. And this means nothing if not learning to deal with emotion by other, healthier means.

As AA taught us from the beginning, the first step is to recognize the problem. Counselors can hardly do this if they see *all* of the drinker's drinking behavior as nothing but biochemical insanity. Properly understood, the thought "One won't hurt" (or "F--- it") can be an "open sesame" to the world of feelings and how to deal with them. We may start with our client by defining his or her problem as having the urge to take a drug that changes feelings. This connection between a desire to drink/drug and a desire to escape emotion makes practical exploration possible. It invites the alcoholic/addict to examine their feelings and the part emotions play in relapse. For example, "Let's look at what you were feeling at that very moment." Merely telling the relapser, "Don't take that first drink" may often help. But it does not tackle the remaining problem the person is stuck with — *what do I do about my feelings now?*

To increase understanding of the above section, complete Recovery Exercise #11 at the end of the chapter.

The Wish for Wishes

AA spells out its own theory of the emotional/psychological core of alcoholism in Chapter 5 of the Big Book [4]. "Self-will run riot" (p. 62) is presented as an attitude toward life at the heart of the problem. This attitude sees the world as a stage on which I am director, scriptwriter, casting agent, props man, special effects, etc.:

> *Didn't Shakespeare say that all the word is a stage and each must play the part I assign? This is the world I want to live in and, in my bones, I assume that I do or believe that I should live in it. It is, of course, a world without frustration — I get what I want because I direct what I want. This is the "ism" in alcoholism, an unspoken world view which sets myself at the center and my desires as supreme. It is a world view that dooms me to a sense of failure at my actual limitations, as well as outrage or dismay when reality dares to deny my wishes. My grandiose pendulum swings between fearful, depressed inadequacy and bitter resentment.*

Alcoholics Anonymous does not spell out that much of this self-will operates in the unconscious mind. The person does not even know they have it! AA does not consider that a large part of it may be inherited "temperament," a congenital way of reacting to frustration or threat that creates a need for relief. Nor does the Big Book spell out how alcohol/drugs satisfy the desire for omnipotence so clearly implied in "self-will run riot." This requires looking at what happens after so many addictive drinkers drink, and there is a taboo against this in the field. Our ingrained

codependency does not like to embarrass people, especially if we are vulnerable to the same embarrassment.

Fantasy.

Many alcoholics will describe, if given the chance, how alcohol blurs the line between fantasy and reality for them. A former patient, obviously in relapse and living in the street, once challenged the author, "What have you got that I want? When I drink I can be anything I want, brain surgeon, CIA agent, test pilot. Sober, I was just another attorney!"

Fantasy.

A middle-aged family man with a middle class income and an ordinary job sits in a gin bar and watches football on TV. As the quarterback drops back in the pocket, he *is* the quarterback, reliving his "glory days" of high school.

Fantasy.

A physician's wife boasts how she floated naked in the pool in the moonlight. Her husband had to tell her it never happened, that she never left the couch where she had passed out.

Fantasy is imagination, the fulfillment of wish by the mind in isolation from reality, by pretending.

> In my imagination, I dictate who is present, what they do, what I get, and all that happens. I am director, script-writer, casting, special effects, rolled into one. In fantasy, the world is my stage and self-will runs riot with nothing to trip it. In fantasy, I am God. Every wish is my command, and beggars can ride. In alcoholic fantasy, my horse is named John Barleycorn or Spuds MacKenzie or Ernest and Julio.

As we have already seen, "one won't hurt" is the claim of a mind already "choosing" wish over reality. And by that choice, it releases a further flood of fantasies that alcohol makes still more vivid and more powerful. It may be that alcoholics are people for whom alcohol makes fantasy more real due to neurochemical interactions. It is logically just as possible that alcoholics lack the power to sustain their own fantasies, possibly for similar reasons. A codependent who is "in love" again with another person who "needs me" is every bit as caught up in fantasy. Yet the codependent brain needs no alcohol or drug to make the fantasy so real it controls judgment and behavior...the fantasy *is* the drug!

Practical implications?

Fantasies themselves may be indicators that a relapse is developing, like thunderclouds before a storm breaks. The most direct approach is to routinely ask clients what fantasies they may be having. Assessment interviews might also include typical fantasies the person has while drinking/using. But don't push it — this is embarrassing stuff and it can wait.

Once a fantasy is reported, the idea is to get it reconnected to reality. What does the fantasy say about what the person wants? What is the wish in my wishful thinking, if it was not for a drug? Is there a way to get it? If so, what is the plan? If not, how will I cope with the frustration? In addition, fantasies, like other cravings, have triggers. What is going on in reality that the fantasy might escape or "solve?" The most dangerous thing about fantasies is their ability to take over consciousness and behavior. We "act them out" — it might be more accurate to say that they act out *through* us. The helper must remain on the alert for fantasy bubbles, with a little stickpin in hand. It is called "Reality." And the recovering alcoholic/addict who understands and recognizes fantasy is less likely to get "blind-sided" by one.

To increase understanding of the above section, complete Recovery Exercise #12 at the end of the chapter.

Euphoria

So far we have looked at the statement "one won't hurt" as a piece of thinking. We have scanned it for logic and for belief, as well as for perception that is skewed or lacking. Emotion has been dealt with as a problem and a "link" pretty much by deduction. But what is the drinker who is about to have "just one" actually feeling? It turns out that the feelings this person does experience may hold the key to effective treatment and prevention. Thinking may be dealt with logically, after relapse. But the person who says "one won't hurt" seems frequently to be in an unrecognized emotional condition, one that makes healthy use of logic virtually impossible.

One of these conditions is called "euphoria."

Example: L. is on probation at her job for an alcohol-related problem. She has complied with a treatment contract set up by the Employee Assistance Program (EAP). Many living problems persist, including indebtedness and the necessity to live with a wacky, codependent father. She also has a long history of shyness and relationship problems. Yes, she is an adult child of an alcoholic. Friday night she is driving several hundred miles to visit high school friends and get away for the weekend. She "decides" to drink on the way. Needless to say, she gets arrested for drunk driving, and she will be fired if she has to miss any work due to drinking.

"I can't believe I did that," she says to her counselor afterwards.

The counselor's first response is to recognize her dismay, then to explore what she was thinking and feeling as she made the fatal decision. It turns out that before she decided to have "just one," she felt "free," a state she can label as "excitement." Most of us would recognize it as an intense case of "thank-God-it's-Friday," the feeling of relief from the constraints of workplace: boss, machine, clock, and role. It is the elation of now being able to "do what I want to do." This condition is highly dangerous to the health of recovering alcoholics — relapsers are often able to describe this paradoxical sense of "freedom" and "power" at the moment of weakness, if the right questions are asked. It turns out that these feelings are the emotional opposites of the "powerlessness" the person must accept in order to recover.

> *I may have "thought" I was powerless over alcohol at one time, but in euphoria I do not feel powerless over alcohol or anything else. In fact, euphoria seems to be pretty much the same feeling, whether I feel it because of a drug or an emotional reaction. Because the effect is similar to at least a few drinks, to prevent a relapse at this point is like trying to stop me after I have already had two or three. Once euphoric, I am already "under the influence."*

A real patient, euphoric prior to his relapse, put his finger on what makes the feeling so deadly. "I was already high and I didn't want anything to bring me down."

Apparently, reality becomes an intruder that chills the glow of euphoria, the "iceman." Alcohol, on the other hand, allies itself with this energized state, stoking the fire and keeping it burning.

The alcoholic in euphoria has lost the First Step (being "powerless") of AA and doesn't want it back! Forgotten is any treatment education — mental access denied! If the information does try to return, it will be angrily rebuffed or cheerfully ignored. Mr. Hyde seems firmly in control and Doctor Jekyll hasn't even taken that first drink!

☞ Many alcoholic/addicts say, "I drink when I feel good." Look for euphoria.

Many say, "I was too complacent or comfortable." Look for euphoria.

Many say, "I just like to party on weekends (denying any connection to feelings or problems)." Look for euphoria.

Many people say, "I didn't have anything bothering me." Look for euphoria.

☞ What can we do if we find euphoria? First, alcoholics and

addicts need to know this is a dangerous condition for them, and why. Like the thought "One won't hurt," it is a symptom of the disease, to be feared and not enjoyed. If they are AA members, it will be easier to explain, as above. In fact, Chapter 17 of AA's book *Living Sober* [11] is called "Looking Out for Overelation." And it may help to read Chapter 3 of the Big Book, which concludes with the relapse story of an early member. This man drinks after a completely successful day, "...not a cloud on the horizon" (p. 41), probably euphoric. For at least some alcoholic/addicts, the aversive conditioning programs might retarget their conditioning. It might increase their recovery rates to try associating the aversive consequence with the thought "one won't hurt" and/ or the feeling of "euphoria." In general, a daily meeting with AA and/or sponsor or other recovery reminder may serve to keep bringing a person back down to earth.

Treatment of euphoria is going to first consist of detecting it, bringing it to the person's awareness. Defining it as an issue to work on and looking for what triggers it come next. Euphoria appears to be a form of anxiety, either a letdown effect or "delayed stress" as in the case of "B" above. Sometimes it is a child-like response to helplessness, and euphoria also seems to be triggered by success in those who feel inadequate. Such a person may become elated just from getting a desired result — a sale, a solution, a compliment or date. Those who take their competence for granted take success in stride, expecting the fruits of their labors. Those who feel inadequate and/or expect to get "screwed" may overreact to trivial accomplishments. The resulting excitement and exaggerated sense of power are what we have here called "euphoria." They lead to behavior which fulfills the inner "prophecy" of inadequacy, failure, and losing — snatching defeat from the jaws of victory. The connection to adult child issues should be obvious, not to mention the direct connection to relapse.

To increase understanding of the above section, complete Recovery Exercise #13 at the end of the chapter.

Boredom

"Boredom" is another feeling that often occurs with the deadly self-deception "one won't hurt." But what *is* boredom?[2]

> *I have time.*
> *I could go fishing. Nah.*
> *I could read that book I've wanted to get to for two years. Nah.*
> *I could call Jack, or Jill. Nah.*
> *Damn, there's nothing to do.*
> *Might as well go down to the bar.*

Here is a person with a seemingly endless list of things to do, yet unable to get interested in any one of them and to choose it. Lack of enthusiasm and inability to decide appear to be the essence of boredom, accompanied by a fatal lack of any sense of danger.

If you think about it, no alcoholic/addict in recovery should ever lack a sense of danger, always being one drink/drug away from disaster. Realizing there is a deadly force within you, ever ready to catch you with your guard down, at a weak moment ... or a bored one.

And then where has the energy gone? Certainly, we all fluctuate in our energy levels, but it is generally true that this sort of boredom is the result of emotional shutdown:

> *I am blocking something, an urge to drink, anger, frustration, even joy and enthusiasm. I do not feel my energy because I am not letting myself feel at all. Perhaps treatment or abstinence itself is awakening some of the monsters that live in my emotional basement. They are, so to speak, pushing on the cellar door. In knee-jerk fright, I slam the door so hard it takes all my grim energy to hold it there, and I don't even know I did. "I'm just bored."*

---

[2] Anatomy of boredom first heard in a Gestalt Therapy demonstration in 1977.

Why does "just one" appeal to the alcoholic/addict who is bored, when nothing else does? Why is the almost unlimited field of possibilities narrowed to one chemical self-alteration? How does even the thought of "just one" relieve boredom? Many alcoholic/addicts get excited just fantasizing about that first one. Already, boredom is lifting, but what is so exciting? In addition to the euphoric recall of past exciting events, the drinker knows that alcohol disinhibits. Boredom may be emotional shutdown:

> *Alcohol is a way of opening the cellar door while seeming to put the monsters to sleep in my emotional basement. It seems to provide a way to have my emotional cake and eat it, too, to feel alive and not feel pain. However, my mistake is the monsters do not sleep when I drink. They rise out of the cellar and attack those closest to me. Passed out by the cellar door lies the exhausted Doctor Jekyll, worn out trying to hold that door shut. He is the part of me now passed out drunk, but what Dr. Jekyll does not know won't hurt me, will it? No! Not until I realize the semi-conscious game I have been playing, and take responsibility for what the monsters do. The price of controlling Mr. Hyde will be to realize that crooked face in the mirror is me.*

☞ One metaphor the author has used with "bored" alcoholics is this: to be a sober alcoholic is to live with a loaded gun at your head. (Counselor points a finger at temple.) True, your finger is on the trigger, but the problem is that you have a spastic trigger finger. (Counselor twitches finger convulsively.) Picturing this condition as vividly as possible may help some people to see it. The image also tries to stimulate the positive anxiety needed for working continuously at recovery.

Sometimes "boredom" complains specifically about Twelve Step meetings.

"Same old stuff, over and over."

☞   *There is plenty of repetition in AA, and if I submit passively*
to the repetition, I may well become terminally bored. What is
the antidote? — take a risk! Create some anxiety for myself by
sharing something embarrassing or for which I don't have the
answer. Take a risk for the thrill of growth instead of for the
thrill of escape. But first, I must recognize boredom for what it
is, another dangerous symptom, and take responsibility for
protecting myself against it.

Sometime into serious sobriety, boredom with the program may
appear again. New ways to serve may help, but new ways to grow
may also be in order.

Exposing my interpersonal blind spots in a therapy group
may counteract stagnation. Such professionally facilitated
"cross-talk" is a lot riskier and a whole lot less comfortable than
the protective structure of a Twelve Step format. It is hard to
be bored on the hot seat. Couples and/or family therapy may
be growth options for which I am long overdue. I might even
take those blind spots one-on-one to a professional, one who
specializes in nothing but the gentle removal of blinders. This
should be a process which is anything but boring. I mean, how
can I tire of the most fascinating subject on the earth, my "self."
Besides, the intimacy and vulnerability involved seem as fright-
ening as they are healing. I'd rather go skydiving!

A third attitude/link, often found in large quantities at the moment of a wishful relapse and closely related to boredom, is often
described as "complacency." This is a deadly sense of being okay
and out of danger, cured, for all practical purposes. If there is no
danger, there is no reason to protect myself, whether by continued
AA, CA, NA, etc., or by therapy. This sort of complacency seems
almost inevitable and particularly "normal." Physically, addiction
is a disease that does not remind you of its continued presence
until after you relapse. Unlike arthritis, for example, (some)

diabetes, angina, amputation, alcoholism does not tweak the body with pain between episodes.

It is like "the silent killer," high blood pressure. And the killer lurks behind the cloak of delusion — "gee, I don't feel sick, how can I be sick?" The name stitched on the cloak is "complacency," and the antidote for complacency is anxiety.

The chemical dependency field generally regards anxiety as a taboo, seldom admitting the role it plays in drinking or abstaining. As the field comes of age, perhaps we will borrow a page from the psychotherapists. They have long used constructive button-pushing to keep their clients working in therapy. AA seems to understand the need for healthy fear, which is one reason for so much emphasis on "drunkalogs" of how bad it got (and will get again, if I drink). "People who don't keep coming back to meetings don't get to hear what happens to people who don't keep coming back to meetings. Working with newcomers also keeps memory (and healthy anxiety) fresh.

To increase understanding of the above section, complete Recovery Exercises #14, #15 and #16 at the end of the chapter.

The Hidden Guilt

Whatever else "one won't hurt" and its variations represent, it is clearly a rationalization and/or justification. Social drinkers who are about to have "just one" have no need to reassure themselves about it. If one part of my mind is forming an alibi, another part has some sense that what I am doing could get someone hurt.

Shame, guilt, anxiety: the voice of reality does sometimes speak in "negatives." But their presence confirms that some part of the relapser knows better, even if it's voice is drowned in sweet assurances. The alcoholic/addict who can understand this fact intellectually is sometimes able to connect emotionally with his or her real feelings. The task then is to strengthen and nurture the connection:

Shame, guilt, and anxiety can save my life if they are truly my own and I know it. I "do it for myself" because I can't stand doing it the old way any more. The Twelve Steps and psychotherapy both offer different but overlapping and complementary ways to face my shame and guilt, to turn them into motivation and humility instead of running away.

External Links: Living Problems

So far, we have talked about what goes on inside the skin of the abstainer who says, "one won't hurt." What about living problems? Where do they fit in the chain?

Joan Doe has been sober eighteen months. She successfully completed residential treatment and has become an active AA member. Yes, she has problems. Yes, she has holes in her program of recovery. Who doesn't? But today, she has been thinking "one drink won't hurt anything," for the first time in over a year. She has not yet acted on it and reports it in aftercare. One of the most practical questions we can help her ask herself is, "why is this happening now?"

We start by working with the urge itself. When did it start? How intense is it? How often does she think about it? What are the specific thoughts and feelings she experiences about having "just one"? What tools has she tried, if any, and how are they working? Are there any tools she is specifically avoiding? It may be that she was triggered by a "cue," such as the sight of her favorite drink. Dealing with that kind of craving is a specialty in itself, one that is beyond the scope of this particular book or chapter. Here, the cognitive behavioral therapists and researchers seem to be making the biggest contributions.

For the sake of this example, we expand from the urge itself, directly into whatever feelings have appeared. If she is aware of anything bothering her, we look at the problem and any feelings that seem overwhelming. With her help, we look carefully for any point at which she is stuck. If she has to accept something, we see if we can get her working toward that goal. If there is something she can change, we look at what is stopping her and try to help get her unstuck.

But how do we know if we are dealing with an urge that was triggered by a problem? We can be reasonably certain if talking about the apparent problem/trigger reduces the urge. There would seem to be no reason a biochemical craving would fade in response to talking about an unrelated living problem. Surprise, expressed by the client — "I didn't know how much this was bugging me!" — with relief visible in the face — *that* is a pretty good clue that we are in the right ball park. What if we can find no trigger problem? We may look some more, using common tools of experiential therapy. What if we still can't find a trigger? We focus on whatever tools, physical and mental may help protect our alcoholic/addict from the urge. And we engage the client in continuing to look on his/her own — by noting when urges appear, journaling, bringing in current fantasies, dreams, etc.

The initial trigger may have been a living problem that was readily identified. And it may also be that physiological process contributed to the intensity of the person's craving reaction. Helpers do not have to think in all-or-nothing terms. Anti-craving drugs and attention to physiological influences (diet, vitamins, exercise, etc.) often help, *regardless* of the "trigger." Spiritual and psychological helpers are better equipped to tackle a real living problem than a metabolic shift. Yet even dealing with such a shift requires helper and person to develop self-awareness, and the active sort of responsibility described in the chapter on "Ownership."

If the ownership link is missing, I will not proactively deal with my ups and downs, no matter if they be emotional or biochemical. If I am actively self-aware, I will work with my problem until I find what works, whether it is a new therapist or a new vitamin.

As a clinician looking for emotional triggers in the real world of the client who says "One won't hurt," the author is seldom frustrated, especially if immediate cues are first ruled out or in. The difficulty is to get the client sharing the urge *before* drinking/drugging.

Even when a specific living problem emerges from the exploration of an urge to drink, we may not be finished. What made this problem so intolerable that (1) the person was unable to let themselves be aware of it, and (2) the only option the person's psyche came up with on its own was the old knee-jerk "solution?" Stress overload and organically impaired coping will account for some of this. But the longer a person has been sober, the more necessary and possible it will be to locate the source of overwhelming pain, the distress and anxiety that blocked out almost everything recovery has taught. The current living problem has often poured salt in old wounds, stirring up old rage, grief, and fear. This should hardly come as a surprise, given the fact that fifty percent of our clients are from alcoholic families. Why wouldn't they have emotional hang-ups? Again, biochemistry may be a necessary condition for developing some addictions, but the psychology of accepting the disease and of resolving old wounds seems critical in preventing relapse. The longer the person is sober, the more this is true.

Is the abstinent alcoholic/addict who is beginning to think, "One won't hurt," aware of boredom, complacency, euphoria, or shame/guilt? Sometimes:

> *Do I connect the emotional state with my desire to drink? Less often. Do I connect the emotional state with triggering events and blocked emotions in my current life? Even less often. Am I actively looking for alternative ways to deal with the triggering events and my upset about them? Almost never. How about working from the salt of the triggering event to the wounds of prior experience, even childhood? Reader's guess.*

☞   Whose job is it to help me make these practical connections?
The helper's.

Is the job getting done? Not as often as it might!

Why?

Why, indeed?

To increase understanding of the above section, complete Recovery Exercise #17 at the end of the chapter.

Psychological Core Links

The following article was published in *Alcohol, Health and Research World* in 1984 [12]. It connects the empirical observation of adult alcoholics saying "One won't hurt" with a readily observable form of childhood behavior. As our ability to work with the "inner child" grows, the article seems even more relevant today:

Article: In his classic study, *The Ego Factor in Surrender in Alcoholism*, psychiatrist Harry Tiebout [13], developed a simple model of alcoholism and recovery. It was based on years of experience with treatment failures followed by witnessing some of the very first AA "conversions." In Tiebout's view, buried alive in the drinker's unconscious dwells an infant, one who still feels entitled to all the privileges of infancy, starting with a demand feeding schedule. This unconscious and childlike view of the world is Tiebout's account of what the Big Book calls "self-will run riot." "I want what I want when I want it!" is precisely the attitude of an infant. Tiebout invoked Freud's charming phrase, "his majesty the baby," to emphasize the attitude of demand and entitlement.

Many people working in the field of addiction do not respect the reality of the unconscious mind. They are neither trained nor interested in methods to look inside. Some professionals seem to join AA in seeing an inert substance, alcohol, as literally "cunning, powerful, and baffling." The victim's mind, passively and innocently, suffers from all this chemical chicanery. In addition, addiction treatment and research people deal mostly with adults. We see infants in our own homes and in public, if at all.

One such public place this writer observed "his majesty" in action was a Sierra Club hike for families in Thousand Oaks, California. This only happened once and there was no control group.

A small boy, about three years old, walks the trail on Wildwood Mesa, one hand in his father's and the other clutching a small treat.

"Daddy, can I eat it now?"

"No, son, it will make you thirsty."

"No-o-o it wo-on't." The "o" sounds are prolonged with seductive three-year-old conviction. "I just want one piece."

"You better put it in your pocket, son. It may melt in your hand."

"No-o-o, it wo-on't."

Again, son is more convincing than father.

Describe this scene to a group of sober alcoholics and they get the point immediately. Alcoholism is a disease of much stereotyped thinking and behavior. And the most common and deadly of all the inner dialogues typical of so many alcoholics often goes something like this:

"A drink would sure be nice right now."

"You'll just get in trouble."

"No, I won't."

"You better not. You know what always happens."

"Oh, no. I'm just going to have one drink this time."

The drink is then taken and the dim voice of reality is drowned completely. What we in the field hear and see over and over again is the desire for the "treat" and the denial of the inevitable consequences. This sadly continues long after the adult has been educated by our purely medical disease theories. It is simply unbelievable to a person in this state of mind that he or she could want something so badly and not be able to have it. Why? Because I want it, goes the infantile logic.

No one is going to make a case at this late date that psychoanalysis is the treatment of choice for addictions. Tiebout's point was that he failed as an analyst until he studied and understood the AA conversion experience. He then returned to treating patients, but with a different clinical approach. His interventions now had two functions — to stop the infantile "Ego" and to help it accept "messages from reality."

Tiebout let go of much of his psychoanalytic technique, without giving up the attempt to understand and tame the awesome power of the unconscious. Yes, Virginia, he still worked with dreams and defenses. Unlike many burned-out therapists and "if-you-can't-count-it-it-doesn't-exist" researchers, Tiebout did not throw the baby out with the bath water.

To increase understanding of the above section, complete Recovery Exercise #18 at the end of the chapter.

Instant Regression and the "Adult Child" Connection

Some characteristics of "regression" are:
- Belief in wish over facts.
- Absence of past experience or thinking through of consequences based on such experience.
- Sometimes, euphoria or excitement.
- Preference for a fantasy world, a state of omnipotent imagination.
- Commonly, avoidance and suppression of problems that seem too overwhelming to be dealt with any other way and feeling too small to cope.
- Impulsiveness.
- Following the Pleasure Principle, rather than the Reality Principle.
- Putting hand to mouth.
- Difficulty putting off gratification or relief.

This list often fits our alcoholic/addict who says "one won't hurt" and proceeds to drink. It also fits the age-appropriate behavior of three-year-olds. (Of theoretical interest, it also overlaps considerably with the reactions of the "old brain.") In work with adult children of alcoholics, we routinely recognize "instant regression." When upset, some alcoholic/addicts will start suddenly wishing for "a drink," even right in therapy sessions. Here-and-now exploration of the sudden wish often reveals feelings of childlike helplessness. *Feeling* like a child in an adult body and an adult world, desiring to escape to a different world in which alcohol "makes me feel like superman or King Kong." This is a direct quote from more than one person, whether exploring a sudden wish triggered by therapy, reliving a moment of relapse, or doing the Dr. Jekyll and Mr. Hyde exercise.

The author does not claim to know precisely where physiology fits in all this. But that won't spare the reader from further speculation on the subject in later chapters, especially the last one. The importance of physical pleasure centers in addiction and the observable dominance of the Pleasure Principle over behavior can hardly be coincidence. Yet nothing that comes out of the research laboratory will delete this *experience,* that of feeling like a child, which many alcoholic/addicts have at the moment of relapse. This reaction link is real. It seems very clear that this particular sort of relapse is based on sober regression to a childlike state of experiencing and deciding. The question becomes how to block this from happening and/or to cope when it does. It seems we are going to have to help grown people to recognize and to handle their childlike states. Paradoxically, this generally requires active eliciting of the "child," overcoming the shame of having such a "child within." If the person takes care of this child in direct and healthy ways, he or she will be far less controlled by "it." If the person neglects the inner child, this self-abandonment will be paid for dearly. The wish for relief and omnipotence will grow as adult ego shrinks. Finally, all that will be seen or heard is the innocent, childlike whisper, "One drink won't hurt anything. Yeah. This time will be different!"

Of course, *some* people's inner child says those naughty words: "F--- it." We'll look at those in the next chapter. First, we will take one last look at the wishful relapse, as it develops over time.

Links Over Time: The Process of the Wishful Relapse

So far we have focused on links in the reaction of a sober addict/ alcoholic at the moment he or she says "One won't hurt." We have hopefully shed some light on the thinking itself, on defenses, physiology, experience, desire, feelings, unconscious and childhood links. But if relapse is also a "process," that means that something changes over time, sequentially and/or progressively. The practical question becomes "what changes?" And how do we help the relapser see his or her own change, much less prevent it from happening again?

 Try this exercise with yourself, an individual, or a group:

1. Identify a *temporary* period of abstaining from alcohol, drugs, anything you know isn't good for you. Make sure it is one that ended, a relapse.
2. Draw a straight line across a piece of paper (individuals) and/or on a whiteboard (for a group.)
3. Mark the left-hand end as "Beginning;" "Ending," on the right. Mark a spot somewhere near the center as "Middle."
4. Go back to the period of abstinence you have chosen and picture yourself at the very beginning. Now rate yourself on the following ten-point scale *the way you would have that day*. Notice that the scale measures *strength of belief*. "1" is minimal and "10" is unshakable conviction.

5. *ADDICTION CONVICTION SCALE: I cannot take so much as one drink/drug without losing control.*

6. Enter the rating you gave yourself at the beginning of your abstinence on the "Beginning" of your (individual) line.

7. Now rate yourself at the "Middle" of your temporary period of abstinence and enter it at that point on your line.

8. The last rating is for the day of the relapse *when you first awaken.* In other words, rate yourself *before* you take the first drink/drug/whatever. Enter this number at the "Ending."

9. Did your numbers change?

10. Make a simple freehand graph (on paper for individual, whiteboard for group) as follows: write "10" on the left, with each next smaller number in a column below it, down to "1." To the right of your numbers column, mark three separate parallel columns as "beginning," "middle," and "end."

11. Now comes the fun part. Enter a mark to the right of your numbers (or the other person's, group's) for each of these columns.

Your individual dots will likely follow one of three patterns. When a group does this and graphs their collective answers, the three patterns form a backwards "Z." The typically small number across the top of the "Z" will be people who started with a strong conviction and stayed there. By definition, they could not have said "One won't hurt" — they had to say "F---- it" and their relapse will be dealt with in the next chapter. The typically small number forming the bottom line of the "Z" will be people who started low and stayed *there.* Hopefully, they are back in treatment with more conviction and with more awareness. But a very consistent two-thirds majority will start abstinence with a "strong" (8–10) conviction and be down below 5 by the day of relapse.

This last group, who started high and ended low, have graphed the process of a wishful relapse. They have begun to answer the question, "What changed?" At the very least, belief in loss of control with one drink/drug appears to have changed markedly. Another word for this link is "acceptance (of the addiction.)" A similar scale for memory (of suffering due to use) would show a similar plunge. So what do we have to do to prevent this from happening again? Accept the addiction, preserve the acceptance, and *not forget the suffering*! Most groups can readily list the Twelve Step and other tools designed to preserve acceptance and memory. This is a good way to conclude the exercise, emphasizing the connection between their personal experience and the tools designed to protect them from a repeat.

What the "Addiction Conviction Scale" adds to the present text is a way of tracking "links" over time. It is part of a "Learning From Relapse" questionnaire that tracks five links over time. This questionnaire, provided at the end of the chapter on the "Relapse Post-Mortem," also tracks belief in "willpower." That belief also deteriorates over time, but it does not so consistently start high.

At its best, this scale gives the wishful relapser a visual image of what changed during the process of their relapse. It spells out, in black-and-white and in terms of a person's own experience, the problem of *preserving* both acceptance and memory of suffering, the very reason to stay clean and sober. It seems to be "remotivational."

> *In other words, if I can believe, accept, realize, own my addiction one day, and then lose that over time, I must need something to maintain or nurture belief. AA understood my memory problem from the beginning. To this day, it is the only system of "relapse prevention" which will give me that memory "booster" on a lifelong basis, unlimited by grant or insurance moneys.*

Theoretical note: There seems to be a theoretical value to this exercise, as well. What it graphs is the progressive loss of memory, of judgment, of reality testing. To look over the brink of a two hundred foot cliff and to see only a one-foot drop, would be fatal. An alcoholic/addict thinking of "only one" suffers a comparable impairment of judgment. We have already seen the disconnection from experience, feeling, desire, and pain that so often precedes "One won't hurt." What has the power to *do* that? There is no drug in the brain and yet the "mind" is changing. The "wish" for the drug in the drug-free brain is apparently so powerful it can literally reverse the person's grasp of reality. It can dissociate experience and feeling, pain and judgment, leading to devastatingly self-destructive decisions.

What draws the alcoholic/addict moth back to the flame of drugs? As mentioned earlier, a "wish" of this magnitude earns the name "craving," even though the victim may experience and report no such thing. Though this author works with "psychosocial" links, it is hard not to see a place for neurochemistry in this process, just as it is hard not to see a role for the unconscious and its defenses.

Subliminal craving.

Increasing over time, invading the healthy mind, perverting and corrupting its functions.

The *process* of the wishful relapse in the bio-psycho-social disease of addiction.

To increase understanding of the above section, complete Recovery Exercise #19 at the end of the chapter.

References

[1] DuWors, G. "One Won't Hurt, Anatomy of a Common Alcoholic Relapse." Alcohol, Health, and Research World, Winter 1982/3.
[2] Beck, Aaron T., Wright, Fred D., Newman, Cory, F., Liese, Bruce J. *Cognitive Therapy of Substance Abuse,* New York: The Guilford Press, 1993.

[3] Jellinek, E.M. *The Disease Concept of Alcoholism.* New Haven: Hillhouse Press, 1960.

[4] Alcoholics Anonymous. *Alcoholic's Anonymous, The Story of How Many Thousands of Men and Women Have Recovered from Alcoholism,* New York: Alcoholics Anonymous World Services, Inc., 1955.

[5] Thomas W. I. *The Unadjusted Girl.* New York: Harper and Row, 1967.

[6] Diagnostic and Statistic Manual of the American Psychiatric Association. 1995.

[7] Anonymous. *'Pass It On' (The Story of Bill Wilson and how the A.A. message reached the world).* New York, N.Y.: Alcoholics Anonymous World Services, Inc., 1984.

[8] Stalcup, Alex. "Contemporary Approaches to Treatment for Substance Abuse" Workshop Seattle, WA, 1996.

[9] Beck, et al, as above.

[10] Kim, Eleanor, Marlatt, G. Alan, and Dimeff, Linda A. "The Road to Relapse," in Professional Counselor, June, 1996.

[11] Anonymous. *Living Sober.* New York: Alcoholics Anonymous World Services, 1975.

[12] DuWors G. "His Majesty The Baby." Alcohol, Health and Research World, Winter, 1984.

[13] Tiebout, Harry. "The Ego Factors In Surrender In Alcoholism." Quarterly Journal of Studies on Alcohol, Volume 15, pp. 610-621, 1954.

Recovery Exercises

1. Review the list of different words for the wishful relapse at the start of the chapter. Check each you have experienced and write the number of times (rough estimate OK). Write, share, discuss how you feel doing this, as well as what you see about your disease.

2. Read the first three chapters of the AA Big Book. Underline anything you find about relapse thinking, examples as well as explanations. How would working Twelve Steps correct this kind of thinking?

3. How many times, would you estimate, have you been told that the key to recovery is not taking the first drink/drug? If you have had at least one wishful relapse, write, share, discuss what it means to you that you have not been able to believe this.

4. Make a list of the 3 (5, 10, more) most painful experiences in your life, since you started drinking and/or drugging. What percentage of that total pain would never have happened if you had never had a drink or drug? Write, discuss, share. You might try giving each painful experience a score from 1 to 10, with "10" being the most painful. Add up the points for all of the experiences you list and then subtract any points that would not have occurred if there were no drugs or alcohol on planet Earth.

5. Borrow a copy of the Diagnostic and Statistical Manual, or at least the relevant xeroxed (with any required permission) pages, and read the criteria for "dependence" on your drug(s) of choice. How many fit you? Document your specific symptoms or behavior. Which ones would describe an alcoholic/addict saying "One won't hurt?"

6. Read the "Exhaustion of the Obvious" exercise. What is your reaction to the author putting so much emphasis on taking a drink/drug when there is no chemical yet in the brain. What does this tell you about your understanding/acceptance of your disease? Write, share, discuss.

7. When did you first think of yourself as an alcoholic or addict? How many times have you said "One won't hurt" or its

variations since then? What does this tell you about your level of acceptance or understanding of your disease? Write, share, discuss. Did you have any sort of emotional reaction to the section, "Denial of Denial?" If so, write it down, as well as what you think it means. Be sure to share and discuss.

8. Look again at the section, "Desire, a Missing Link." In your experience, if you have said "One won't hurt," is it true that you wanted more than "just one?" How do you know? Write and discuss your answers and any emotional reaction to reading the section.

9. If you have said "One won't hurt" and relapsed, sit down and objectively look at one to five actual instances. For each one, try to gently answer whether you realized — whether these things were real to you — *at the time:*
   - how much alcohol/drugs really do hurt you, including past memories
   - how much you wanted to drink, the actual desire
   - how upset you were about any living problems at the time
   - the reality of being an alcoholic and/or addict
   Write, share and discuss.

10. Think of how badly you did not want to be an alcoholic or addict. Make as long a list as you can of what you wanted to be instead. Write, share discuss. For each item, describe how you might or might not attain that if you never have another drink or drug.

11. List 3 (5, 10, more) things you drank or drugged over. For each, what were your feelings at the time. Which feelings will you have to work with the hardest, if you are not to relapse again?

12. Write down 3 (5, 10, more) fantasies you had while drinking or drugging, especially any recurring ones. What does each tell you about what you seem to want? What might you do to attain these things in reality, or to accept that they may not be attainable? Write, share, discuss.

13. Have you ever relapsed when things were going very well and/or you felt very "good?" If so, how many times? If even once, reread the section on "Euphoria." Which explanation or description fits your kind of euphoria the best? What will you do to cope with it and not relapse, should it return?

14. Have you ever relapsed when bored? If so, pick one (3, 5, 10) instance(s) and try to identify if you were "shut down" about something and, if so, what. How aware were you of this each time? If you were or had been aware, what might you have done instead of drinking/drugging?

15. List three (5, 10, etc.) experiences that would make you nervous or uncomfortable to share in a Twelve-Step meeting and/or in treatment. If you get bored in recovery, share the first one. If you are still bored, or become bored again, share the second.

16. If you grew bored in recovery and eventually relapsed after working the Steps, having a sponsor, etc., list three areas in which you needed to improve *at the time* and what you might have done to work on them. What risks and/or discomfort were you avoiding in "boredom?" Hint: it is usually relation-ships, or relationships, or relationships. Then again, it could have been relationships!

17. If you have had one (3, 5, 10) wishful relapses, pick at least one and examine your living problems at the time. Were you

dealing with them? If not, did they contribute to your saying "One won't hurt" when you did? What is your plan for learning to deal with what is bothering you? Write, share, discuss.

18. If you have had a wishful relapse, put yourself back to the moment of "deciding" to pick up the first drink? How old did you feel emotionally at that moment? How many of the symptoms for "instant regression" were you experiencing? How will you deal with feeling like a child in an adult body when this reaction occurs again? Write, share, discuss.

19. If you have not already done so, do the "Addiction Conviction Scale" for your most recent period of temporary abstinence. If your "conviction" dropped from "8" or above to "7" or below, make a list of the things you were doing during the month before relapse to preserve your memory/acceptance. Then make a list of tools you were not using that might have kept your memory fresh and strong. From that list, pick the ones you will do this time and/or the ones you find hardest. Ask for help with the ones you feel are hardest for you.

4

The Links of the White-Knuckle Relapse [1] (F--- it)

From Questions to Observations and Back

In the previous chapter we explored reaction links connected to saying "one won't hurt" with the first drink/drug of physical relapse. We called this reaction the "wishful relapse."

In the present chapter, we look at common links in the moment of relapse signaled by the words "F--- it." We start by exploring the point of view of the person saying them. We will focus for now on the experience, on issues that "F--- it" seems to carry with it, less on specific tools. "What does it mean?" and other questions seek to understand rather than to treat or prevent the "F--- it" relapse — that job is addressed in later chapters. However, the questions raised are not rhetorical. They are themselves "interventions", designed to chip away at denial and encourage self-acceptance.

Questions must be asked in context — the ideal question builds from what the person already knows. The idea is to help those who suffer relapse take a small, tangible look beyond what they have so far faced. It is hoped that the discussions here may aid the helper in recognizing the most useful question for any given client. If you are reading for your own recovery, "take what you can use and leave the rest." If anything you find triggers a reaction, be sure to write and share about it.

Imagine a cardiac patient clutching his or her chest in the pain of another heart attack and saying, "Oh, I'll just have a little one this time." However, the moment a seemingly stable cardiac patient goes back to steak and potatoes, you may be sure we would routinely hear "F--- it" and/or "One won't hurt." Likewise, when a cancer patient goes back to smoking or when a diabetic starts eating sugar again. And for the same reason — the person is aware, at some level, of needing to justify the behavior, or to dispense with justification altogether.

I know, however dimly, that I am doing something unwise, if not just plain wrong. I am rebuffing a part of myself that is trying to say, "Stop!" But this knowledge is buried too deeply to have a deciding voice in my behavior. "F--- it" is the sound of the very last shovel of mental dirt to cover it up.

The helper's job is to help alcoholics/addicts dig up their personal truth, to help them rediscover their own conscience and their own wisdom. The relapse victim's job is to use the mental "shovel" to dig things up rather than tamp them down. One place to start is by looking at the shovel itself and whatever is stuck to it. But when we examine those two words, "F--- it," with this in mind, we confront an immediate puzzle. Taken literally, the words are virtually meaningless. The person is not about to have sex, and "it" appears to be a pronoun without an antecedent.

Here I am about to do the single most meaningful negative thing I can do about my addiction: take the first drink/drug of relapse. Yet my mind is saying something utterly meaningless. What is wrong with this picture?

Apparently, the only way to make sense out of "F--- it" is to look at the context. This will inevitably include both the inner experience of the speaker and the person's environment.

☞   So we ask alcoholics/addicts who have said "F--- it" and relapsed how *they* would translate their own words. "Right as you were saying that and reaching for your first drink/drug, what did you actually mean?"

The same answers emerge from many different groups and individuals. The translations are related and overlapping, but we can look at them, one by one. Each may be isolated and observed as a link in the chain that leads to "F--- it." Sometimes the links occur together; sometimes, separately. Generally, we will work with whichever one a person identifies with the most.

"I Quit"

"I quit" comes up consistently as one of the translation of "F--- it." But if I "quit," that means I was trying to accomplish something, to get somewhere. I had to have a goal!

To have a goal means working to get something you do not yet have. To live with your goal while you pursue it is to live with the perpetual frustration of not yet having what you want. In this way, a long-term goal can set up perpetual frustration! A person who cannot tolerate that frustration is going to have to give up the goal or go nuts. And the thought at the moment of giving up is likely to be "F--- it."

If the person is alcoholic and fortunate, they eventually make it to treatment and/or AA. Once there, one of the first things they learn is how to do short-term footwork for a long-term goal, "one day at a time." Physical abstinence is only the first such goal, but it teaches the tools and attitude for all that follow in recovery. The Twelve Steps themselves further help the person in recovery tolerate the perpetual frustration of not being at some future destination.

> *I mean, if the "New Employer" I signed on with in Step Three wanted me to be the CEO, I would be. So what does this same "Principal" want His "agent" to do today?*

It is true by definition that the capacity for living with an unfulfilled goal — deferred gratification — is a function of emotional maturity. Yes, that apparently low level of "maturity" in many addicts/alcoholics may be a mere label for behavioral reactions that are set up by a genetic "temperament." This would be most clearly the case in those addicts/alcoholics with Attention Deficit Disorder. Yet many other drinkers report they are the kind of people who can't stop working on a job until it is finished. This apparent "compulsivity" may be nothing more than the drive of a childlike mentality. One that must close the gap between intention and result before it can sit still again. Such people cannot afford to take on long-term goals.

However, many alcoholics/addicts have fulfilled long-term goals and established successful careers. They apparently tolerated years of preparation and training. AA was founded by a physician and a stockbroker — their first successful recruit was an attorney! But many such alcoholics had to have chemical relief during the long grind before the American dream came true. And by the time it does come true, middle stage alcoholism may accompany middle class success. The prop that made the long struggle tolerable may knock itself out from under the person who finally "made it." In one sort of alcoholic the "child" side of the personality appears to dominate from the beginning, possibly with a large boost from heredity. In the second sort, the one who appears to defer gratification, the immature elements seem to be blocked out but bottle-fed. Strategies and tools may vary somewhat for these two kinds of alcoholic. But the necessity to face and live with frustration, without saying "F--- it," is the same for both.

☞   Many people have never systematically looked at their "F--- it" relapses as "quitting," even the ones who volunteer "I quit" as their personal translation! They have never even asked themselves what the specific frustrations were.

"What was I quitting? What made me think it was hopeless?
And, if it was, what made that so intolerable I had to drink/drug?"

Nor have they asked,

"How often have I done this? What are the examples? And when have I not given up — what are my strong areas and where do I seem vulnerable?"

They were not in tune with the actual feelings involved. And no one ever told them there might be such a thing as giving up gracefully.

Many drinkers have to get drunk in order to get fired from a job they want to quit, or to get divorced from a spouse they cannot stand. Alcoholics Anonymous may help people to accept being "powerless," to learn to "turn it over," and to "accept what I cannot change." But the practical and emotional connection from these general principles to actual upsets and choices does not seem to happen automatically. There will always be a place for counseling, including sponsorship, that ties things down to the concrete and specific. Accept what? Change what? Turn over what, exactly? Even then, the question remains wide open:

How does the decision of "quitting" lead so directly to drinking? What is there about the frustration of my attempt to untie my hopelessly knotted shoelace? What makes getting intoxicated seem like such a "natural" solution? Indeed, the only one?

The author had to probe for the connection between quitting and drinking many times to develop the sort of understanding that might lead to practical help. In the beginning he had to accept the defensiveness triggered by these kinds of questions. And this led to yet another question: what nerve was hit by naively asking why giving up on some goal or desire seemed to call for drinking?

The answer to this last question that makes the most sense seems simple enough — a good question threatens denial. As developed further in the chapter on the subject, denial functions by "not thinking about it." Almost all discursive problem-solving proceeds by following our questions.

What is that noise in my engine? I lift the hood. Where is it coming from? Ah, a fan belt. Is it loose, severed? How bad is it? What will it take to fix it? Do I need outside help? Where can I get it?

Each question leads to the next if the problem is ever to be "solved." Denial is the mental posture of blocking all questions about whatever is being denied.

"You don't understand. You're not an alcoholic," for one example, or "You forgot where you came from," for another, are client responses that discount and block an external question. It happens to be a question that briefly focuses my attention on exactly what I don't want to think about. The same person blocks internal questions with "I don't want to be bothered," or "I just won't/don't think about it."

The process of staying with these questions needs to combine two precious qualities: the persistence of a Socrates and the attentiveness of a Carl Rogers [2]. A person's life is at stake.

I will die if I do not smash the knee-jerk connection between "F--- it" and quitting-by-drinking. After all, if I cannot see a target, how can I ever hit it?

As we might expect, the connection lies in heartfelt feelings and attitudes. Feelings like anger and resentment — "F--- it" is an angry quitting, far from the "surrender" of AA. Another translation of the two words might well be "I will **not** accept" whatever "it" I may be saying "F--- it" about. The Big Book seems too politely written to use the words "F--- it." But it minces no words about "resentment," ...which .... "destroys more alcoholics than anything else" (p. 64). Even with resentment, there are usually other links in the thought/feeling chain, feelings like failure and inadequacy, impotence and weakness. Fear, pain — the sting of today's broken shoelace so often pours salt into yesterday's unhealed wound: rejection by a parent, abuse, neglect, etc. Even if the drinker is acting like a spoiled child who must have its way, who spoiled the infant? And isn't spoiling a child as abusive as neglecting one, since it trains him or her to be unfit for adult life?

Once the emotional cards, specific, concrete, and personal, are out on the table, helper and relapser can both look at them to see how they played into the relapse. This may already begin to reveal how else they might be played. How does alcohol "solve" the feeling of inadequacy - the issue of power and drunken Ego reappear? What does it do for resentment or depression or fear? And how else do human beings deal with these things, especially those who used to say "F--- it" and relapse? Above all, what blocks healthier ways of handling real frustration and makes getting loaded seem like the only alternative? What happened to all the other choices?

The first choice, of course, is to talk to someone else about the pain. What stops many an alcoholic/addict from doing this? In the chapter on "talking and drinking" the importance of talking is spelled out. In the chapters on acceptance, the "taboo" against it will be described. The person who says "F--- it" is caught between the rock of addictive drinking and the hard place of talking about feelings. *One of the first ways to help such a person is to help them talk about how difficult it is to talk about difficult things.*

Frequently, the "I quit" of an "F--- it" relapse takes on an interpersonal flavor. It is really "F--- you!" The relapsing alcoholic/ addict may report a sense of having tried "so hard" to do what he or she "should," or of doing what some/everyone else wants. Empathic and concrete exploration of these feelings brings out a sense of being externally controlled, a lack of choice, feeling like a "puppet" or a "robot." Psychologically the person feels he or she is no longer "my own person." In effect, they have no self. Not only have they lost track of their own part in their experience. The very last thing they will seek in this state is a chance to "open up." What!? And become vulnerable to "support" (which seems like influence and control) of others! The fact that healthy adults face and solve problems by sharing them is not even a distant theory in the person's mind.

What does alcohol do?

It creates an illusion of freedom.

How?

By its specific chemical action on the brain, it knocks out part of the brain that cares about social appearances and rules. It puts the Emily Post in us asleep. Unfortunately, it also knocks out the Good Samaritan and the lifeguard, not to mention the Cassandra. You all remember Cassandra — destined to always tell the truth and never be believed. She was a mythological equivalent of the "Holy Spirit," the voice of truth within each of us.

The experience of alcoholic freedom often feels like relief from "self-consciousness." In fact, this painful and inhibiting condition arises from an excessive consciousness of others, from a real or imagined perception of their judgments. I dance better drunk because the people-pleaser between my ears is now asleep. It can't scan the audience for critical looks, a grin of contempt or pity. What I don't know won't hurt me, at least not until the next day. Then I can say "it wasn't really me. I was drunk," an excuse that should only be allowed once in a lifetime. After that, I know what happens when I drink. If I do drink, I am choosing to be this "not-myself." Of course, if my dancing was a hit and I didn't throw up on anyone, I can glow with my newfound social spontaneity.

Alcohol works.

The darkest side of the "I quit" relapse, exquisitely interpersonal, may reveal my true motivation for sobriety.

☞   *If I abstain because you say I should, that means I can still live with my drinking. You are the one who finds it intolerable. Maybe, I quit drinking to "get you off my back," so you don't divorce me, fire me, or put me in jail. That makes my "sobriety" contingent on my belief you will catch me if I drink, and that you* will *swing the sword you have poised above me. There is also a contract implied: you owe me something for my absti-nence. All it takes for me to drink now is an opportunity to not get caught or a willingness to test you. An angry decision that you have broken our contract will also serve. Getting drunk "at you" is a perfectly logical consequence of depriving myself of alcohol "for you." Naturally, the greater my sense of depriva-tion, the more persistent and outrageous my attempts to pro-voke your breaking of the "contract." However, if you are a smothering codependent, it won't take much. The very fact I have a mind of my own is all the provocation you will need to express your disease. It is then only just that I should, once again, express mine. What a team!*

Wanting to be an autonomous self is healthy. If we can rec-ognize and validate this drive within the alcoholic/addict, we can join in finding a better way to fulfill it. When the relapser says, "F--- it, I gotta be me and alcohol is the only way," we must re-spond "Yes, you gotta be you. But that isn't your true self that comes out of the bottle. In fact, the only way to really be you is to quit drinking and start facing the self you hid from in the bottle."

In his classic treatment film, "Guidelines," Father Joseph Mar-tin [3] graphically pictures the moment alcoholic denial collapses. He calls it "God's greatest gift to the alcoholic" and describes it as "the pain of looking in the mirror of self and wanting to throw up." The problem with people-pleasing is that it looks in the "mir-ror of other" instead. External "shaming" does not work because your shaming me does not permanently disturb my ability to live with myself , to exist inside my own skin. The fact my drinking/ drugging bothers you is embarrassing and inconvenient. However, if you can help me face my *own* shame, that is another story. This would mean helping me to perceive both my out-of-control behav-ior *and* how it effects the people, places, and things I care about.

The chemical dependency field seems to have become increasingly more effective and professional in this effort over the past fifteen to twenty years. Autobiography, intervention, and professionally facilitated peer groups, all go beyond the pioneering "program of attraction" that AA gave to the world. Various therapies try to reach the alcoholic/addict who has not yet suffered enough to be attracted by those who have. Psychodrama and Gestalt Therapy have been used to help the drinker feel that personal wall of denial, as well as what is on the other side. More recently, family systems theory has brought an increasing awareness of the dynamics of shame. The "Adult Children of Alcoholics'" movement that grew out of family therapy has much to offer our understanding of at least fifty percent of alcoholics/addicts. What greater shame and consequent denial than being an alcoholic "ACOA" who swore "it will never happen to me" [4]? The more bitter the pill to swallow, the stronger the gag reflex. In addition, "Remotivational Therapy" [5] appears to take the person as she or he is. Along with "Solution-Focused Brief Therapy"[6] , it avoids triggering shame about not being someone else. Cognitive therapy [7] simply engages the person in dismantling the ideas on which the shame is based.

To increase understanding of the above section, complete Recovery Exercises #1, #2, #3, #4, and #5 at the end of the chapter.

"I've Had it!" (With a Feeling of Snapping)

This translation of "F--- it" seems similar to "I quit." But it implies some sort of "straw" breaking some sort of inner "camel's back."

Something has built up to a critical point of overload. To put it visually, in the beginning of my relapse process, "it" was about waist level. At the mid-point, perhaps, "it" was chest high. But the day I said "F--- it," with that feeling of snapping, "it" was apparently above my nostrils and I couldn't breathe. So what was "it"?

Most groups of alcoholic/addicts are able to come up with various names for the practical answer here, "emotional pressure." They recognize their own words as synonyms for this phrase, and this enables us to look at an utterly practical question. What can I do to reduce my emotional pressure before it builds to the snapping point? And most groups are able to come up with the practical solution, some form of venting, verbalization, "getting it out." The author's clinical term for this highly effective relapse prevention tool is "sharing." What many "I've-had-it" relapsers have never thought through is the mortal necessity for sharing their own feelings to prevent their next relapse. And most have never addressed the barriers that have so powerfully blocked their ability to share, to reach for human help instead of chemical relief. Such blocks include everything from the John Wayne syndrome to parental betrayal. Nowhere is the potential for the professional clinician to help the addict/alcoholic prevent relapse greater than here.

"What's the Use!"

Another translation relapsing alcoholic/addicts give for the true meaning of "F--- it," is "what's the use?" The feeling is one of futility — the sense that their actions and efforts make no difference to the outcome. No wonder "I quit!" But this translation can lead the helper to ask a slightly different set of questions. For instance, what was the real, concrete difference your actions and efforts sought to produce? What has happened to tell you your efforts have been and always will be futile? What is your view of reality that says you could or should have been able to make this difference happen? And if you truly realize that nothing can be done, what stops you from simply accepting this fact of life and moving on? What is there about this experience of ineffectiveness, of not controlling these particular results, that calls for drinking alcohol? What will alcohol/drugs do for you now?

Futility and Serenity: As we explore the meanings of "F--- it," guided by the above questions, we may encounter an enlightening contradiction. "F--- it" is also humorously described as "the short form" of the Serenity Prayer! ("God, grant me the serenity to accept the things I cannot change, etc.") This is one of the most cherished and effective of all the Twelve Step tools. Apparently, one person may say "F--- it" and relapse, while another person, with the very same disease, says "F--- it" and *relaxes*. What on earth is the difference!?

The words are the same.

The behavior is different.

So apparently are the attitudes and other links of feeling and thought. The "F--- it" of the person who deals with frustration without chemical relief translates as:

> *"What's the use of beating my head against a stone wall? I have better things to do and I'm going to do them. If I need to do some footwork to take care of my feelings, I accept responsibility for doing that."*

The effective meaning of the relapsed person's "F--- it" seems to be:

> *"What's the use of beating my head against a stone wall? My inability to soften it with my head is intolerable. The stone wall has no right to exist or I have no right to fail in my efforts to soften it with my skull. The only thing that makes sense is to drink. At least, I can make my poor, bruised head feel better." A further elaboration might read, "And any disastrous consequences of my drinking are the responsibility of the wall. What I do makes no difference anyway. So how can I be held responsible (or asked to even care?)."*

Many things we try really *are* futile — to say "F--- it" and accept the facts of life seems healthy. But if we have truly accepted "defeat," our "surrender" does not call for drinking, or any

other pleasure, escape, or compensation. Why? Because the very
☞ definition of acceptance is to be at peace about something that
once troubled us. Whatever else it means to be at peace, the experience is recognizable by a lack of any sense of being owed
anything. And the state of peace includes no impulse to "fix" the
way it feels to be in it — being at peace is good enough!

This seems like a good time to introduce a vital principle of
living.

☞   *DuWors' Law*: *There is no situation so bad that I cannot make
it worse by the way I handle it.*

This left-handed, tongue-in-cheek aphorism is actually a restatement of the Serenity Prayer. It is not something you want to
say to someone (including yourself) who is still beating him/herself up. What it does do is focus an inescapable responsibility on
all of us, even when we are truly victims, even while acknowledging our lack of control. Apart from the irony that tends to make it
memorable, the aphorism focuses my attention on me, on my part
of the problem. It implies realistic choice and action, making it
neither hopeless nor helpless.

There is a very concrete way to work with this principle. Make
☞ a list of what was "bad" about a situation. Then look at what you
did or might do to make it better and/or worse. The principle can
also be used sympathetically to engage someone in crisis counseling: "You really seem to be getting screwed and have every reason
to be upset. One of our jobs is to make sure you don't do anything
to make it worse — the last thing you need is to be screwing
yourself. Any ideas?"

Futility and responsibility: Exploration of futility also brings
us to a recognition of the connection between hope and responsibility. Hope is the spiritual opposite of futility. Let us say the doctors carve open my chest, take a peek at my tumors, and zip me
up: "Sorry, three months at most," they tell me. They are not going

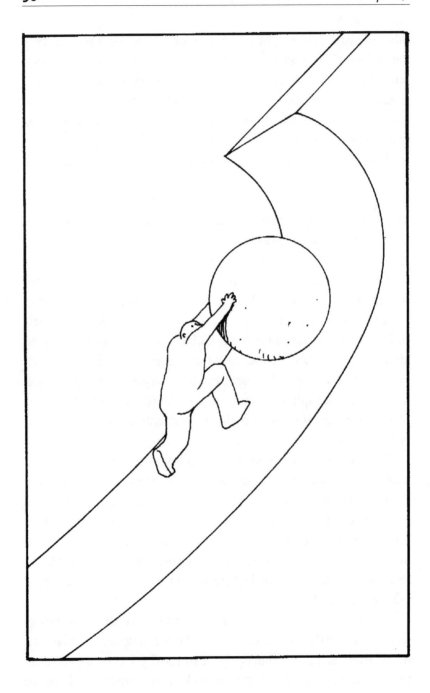

to harass me to quit smoking. What is the use? As a lung cancer victim, I am a hopeless case. (This most emphatically does *not* mean that I am hopeless as a human being.) But if the doctors find only minor, early stage emphysema, it's a whole different story. They and my wife and kids and friends and boss are going to demand or plead that I quit smoking. They will be angry and disappointed if I do not, because they know I hold my health in my hands. The responsibility is physically mine and no one else's. *Because there is hope.*

Alcoholics Anonymous is the bane of the "hopeless" alcoholic. By sharing "strength, hope, and fellowship," AA has proven over and over that there is a choice, there is a way to recover. No wonder a few meetings can spoil a drinker's drinking for life.

> *Oh, I may well continue to drink/drug. The problem seems to be that each of us wants to assume we are doing the best we can. How can I do that with the living proof of so many ex-drinkers who are doing so much better than I? The two things that may still temporarily work are my old friends, alcohol and denial. But the worm of hope has planted the seeds of guilt. What a strange and wonderful butterfly this mating can make!*

☞   The key to understanding a particular "F--- it" relapse, then, is to open up the stereotyped, meaningless words. For the person to realize and start dealing with their own unique meanings and feelings. Then we can connect to the tools of therapy and recovery. One of the biggest obstacles to this exploration is the word "just."

> *I "just" wanted to drink. That's all.*
> *Or, I "just" couldn't take it. That's all.*

☞   The effective meaning of "just" in a sentence is: "all that follows in this sentence is so insignificant there is no reason to think about it. Only a fool would question it further, as if there were something more to it."

The word "just" plants a sign in front of the alcoholic wall which reads:

"Keep out. This wall is very small and there is nothing of interest behind it. Keep out."

When an outsider tries to get past the word "just" the wall mysteriously seems to grow larger and grow more menacing.

Is that boiling oil up there?

Patience, persistence, a willingness to understand the shame that is the foundation, brick and mortar of the wall — these are the things that are needed to understand and to help. We can take small, intellectual steps at first. Many people will respond to gentle explanation of what "just" implies. Group members can help each other to see there is more going on than "just" drinking/drugging, having lived it once or twice themselves. We can ask no question that has not already haunted the person a thousand times from within. That is the precise nerve we irritate with the probe of our external questions. The ghost of felt truth languishes inside the person somewhere. Even in the most defiant and antagonistic alcoholic, this moral ghost is dying to come back through that wall, back to life. The helper's job, whatever hat we are wearing, is to reach through and lend an invisible hand.

Perfectionism and Futility (The Koufax Principle): No discussion of futility can be complete without addressing its number one source: perfectionism. We are talking about the attempt to be what I am not, to do what cannot be done. This willful struggle can have only one unvarying outcome, falling short.

But "perfectionism" is just a label. What specific idea of being perfect hypnotizes the relapse victim? The relapser is not going to exorcise his or her devil without looking it in the eye. No more than a surgeon can take out tonsils with a blindfold on. The label "perfectionism" may be a crucial section in the addictive wall, one that sensitive treatment hopes to turn into a gate. But we may have to take a closer look at some of the stones, before we can loosen them.

> *Do I wish to be the perfect son, daughter, Catholic, or disc jockey, etc.? What is my personal idea of perfection as son or daughter? Do I even know what standard I am killing myself to live up to? And what makes this seem to be a matter of life and death? So much that falling short seems to make my life no longer worth living? What do I think is so wrong with the real me that is, admittedly, so far from perfect? Whom do I seek to impress? And what do I think will happen if I succeed? What is my personal carrot and what is my personal stick?*

The author found an intriguing and revealing example of "recovery" from perfectionism, far from the halls and offices of chemical dependency treatment. Hopefully, it may still teach us all something.

Baseball legend Sandy Koufax [8] told this story to the *Los Angeles Times*, long after his great baseball pitching career was over. He described how, early in his career, he almost failed to make it in the big leagues. And he emphasized that the changes he had to make before he could succeed were mental, not physical. It seems he was trying to never get hit by the best hitters in the world of baseball. Not even once.

In order to literally be perfect, he tried never to throw the ball where it could be hit by anybody. Unfortunately, this made him give up too many walks. One day, the young Koufax realized he must throw the ball in the strike zone. He must pitch to locations where a good hitter, on a good day, might hit it.

When Sandy tried this approach, a terrible thing happened. The opposition started hitting him — two, three, sometimes five or six times a game. In his whole career, he only pitched four no-hitters. This, from a young man who started out wanting to throw a no-hitter on every pitch, to every batter in every game, against the best players in the world!

What happened? Koufax lowered his standards and raised his

performance. [9]. He gave up the absurd struggle for a specific and absolute perfection. He gave himself a chance to find out how good his real "stuff" was. The Grand Canyon separates "doing your best" from "perfection." If we try for perfection, we try too hard. We fall into the abyss between will and body, and do far less than our best. If we do only "our best," we may find out that we are not Sandy Koufax. We may even have to take up a new line of work based on our real talents. But an uncontrolled perfectionism will always produce less than our best. We try so hard and don't even do what we could have done. What, indeed, is the use?

This illustration does not have to answer the question of what seemed to make it a matter of life and death for Koufax to never get hit. The stakes for winning and losing in professional baseball are given. He simply faced the specific fact that what he was trying to do was impossible. He "realized" it, in the most literal sense of the word. The reality of what he was doing became more "real" to him and *it changed his reaction.* After much frustration, struggle and futility, he had a classic "aha" experience. There was now a different "link" between his ears when he went out on the mound. He could not *not* give up the effort to do something which now seemed so absurd, and giving up the effort to be perfect corrected the problem. It is not always so simple for someone who has a perfectionism based on a "need." Some alcoholics/addicts "need" to please a long-dead parent about the most trivial of details. Others may struggle vainly to please a particularly demanding and literal concept of "God." Yet the principle seems to be the same:

When perfectionism impairs performance,
☞ *lower the standard to raise the performance.*

To increase understanding of the above section, complete Recovery Exercises #6, #7, #8, #9, and #10 at the end of the chapter.

"Who Cares?"

A fourth common translation our "stinking thinkers" give of "F---it" is, "I don't care." Variations include, "Who cares!" "No one else cares — why should I?" "Who gives a ---!"

- *I don't care about the consequences, which I implicitly know will be bad.*
- *I know I will lose control and I don't care.*
- *I don't care about my recovery or sobriety, or the effort it takes.*
- *I don't care what anyone thinks of what I am about to do.*
- *I don't care about anything in this life, so I have nothing to lose anyway.*
- *I don't care about me.*
- *I don't care about you.*
- *Least or most of all, I don't care about whatever it is that I am about to drink or drug over!*

This is someone who is quitting, who is giving up and perceives all of their effort as futile. Why would they feel they have any emotional stake in what happens? And if they have no emotional stake, how could they possibly keep going?

But why not just quit and let it go at that? Why drink or drug?

If a person really does not care, there would seem to be no reason to do anything at all?

☞ It is crucial to understanding the white-knuckle (F--- it) relapse to see how someone can "not care" and still feel need for chemical relief. First, we have to understand the protective nature of this "not-caring." Like "One won't hurt," it is the voice of denial.

Just as I denied my addiction, the fact of my life that guaranteed one would hurt, I now deny the very caring without which I would have no pain.

The principle is this: *Emotionally, I can only be hurt if I care.*
I may hear on TV that a ten-year-old is hit by a car and dies. I
feel a twinge of empathy before hitting the remote and resuming
the channel surf.

> *But what if the ten-year-old turns out to be my own child,*
> *or grandchild? I would immediately collapse into grief and so*
> *would almost anyone reading this book. Slowly, over a period*
> *of more than a year, I might regain my balance as I shed my*
> *tears. I would rail at God and threaten to withdraw the vote of*
> *my belief, to put a stop on all my tithing checks. Calmness and*
> *energy may eventually return, if I let them. But there would*
> *always be a hole where the child used to be. A not-quite-healed*
> *wound that would flare up at Christmas, birthdays.*

We all know this is what would happen, if it were a child we
cared about.

But we may not have appreciated the single necessary condition
without which this devastating pain would never be born: *Caring*

> *If I don't care about the child, I continue channel surfing*
> *and get on with my day. Oh well, one less child to support, or*
> *to support me.*

The alcoholic who says "F--- it" and means "I don't care,"
knows intuitively that caring is causing the pain. Solution? Eradi-
cate your caring. How?

My old friends, denial and alcohol.

"F--- it" (I don't care) denies emotional reality every bit as
much as "One won't hurt" denies the physical reality of addictive
disease.

> *The truth is that I am denying that I care because I care all*
> *too much. So much that the pain of what is happening with*
> *what I care about has become intolerable. So much that de-*
> *nial alone cannot sustain the necessary self-deception that I*

don't care when I do. Chemical help is needed. A chemical that
anesthetizes the cerebral cortex, that puts the part of my brain
that cares what I care about to sleep.

An alcoholic parent bursts into tears at the idea of losing a child due to drinking. Yet the very same person spent the entire three days of the binge on a bar stool saying "F--- it."

When life gets so painful that we can't stand the price of caring anymore, we sail off to a safe island called "I-don't-care." We are not saying "Au revoir" as we cast off, and don't drop a match in the liquid surrounding the island! Perhaps this strategy works better for us because we have a hereditary reaction to alcohol, one that knocks out our caring more thoroughly than it does other people's. And there is apparently some evidence that our neurochemistry may be shorting us here. It does not provide physiological relief for stress the way it may for others. Once again, we glimpse the interplay of the emotional and the physical. One thing remains true, regardless of theories and causes. Our physical sobriety won't last long if we don't find ways to deal with the inevitable pain of caring.

Steven King, in his novel *Cujo* [10], creates a character who spends his time drinking vodka and saying "F--- it." This fictitious man is a Korean War hero traumatized by combat. The battlefield is a very expensive place for personal caring. One can well appreciate needing the relief provided by a shot of denial with a chaser of booze. This particular veteran spends the rest of his life drinking and saying "F--- it," even as the rabid Saint Bernard tears out his intestines.

- *I may care about my car and someone dents it.*
- *I care about my work and someone criticizes it.*
- *I care about my health and I have a disease.*
- *I care about my tennis game and I am in a slump.*
- *I care about my kids and they are rebelling, seem not to care about me.*

- *I care about my looks and I see a wrinkle.*
- *I care about your approval and you don't think I am the greatest thing since sliced bread, having only just met me.*

Once we care, we are vulnerable to being hurt. How? By all the things we don't control that can affect what we care about. There are really only two solutions to this fact of life — stop caring or handle the hurt when it comes. Recovery from relapsing alcoholism (or food addiction, cocaine, marijuana, etc.) would seem to require a judicious combination of both. Both psychotherapy and the Twelve Steps can help us sort out what we care about, to realize that some of it has to go. But treatment and the Steps also offer ways to cope with the inevitable pain of living and caring. To feel it, work with it, and grow from it.

Wishing and Not Caring: There is, at least, one point where the wishful relapse and the "F--- it" relapse seem to be based on the same reaction links. Some alcoholic/addicts will translate "reality" as the implied antecedent to the pronoun "it" when they said "F--- it." And how do you "F---" reality? By leaving it, of course! And where does one go when one leaves reality? To the Big Rock Candy Mountain called Fantasy, the land where there is no frustration because all wishes come true. Small wonder that many relapse patients say both "One won't hurt" and "F--- it" and are gone.

Two brief, meaningless words, "F--- it," but they can lead to the emotional truth without which spiritual truth cannot become real.

To increase understanding of the above section, complete Recovery Exercise #11 at the end of the chapter.

Author's Translation: "I Can't Cope"

☞ *All* of the patient translations of "F--- it" may be summarized in one way. "I cannot/will-not/should-not-have-to *cope.*" The minute we recognize this, we have a handle on what led to this relapse. Seizing that handle is crucial to preventing the next one.

Those who relapse know when their thought at that moment was "F--- it." Most who started to drink/drug that way can usually identify being upset about something. Sometimes it seems to be the struggle with craving itself, but much of the time it is a living problem. As Alex Stalcup [11] says, "Stress triggers craving." That is why several chapters of this book are devoted to that problem — what coping is and how to do it.

For the current chapter and discussion, it is enough to understand one thing. The person who relapses with "F--- it" has suffered a breakdown, a collapse of the ability to cope. Most important, they are still sober when it happens. This is the piece that ☞ alcoholic/addict and counselor and sponsor all need to register. If my *sober* coping ability breaks down, my *sober* coping is what needs fixing. And this creates the "Catch-22" of early recovery:

> I need to learn how to cope in order not to relapse, which takes time, a lot of time. So I need to avoid relapse long enough to learn how to cope. In other words, I have to do what I don't know how to do long enough to learn how to do it!

This may all seem self-evident, but it is often not at all clear to the person who is living it. Many relapsers know full well what happens after the first drink/drug. They even take comfort in seeing addictive loss of control as a "disease." But a subtle denial prevents them from seeing what it really means to be "powerless" over their drug of choice: abject failure to cope effectively enough with sober reality to avoid that first drink/drug, even "knowing" it is a very real disease.

☞ There is one obvious difference between those who have faced this and those who have not. The ones who know they do not know how to cope are open to learning how. They will work at it. Those still blinded about their own impaired coping will not — a strange lethargy retards their recovery. They see no need to spend time in safe havens, places that will protect and nurture impaired coping skills. Nor to attend meetings or groups devoted to learning how to "meet life on life's terms." Therapy? What for?

The field of chemical dependency treatment itself has come a long way in addressing the issue of sober coping. Following the lead of AA, Gorski's CENAPS model [12], cognitive therapy [13], rational-emotive therapy [14], reality therapy [15], solution-focused brief therapy [16], all work with the current adult living situation. Each has something to add. The NIDA "Relapse Prevention Technology" [17] systematically prepares the addict for predictable trigger situations. The list of "class topics" from NIDA parallels the AA book, *Living Sober* [18]. "Peer therapy" is used extensively and appropriately.

☞   The treatment of coping seems to require two levels of intervention.

> *The immediate issue is current problems which exceed my ability to cope. If we don't get my reactions to those under control, nothing else much matters. Then comes the hard part, to identify my particular vulnerabilities. Where are the gaps inside me or in my coping skills, the things I don't seem able to deal with? And what will it take to:*
>
> *1) protect me from these deficits and*
> *2) reduce them before they lead to another relapse?*
>
> *In short, I have to get a handle on the living problems that led to my relapse. Then I need to increase the coping skills that fell short.*

Two little, meaningless words.

"F--- it."

To increase understanding of the above section, complete Recovery Exercise #12 at the end of the chapter.

The Three P's: Partialization, Perspective, and Prevention

Meanwhile, all of this intellectual understanding goes for naught if the alcoholic/addict does not realize that "F--- it" is a state of mind, one in which these explanations themselves are of no interest! Recognition and avoidance of the "F--- it" state of mind must become a top priority. Perhaps, the words "too much to ask" precisely summarize the attitude in this state. Too much effort, too much pain or deprivation or anxiety, too many frustrations or choices.

Some relapsers can describe both their living problem(s) and the inability to break them down into manageable pieces, to "partialize." They are so overwhelmed they can't even make a list, much less decide where to start. In early recovery some of this is due to lingering toxic effects of alcohol/drugs on the brain. A person who sees only a forest is going to feel far more overwhelmed than one who can pick a particular tree for his or her ax. A person who can swing his or her lasso for a lead steer will fare better than one who sees only an on-rushing stampede.

The person in the "F--- it" state of mind can think of only one thing, *doing* something to get relief or comfort.

Not only can I not partialize and handle this problem, I have forgotten I even have other problems. Some are, perhaps, worse, and some I might care about more, if not consumed by the inability to control this one. I have lost perspective, and with it goes the will to cope, as well as any reason or means to get it back. "Ownership," as described in the chapter on the subject, is irrelevant — "you" or "they" have driven me to it. If I am

both desperate and fortunate, I put myself in the hands of a
helper. Sponsor, therapist, minister, counselor, friend — anyone with an outside perspective — *if my helpers can help me*
see with their eyes, even for a moment, I may have a chance.

Never far away from the "F--- it" state of mind are the "others,"
Those who should not expect "too much." These may be living
people who expect one not to get drunk even when they don't submit to one's will. "They" may also be the "inner mother" and/or
"inner father" that every "inner child" drags around with him. And
you thought Linus' blanket was dirty and heavy! "F--- it" has an
audience — it is not a soliloquy — even if the members are long
since dead. The toxic "inner family" seldom seem to have been
paragons of healthy coping themselves, nor did they pass on such
skills to their children. "F--- it" is often a long family tradition.

The feeling of anger, the righteous sense of having been pushed
too far, often dominates the "F--- it" mentality. But why say anything
at all? It is almost as if a plea lies behind the defiance, "They've
pushed me to far now — haven't they?" The enabler, inner or
outer, says "Yes, dear, it is too much." Those who would be part
of the solution must say something else, ever so patiently. "No,
my friend, there is no such thing as 'too much.' Nothing justifies
your drinking, precisely because it is a disease. And for the same
reason, it is your job to learn to cope with your life instead of
saying 'F--- it.'"

As Gorski [19] stresses, lapsing into the "F--- it" state of mind
is a process. He calls this progressively deteriorating attitude the
"I don't care attitude." The person seems to pass a mental point of
no return before actually drinking/drugging. Once past this point,
the alcoholic/addict is no longer able to utilize awareness or discursive thinking. They are *in* the state of mind. The Big Book
would say the alcoholic is, at this point, "without defense against
the first drink" (p. 24).

In this chapter, we are trying to understand the process of relapse

by looking at one of its two climaxes, the one expressed by "F---
it!" We have seen that the person's tolerance for the pain of ca-
ring/wanting-and-not-getting has been reached. They break. How
do we help someone not break down like this again? First, the
alcoholic/addict must understand that recovery requires prevention of the "F--- it" state of mind. This means making sober choices
and actions that keep it from developing and becoming dominant
once more. The more an alcoholic/addict can see and feel and
even taste this need for a "Futility Prevention Program" in his or
her own relapse experience, the better. And the more likely the
person is to make those preventive choices. They will know why
they go to treatment and/or meetings, even when they do not want
a drink/drug at that moment. And even when life goes well.

*To increase understanding of the above section, complete Recov-
ery Exercises #13 and #14 at the end of the chapter.*

Awareness, a Specific Role for Psychotherapy in Relapse Prevention

The white-knuckle relapse thrives on lack of awareness. It is defined by the determination to stay "dry" without making any other
changes.

> *"Emotional work? Ha!" And the more my defensive blind-
> ers — suppression, denial, minimization, intellectualization, all
> of the rest — keep me from facing what really bothers me, the
> closer I am to physical relapse.*

Lists of warning signs appear to help, after the fact and before.
Peer support groups where members keep a watchful eye on each
other are often effective. Likewise, self-help meetings and self-
help readings. But none of these processes directly intervenes to
help the unaware person become aware *here and now.* Any increase

of awareness is a by-product. Psychotherapy, on the other hand, assumes emotional blindness as a fact of life, par for the course. The therapist routinely wonders what is really bothering the person in front of him or her and uses various tools to help them see and feel more clearly.

This is not premature "uncovering" of childhood pain. Rather, it is the deliberate illumination of living problems and issues that cannot be dealt with if they are not faced. Only once they are brought out in the open can other tools of recovery be brought to bare.

☞   One of the author's favorite tools is called "silence." "Silence" works consistently with alcoholics/addicts who say they are doing "great" or "fine," those who, therefore, have nothing to share in treatment. It starts with a brief explanation of exactly what the therapist needs the person to do and why. The person is asked to stop talking or thinking, to let the mind bubble like a pot of stew — just say out loud whatever "boils up" in your mind. With therapist as benign eavesdropper, the person's mind will often begin to fret about something.

"Gee, I did not know that was bugging me so much!"

Q.E.D.

Silence is a seemingly simple tool. It requires a trained and patient listener, one capable of accepting and exploring blocks to even doing silence in the first place. It takes time and individual sessions — few people can let their guards down this much in front of a group. At the same time, it is no substitute for a support group or a "spiritual experience." Yet it seems to work much like some forms of meditation — how can one have "conscious contact" with a "Higher Power" if one is out of contact with self? At its best, silence is a practical tool for bringing problems out in the open, before they build up to saying "F--- it!"

Even proactive therapy does not assure prevention of every relapse. *Nothing does.* Some alcoholics/addicts will never admit they need help to maintain the necessary self-awareness and to stay out of the "F--- it" mental state. Others will have to say "F--- it" many times before they get the point. Every time they say it and survive, the helper has one more opportunity to help the person look at the "choices" made. We must use the most effective cognitive, behavioral and emotional tools we have. The medical team must provide the state-of-the-art physical interventions. In other words, we must do the best we can with what we've got. The one ☞ trying to recover must do his or her part. And if the alcoholic/addict relapses yet again, there is at least one thing left for the helper to say, the short form of the Serenity Prayer.

To increase understanding of the above section, complete Recovery Exercise #15 at the end of the chapter.

"My Way or the Highway": The Spiritual Significance of "F--- it"

☞　　Ask a group of recent relapsers this question:
"How many of you would identify with this translation of "F--- it:"

"If life doesn't give me enough of what I want. Or if it gives me too much of what I don't want, I'm outta here!"

In other words, I am saying to reality, *"My way or the highway!"*

Your will see grins, grimaces, and sheepishly raised hands. If you are reading this out of your own struggle with relapse, read on.

But wait just a minute!
Think!

If this is a moment of relapse, I am still physically sober when I say this. That's my sober mind rebelling against reality!

In other words, "F--- it" is the voice of an attitude in my chemical-free self. It appears to be an attitude that imposes limits and conditions on Reality. It draws a metaphysical "line in the sand," one over which Reality dare not cross. Lest "I" take my life business "elsewhere," with the help of John Barleycorn or some other form of "escape."

☞ *If I am not going to repeat this pattern of relapse, this attitude has apparently got to go. My sober self has to change in a very profound way. For starters I need to see the connection between my sober attitude and my "F--- it" relapse. If I can, I may be ready to hear that my attitude was christened in the Big Book of AA. It was called "self-will run riot." The early AA members used a Shakespearean analogy to explain it — all the world's a stage, and each must play the part I assign.*

The transformation of this attitude to one of humility and acceptance is the objective of the Twelve Steps. Within AA, the change is called variously "psychic change," "spiritual experience" or "awakening," being "reborn." Outside AA, it may be recognized as maturation, metamorphosis, enlightenment, "the Great Awakening," separation/individuation, or just being "born again." In every variation, a self with a demanding attitude becomes a self with a humble and accepting one. "My way or the highway" becomes "go with the flow." The new reactions seem fundamentally different to self and others. It is as if the person had a personality transplant.

The AA word for the act or process by which one is transformed is "surrender." Step One "admits defeat" in the game of Life. Fueled by the hope of Step Two, Step Three embraces the "Power" of the former "enemy." "Life," "Reality," "God," — call it what you will. The (Third) Surrender Step makes a conscious commitment to let this "Higher Power" be "Principal", "Father," or "Employer."

If I relapse with the attitude of "My way or the highway," some form of surrender appears to be a practical necessity. Otherwise, "self-will run riot" remains a chip on my shoulder.

☞   *When Life inevitably knocks it off, I will say "F--- it" and drink/ drug again.*

It may sometimes fall on the professional helper to point this out. If so, the place to start is the person's own "F--- it" relapse experience. Then we must connect the attitude in the sober self and define it as the problem. The recovering reader already has specific instructions from the Big Book. To be sure to talk to the new person about "that strange mental twist that precedes a relapse into drinking." Yours and theirs.

But what if the person is a "wishful thinker" who has never said "F--- it" at the moment of relapse? Is the wishful relapser off the hook when it comes to surrender?

Not by a long shot.

What do we do when we believe what we *wish* to believe? We get rid of facts that jeopardize our wish. Our fundamental attitude is, "to heck with the facts. I'm going to believe what I want (need) to believe." This disdain for Reality, however unconscious, is "self-will run riot." Every bit as much as "My way or the highway." The wishful relapser refuses to let belief be controlled by Reality. The white-knuckler refuses to let his experience be controlled by Reality.

☞   With no more explanation than that, most relapsers can understand this. The reason? Because they have lived it. What they may never have done is to so directly connect their own relapse thoughts to the need for some form of surrender. If we help a person do that, whatever hat we wear, we are truly doing "relapse prevention."

To increase understanding of the above section, complete Recovery Exercise #16 at the end of the chapter.

References

[1] DuWors, G. "Inside a White-Knuckle Relapse." Alcoholism, the National Magazine, June, 1992.

[2] Rogers, Carl. *On Becoming A Person*. New York: Houghton Mifflin, 1972.

[3] Martin, Father Joseph. Film, "Guidelines for Helping the Alcoholic." Carpenteria, CA: FMS, 1976.

[4] Black, Claudia. *It Will Never Happen To Me*. Denver: M.A.Z., 1982.

[5] Miller, William R, Zweben, Allen, DiClemente, Carlo, and Rychtarik, Roberto G. *Motivational Enhancement Therapy Manual* (Project Match Monograph Series, Volume 2). Rockville, Maryland: NIH Publication No. 94-3723, 1994.

[6] Berg, Insoo Kim and Miller, Scott B. *Working With the Problem Drinker.* New York: W.W. Norton and Co., 1992.

[7] Beck, Aaron T., Wright, Fred D., Newman, Cory F., Liese, Bruce S. *Cognitive Therapy of Substance Abuse*. New York: The Guilford Press, 1993.

[8] Sports Page. *Los Angeles Times*. circa 1974.

[9] Koufax, Sandy with Linn, Ed. *Koufax*. New York: Viking Press, 1966.

[10] King, Steven. *Cujo*. New York: Viking Press, 1981.

[11] Stalcup, Alex, MD. "Contemporary Approaches to Treatment for Substance Abuse." Workshop. Seattle, WA, 1996.

[12] Gorski, Terrence T. and Miller, Merlene. *Counseling for Relapse Prevention*. Independence, MO: Independence Press, 1982.

[13] Ellis, A. *Reason and Emotion in Psychotherapy*. New York: Lyle Stuart, 1962.

[14] Beck, as above, [7].

[15] Glasser, W. *Positive Addiction*. New York: Harper and Row, 1976.

[16] Berg and Miller, as above, [6].

[17] NIDA, R*ecovery Training and Self-help* in *Relapse Technology Transfer Package:* PB 95167250/BDL.

[18] Anonymous. *Living Sober.* New York: Alcoholics Anonymous World Services, 1975.

[19] Gorski, as above, [12].

Recovery Exercises

1. If you have ever relapsed with the words "F--- it" or the like ("Shine it," "To heck with it," "What's the use," "Oh well!"), see if you can identify any struggle you were "quitting" at that moment. See if you can spell out what you wanted so badly and what made it seem like giving up and drinking/drugging were the only options. Identify any resentment you may have had, but also the other painful feelings that came with the frustration. If this is a pattern, do it for as many instances as you and/ or your helper think will be useful. Do it with a desire to understand, as you would for a friend or loved one, not to beat yourself up. If this is not possible, set it aside until you are ready to have compassion for yourself. Write, share discuss.

2. If you have achieved some long-term goals, make a list of them. Then spell out the part alcohol/drugs may have played in your tolerating the long wait. Finally, spell out what did/ will happen to each of these achievements if you continue(d) to say "F--- it" and drink/drug.

3. If you are the kind of alcoholic/addict who has not been able to achieve long-term goals, have you been evaluated for ADHD or other problems that may have hampered you? Regardless, make a list of things you have tried and/or wanted to try. What part did alcohol/drugs play in your not getting where you wan-

ted to? What chance do you have of achieving what you want if you continue to say "F--- it" and drink or drug?

4. If you have said "F--- it" and relapsed, did it really mean "F--- you?" If you were mad at someone, what was it about? What tools would you use to handle such anger now, instead of drinking/drugging? For whom were you really staying sober at that time? For whom are you staying sober now? Write, share, discuss — get feedback and *listen* to it!

5. If you said, "F--- it" and relapsed, look at your list of frustrations, resentment, and pain above (#1). To whom were you talking about these things in the period leading up to the relapse? Will you be able to stay sober if you do not increase your willingness and ability to share whatever is bothering you? Try to spell out the attitudes, beliefs and feelings that stop you from sharing. With your group and/or helper, create a plan to reduce these barriers.

6. If you have said "F--- it" and relapsed over a seemingly futile situation, make a list of all the ways that drinking/drugging made things worse.

7. As an experiment, think of something that currently bothers you. Regardless of your beliefs, try saying the Serenity Prayer, slowly and deliberately, as you picture the problem or situation. Repeat this at least ten times, thinking about the situation and what the words you are saying mean. What do you experience? Write, share, discuss.

8. Have you considered yourself a "hopeless" alcoholic? Make a list of things you do not have to do if you are truly hopeless. What happens to each item on the list if there really is hope for you? Share you reaction to this exercise.

9. Look at the list of frustrations you made in #1. How would these change if you were to truly accept (be at peace) about the other person's lack of perfection or your own? If perfectionism seems to be involved, try to identify the "standard" you thought was not met, especially if it was for yourself. What will you lose if it is never met? What will you gain if it is met? Did someone teach it to you? What would they say? Write, share, discuss.

10. If you are a perfectionist, try to spell out in concrete detail how it effects your daily life. How does it make you feel? How does your demanding attitude effect those around you? What happens to the pressure of your perfectionism when you drink/drug?

11. If you have said, "F--- it" and relapsed, meaning, "I don't care," look again at your list in #1. Can you spell out what it was that you cared about so much you could not stand it? With gentleness and understanding, spell out which caring may be unhealthy or unrealistic and needs to be dropped. Then see if you can spell out which caring may be healthy, and how to deal with the pain which it seems to have caused.

12. If you have said, "F--- it" and relapsed as a way to cope with something, reread the section called "Author's translation." What was your emotional reaction to this strongly worded material? Do you see yourself as someone who can cope just fine with adult life, who has no need to learn or improve? If so, rebut the author's "translation" and explain how you came to say "F--- it" and relapse. Write, share, discuss — be sure to get feedback, and listen to it!

13. If you said "F--- it" with a feeling of being overwhelmed or helpless and hopeless, look at your list of frustrations from

#1. For each frustration, try to spell out one thing you might have done, *that day* to either accept or change it, even if the overall problem would not go away. Gently ask yourself what might have happened if you had asked yourself this at the time. Write, share discuss.

14. Make a list of your frustrations the day of relapse, as many as you can think of. Assign each a number, in order of importance. Now make a list of what you lost as a direct result of the relapse, including sobriety itself. Combine the two lists and rank order for importance again. (Another way is to assign each item a point value from "1" to "10," then add each list separately and compare.) Write, share, discuss. If you see a loss of perspective, of what is really important, discuss how you will develop and preserve a healthier perspective, especially under stress.

15. As you look at your relapse(s), how would you rate your level of self-awareness? Did you know how upset you were, how the pressure was building, the things that blocked you from healthier ways of coping, how close you were to a drink/drug? For instance, did you know when you woke up that you would relapse later that day? Rate your self-awareness from "1" (minimal) to "10" (completely in touch with self and reality, virtually no blind spots) during the days before the relapse. If you score yourself low, rate your willingness, from "1" to "10" to participate in treatment specifically designed to increase your self-awareness. Discuss with helper, group, significant others, including "Higher Power." Ask for feedback and *listen*!

16. Whether you said "F--- it" or "One won't hurt" at the moment of relapse, do you identify with "My way or the highway" as the controlling attitude at that moment? If so, do you identify with an attitude in your sober self AA calls "self-will run riot?" If not, what do others think? (Ask them!) If so, reread the

description of the Third Step in Chapter 5 of the Big Book (p. 60—63), including the Third Step Prayer. What is your honest reaction to this "solution" to self-will run riot? Do your peers and helpers think you are ready for this step? If not, what do they think you need to do to *become* ready? Are you willing to follow their suggestions? If you can't see yourself surrendering, how will you keep your self-will from causing another relapse? Write, share, discuss.

5

Three Tough Pills to Swallow — Forging the Links of Acceptance [1]

Acceptance Reaction

"One won't hurt" implies I am not addictive and won't lose control. If I am alcoholic or addict, I neither believe nor accept my condition. "F--- it" rejects something. Whatever "it" is, I do not and will not accept it. If I did, I would not need chemical relief, the artificial acceptance created by the interaction of the drug with my neurochemistry.

Evidently, in order for an addict/alcoholic to not say "F--- it" or "One won't hurt," the person must "accept" the disease. Acceptance, in fact, consists of a powerful experience, usually an upheaval in the personality. It leaves behind a new series of links in the reactions of recovering alcoholics/addicts. The new links replace, control, or override the links of denial and disease. Whatever else it may be, acceptance consists of facing a fact or event. This literally means "making peace," and having peace about whatever had been so disturbing. When this occurs, the reality accepted is no longer upsetting and behavior is consistent with it. A diabetic who accepts diabetes does not eat Hershey bars. Nor is the person still upset, depressed, or resentful about it. The whole reaction has changed, not just the physical behavior.

This chapter describes three milestones in the process of accepting alcoholism and addiction. Each results in changed reactions to the idea of having addiction and to life. Each milestone, however it comes about, is compared to the experience of swallowing a tough or bitter pill. Each represents an experience in which something "revolting" is swallowed and digested. It seems to be so metabolized that it alters the links in subsequent emotional reactions. As we will see, the acceptance itself may prove temporary, unless the person also accepts the necessity to nurture it. The "three pills" are presented now because they connect so directly and logically to the two kinds of relapse. This chapter describes only the content of alcoholic acceptance, what is actually accepted. Chapters 9 and 10 discuss what acceptance itself is and how it works, after we look at its opposite — "denial" is discussed in Chapters 7, 8, and 9.

The Myth of the Overnight Cure

Acceptance is an emotional and painful process that can take decades. Yet it finally leaves the person feeling at peace about what was once denied and resisted. The dramatic moment of "surrender" may be the culmination of a process that has been eroding denial for ten years or more.

Inpatient programs sometimes live in a fantasy. They imagine their "graduates" are truly surrendering in four weeks, ready to live happily ever after. Aftercare is done by someone else and statistics are not kept beyond one year, if that. Usually, statistics reflect only those patients who stay in touch with the program, a self-serving method of accounting at best. Outpatient programs, including drinking driver "schools," often live with the sense of failure and inadequacy. So many "students" are still fighting the existence of the problem that got them there, even two years later. This frustration and futility is the source of much burnout for recovering counselors. Such counselors may share their own "moment" and the personal recovery that has followed, only to see their sincerity scorned and rebuffed.

Time.

 Alcoholism is a chronic disease, usually requiring a long-term struggle for lasting acceptance. As counselors and therapists, we want to be there for the dramatic surrender. We see ourselves as the loving mamas who nurse the new "baby." Scorn, manipulation, and stone-walling are not what we seek — they do not meet *our* needs.

Time.

A patient the author worked with in his first year left the program full of "willpower." He stayed sober two years that way. He reap-peared for treatment the author's seventh and last year working in that program. It took five years for him to get back to treatment. Who knows if he will make it this time? He was certainly more "sweetly reasonable" to work with.

Time.

A patient's husband tape recorded her drunken ramblings and played them back when she was sober. She never forgot. Solu-tion: she locked herself in the bedroom to drink for five more years before something else got her to treatment.

Intervention?

How much time does it take for the family or employer to accept the problem and decide to do something about it, an "interven-tion" [2]? Sure, the drinker goes into treatment. How long does it take before s/he forgives them and realizes "This is *my* problem"? How many relapses?

When this sort of family confrontation is most effective, the drinker has already been softened up by years of suffering. Inter-vention specialist Ed Storti [3] reported several years ago that he had never had a single subject be surprised that others felt there was a problem. The issue in a typical intervention is doing something about the problem. Now. The Johnson Institute long ago learned to extend the preparation for intervention — for some dysfunctional families it could run to months and even years. No serious student of addiction thinks a thirty-day program or an eight-week "Intensive Outpatient Program" does anything more than lay groundwork.

Time.

Alcoholism counselors are acceptance counselors. Our mission, should we choose to accept it, is to assess what level of acceptance the person has. We try to reinforce that. And then we try to help him /her take the next step on the journey of a thousand miles. The steps we help our clients take are usually far smaller than any of the Twelve Steps of AA. At most, we are mandated to help people truly accept the disease, to help them swallow "Step One" of AA. And we generally get to do it in much smaller increments

 than the full integration of even one AA step. Alcohol counselors who want to be exclusively step counselors either burn out or learn. And many of our clients' "steps" can only be taken backwards, in our absence. When they are ready, they come back to treatment for another step or two forward.

Time.

A metaphor from everyday language pictures something difficult to accept as "a tough pill to swallow." Acceptance of alcoholism turns out to involve swallowing many different pills, some of them listed above. Yet, there seem to be three generic issues in the acceptance of any addiction. We may call these the "three tough pills." They must each be swallowed before the person is fully committed to active recovery. The last pill may be identical with

 AA's Step One, "admitting defeat." But these pills are not so much "steps" as they are realizations, three milestones on the path leading to full acceptance. In the beginning, these realizations are very

much against the person's will — is that not what defines the "un-acceptable?" And the will is what must change, if the body is to survive and have a sober life.

Each "pill" appears to involve its own process of shame and denial, of resistance, anxiety, grief, realization, and integration. Most useful to counselors, they appear to be directly associated with the type of relapse a person has. There are three generic pills and only two typical relapses for an obvious reason. Once the third pill has been truly swallowed, there will be no more relapse. On the other hand, relapse after long-term abstinence may just represent a milestone being passed again — going in the wrong direction!

The First Pill — Connecting Alcohol to Problems

In each variation of the disease, we start with active addiction and a stone wall of denial. Even in the early stages, the objective observer can see the symptoms if given access. These include everything from high tolerance to the excessive personal price for an impersonal chemical. The family may be going nuts but not know why, while the boss still thinks s/he still has a real go-getter. And the police may or may not be surprised to pick the person up for the first time. The doctor thinks our hero is a picture of health, until there are some puzzling lab reports.

> *Tell me at this stage you think there may be a problem with alcohol and I will laugh. The possibility seems genuinely absurd, or my confidence in my front is still impregnable. This is the front that says "I am in complete control of myself" — "I can handle all problems" — "Normal!"*

Time.

A couple of years later the laugh may be more visibly forced. ☞ Anger is a good sign that a raw nerve has been touched.

Something in me is already at least dimly aware that "I have a problem." But the front is still too strong: better to counter-attack than to listen to this "attack." Far less do I wish to hear my own nervous feeling that something is out of kilter. But then there is a crisis or two — or fifteen, thirty, or forty-five. Missing work or not being able to get back from lunch, alibied away and attributed to something else. Perhaps my spouse has been asking me to cut down or leaving AA pamphlets around. Why do they have AA pamphlets at those Al-Anon meetings anyway? My mate assured me those meetings were for him/her, not me. And then I really get humiliated — a drunk driving arrest, perhaps. Leather on the tonsils at a Christmas party (worse, I don't even remember the party). Or maybe I make a bonehead mistake at work, the very place that until now has provided daily proof that I'm still in control.

Okay, I say. So I do have some problems and alcohol seems to contribute to them. Yeah, maybe I have "a slight drinking problem." I may even be "a problem drinker" (at times, when I don't get enough to eat or I'm under stress). Guess I'd better go on the wagon awhile, or just limit myself to two drinks, to beer, or to weekends.

 What is happening? The stone wall of denial has developed a chink in it. The impenetrable facade has developed a crack. Sure, the crack is filled with the frantic mortar of qualifications, disclaimers, and minimization. But a lifetime of denial has begun to loosen or crumble. The race is now on. The disease will progress and the acceptance will try to grow, pushing its roots through the mortar in the cracks like a flower in a sidewalk. Acceptance has to have a life of its own now because its owner has not yet claimed it.

The recognition of a pattern: "my drinking/drugging is causing problems for me," is the first huge milestone. It is the first pill to be swallowed. The fight was long and bitter, but acceptance of the disease now has a foothold. Paradoxically, this would also appear to be the birthplace of what AA calls "the great obsession of every true alcoholic," that "he will somehow control and enjoy his drinking."

> *Once I know my drinking causes problems, my initial quest is perfectly logical. I look for a way to get rid of these problems and keep the drinking. In addictive eyes, they appear to be two different cakes. I see no reason I should not be able to have one and eat the other. (Realization of this mistake entails swallowing the second pill.)*
>
> *Whatever else is true, I'm not yet seeking a way to quit drinking and stay quit. I will find most inpatient treatment programs mutually unacceptable. Some programs will accept me with a hidden agenda of changing my goal. They are no doubt often, if temporarily, successful. In other settings, I may be willing to look at my "stress." To start talking about what bothers me. It may be I am a "functional alcoholic," not "always more or less insanely drunk." If so, a flexible counselor may be able to take me a number of steps toward reducing denial. S/he might increase my awareness of emotional pain and of how much I use my drug of choice to cope with it.*

In earlier stage alcoholism, a counselor or therapist who understands alcoholic reaction may be able to begin treatment without insisting on total abstinence. This is not the same as the old trap of ignoring the drinking in a quest for "underlying causes." Drinking/drugging is still an explicit issue directly addressed, as are the things that trigger it. But most agencies will take an all-or-nothing approach. This forces the client to go elsewhere or to lie. Either way, an opportunity has been missed to help take the next step. The opportunity has been missed because of the counselor's need, the wish to work only on steps that are further down the path of acceptance. The lonely flower, pushing its way through the cement, gets no help here. It is not claimed by the alcoholic/addict or recognized by the helper. The counselor may actually step on it!

*The first pill may be swallowed "naturally." Slowly or sud-
denly, I "wake up" to the reality of what alcohol/drugs are doing
to me. I "get it" that I am being controlled, even as I "get it"
that it was my hand on the glass and no one else's. This reality
is also frequently forced down my throat by formal "intervention." But either way, the swallowing of the first pill consists of
a gut level connection. I can no longer keep drinking/drugging
separate from the problems they cause. I see a single strand
running through a quilt of problems — my drug(s) of choice.*

☞   *The beauty of intervention is the way in which it surrounds
me with so many trees at once. My spouse, my boss, my kids,
sometimes other family members and friends and teachers —
each holds up at least one tree that fell on them or on me during my use. They make it very hard to pretend there is no forest.
Most targets of intervention already sense the forest within.
Now I have to face that everyone else can see I am lost. The
collapse of that wish, to at least appear okay, is one of the critical "gulps" of the first pill. "The jig is up" because I'm surrounded by a loving posse who will no longer let me pretend I can
"get away with it." Intervention shatters the interpersonal illusion in which I have been living. No wonder I may be so
angry. "You" have helped me live the lie so long — why are you
abandoning me now!?*

A less orchestrated intervention can work just the same way. A
DUI blasts a hole in the same wall, since it is hard to keep up
appearances in handcuffs. It is also hard to look good having a
seizure, an "intervention" by Mother Nature herself.

☞   Those of us unable to do full-scale interventions may have to
settle for small nudges. Done consistently and sensitively over a
period of time, they can be effective. True, we may never get to
see the final result. But picture a smoker finding a segregated area
to eat or shivering in the cold because the addiction is not permitted in the building. Does anyone doubt that this person is remin-

ded of doing something destructive? Such limited, anonymous interventions on a societal scale have done their part to create over thirty-five million ex-smokers!

☞ Any time the disease has exposed the drinker to the naked view of others, we have an opportunity to pour some therapeutic salt in the wound. It is the sting that makes it harder to forget.

How did your spouse feel about your DUI?

How did you feel in court?

What did you tell your kids?

☞ The effective question focuses attention, however briefly, on how self feels about what others see of self. But the salt of probing in the wound must alternate with the salve of understanding. Depending on the treatment environment, this process may occur in one session, or in many.

To increase understanding of the above section, complete Recovery Exercise #1 at the end of the chapter.

The Second Pill — Eureka! It's the First Drink — How Come Nobody Told Me?

After swallowing the first pill, an alcoholic or addict may say, "Okay, so I better lay off for awhile. All right, no more drinking during the day or during the work week. Sure, I better leave the hard stuff alone." I say it, and at least part of me means it, even if part of me I won't yet listen to knows I am fooling myself.

I certainly try. Sometimes it works for a while and sometimes not at all. Sometimes I forget what my "rule" for drinking was, usually after I have started. Sometimes I come up with a new rule. That's only practical, since the old rule didn't work. I mean, no one can accuse me of not being open-minded about this.

Except on one count. I am not yet open to the idea that there is only one way to avoid these troubles connected to drinking

— quit drinking! Every time I drink now, I can still say "one won't hurt" and part of me, at least, can still believe it.

Then one day I "really" blow it. In actual fact, this may not be the worst loss of control I have experienced. It may not be the worst demonstration of my disease witnessed by family or employers. But this time there is a breakthrough for the flower of acceptance. Why now? Because it has been pushing all along. It has been mixing the powers of truth, shame, self-esteem, and fear of death, all in one potent fertilizer.

The last crisis may have been worse than this one. But it was not quite enough for the flower of acceptance to push through the crumbling mortar of defenses. This time, a root breaks through the wall. It may well feel like some ghoulish, detached body organ in a horror movie. The horror and shame of realization certainly come before the peace of acceptance. But come it does, along with an inevitable burst of energy and excitement.

"Eureka!" I cry.

"It's the first drink! Now I really see my problem" I say, glibly acknowledging my previous denial and already dismissing the possibility that any remains.

"I have seen the light. All I have to do is not take the first drink!"

"How do you do that?" a "negative thinker" may ask.
The question means little to our new convert.

"How do you not jump off a ten-story building? How do you not jump in front of a bus? How do you not pick your own nose, for heaven's sake? You just don't do it — that's all! (Silly you.)"

As described earlier, the word "just" is one of the most "cunning, powerful, and baffling" words in the English language. It is right up there with "but," the three-letter word that allows me to contradict what I have "just" said without pausing for a breath.

I may have been fighting violently against what has just happened for five, ten, even twenty-five years. For just that long, I resisted facing the fact I have just faced — that I cannot drink/ drug without losing control. And I now humbly claim to know the solution, the whole solution, and nothing but the solution. I'm just not going to take that first drink. Say, why didn't you emphasize this more last time I was in treatment?

Make no mistake: the wall of denial does have a major breech. But the quick-setting mortar has already flowed again. The flower of acceptance must send its life juices through a single root, frozen in cement, to the other side.

☞ To realize "I can't drink/drug at all without losing control" is the most crucial requirement for accepting and surviving addiction. Some alcoholics do stay "dry" while admitting and accepting nothing more. Perhaps the most dogmatic single thing that this author/clinician has to say is: no alcoholic/addict can abstain while realizing anything less. An alcoholic who thinks "I can still drink," is going to do just that. An addict who thinks "I can do this one more time," undoubtedly will.

But, you ask, what will I do with myself instead of drinking? Work hard, find hobbies, stay very busy, and use willpower, I say.

"I can do anything I really set my mind to," is my motto.

"Sure, I screwed up drinking, but that was before I understood about the first drink. I mean, I never really wanted to quit and stay quit before."

"What about AA?"

"What for?" I rejoin. "Besides, they think negative and their meetings depress or bore me. I want to be positive about this thing. I know nothing could ever get me to drink again, now that I know it's the first drink."

"What about antabuse?"

"That's just a crutch. I believe in myself. I'm strong."

"Counseling?"

"Listen, I like you. But I don't need to talk to someone else just to do what is right. I know what I've got to do, so how could I possibly not do it? I don't want to waste your time — there are people here who actually have emotional problems. They may relapse if they don't get your help, so I wouldn't feel right about taking up your time."

And so I leave treatment with the tools of "staying busy" and "willpower." I am utterly unaware that something else may be very busy behind my wall, something that seems to have a will of its own. The paradox is that I may have to claim it as mine if it is not to destroy me. (See "third pill" and chapters on ownership/disownership.) And in claiming it as my own, while facing its awesome power, my wall collapses. I will then have the opportunity and feel the necessity ☞ to seek more powerful protection. In other words I am not going to ask for serious help until I see for myself that I am in serious trouble.

The client who has finally swallowed the second pill can be one of the most exasperating for the would-be helper to face. Many of our best interventions bounce right off this person. They seem to collide with a massive wall against having to swallow anything ☞ more. AA cofounder Bill W. clearly describes himself going through this phase of enthusiastic willpower in the first chapter of the Big Book [4]. Can there be any doubt that his friend Ebby would have been scoffed away if he had shown up with a "spiritual solution" at this point in Bill's struggle?

"Yes, I have a problem over which I have lost control. But I have control of myself and need no further help."

☞ The counselor may feel more baffled and/or shut out than he was by the "problem drinker" with five DUIs. If the person can see the problem so clearly, what makes him/her so obtuse about the solution, the one this counseling offers?

The simple answer is that I do not see all of the problem. In fact, I am ferociously maintaining there is no problem of "self," much less an "emotional problem." At most, I admit there is a physical problem over which I lose control after the first drink or drug. I think of it as being literally just like an allergy to strawberries — you don't eat one, you won't get hives!

Here, my denial may get some help from certain voices in the field of chemical dependency. What I am really saying is, "I lose control after the first drink due to something external to me, alcohol. As long as I know that and don't take the proverbial first drink I am okay. There is no problem inside me."

Learn to cope? What's that got to do with it?

Some in the field say "you have a biochemical, hereditary disease, that is, no emotional problem." Lip service is played to personality problems that result from all this drinking. But let's face it — if it's a physical reaction to a physical substance, all you have to do is avoid the substance.

☞ The counselor here may be a victim of his or her own beliefs. We sometimes confuse theories of causation with the life-and-death question at hand in treatment — does this client see his/her problem clearly enough to be able to protect him/herself from it? If not, what can we do in counseling to help the person to see more clearly? The answer may be, get out of the way while the person continues a painful education. But there may be a few things we helpers can try, if we understand what we are dealing with here. In the meantime, we can also rejoice in the gigantic leap forward this person has taken: realizing it is the first drink/drug.

☞ Even without full acceptance, we may also be able to get our customer interested in the problem of learning to handle things without alcohol.

Did you ever drink to relieve stress?

Yes?

Let's take a look at some of those stresses, including the ones you still have to deal with. Let's look inside the feelings and perceptions you experience. Maybe we can see what has made drinking seem like the only alternative at times. Let's look at some other alternatives and see what has made them ineffective up till now. How do you feel when you talk about stresses that actually bother you? How do you feel when you share or ask for help? What were you saying to yourself at the moment you drank under stress? Especially if it broke one of your rules or undid one of your "decisions" about drinking?

☞ Sometimes our questions stir the soil around the root of acceptance. Experiential methods may help some to find out they have already done enough "research." They already "know" the truth, if someone can just help them connect with their own internal reality. But the person who has truly swallowed only the second "pill" does not "have ears to hear." S/he won't even listen to the feeble voice of personal experience, trying to penetrate the wall of confidence and conviction. So the person swallows the second pill and eagerly charges back to daily life, full of faith in the new-found insight.

Now what happens to Mr./Ms. Willpower?

> *Sometimes, I hang on for the rest of my life. I never concede that my denial and/or drug dependency were more than an accidental, physical aberration. I trouble treatment centers no more, though my family may keep many a therapist in business. And I certainly would have no reason to read a book such as this, more's the pity. But in most cases, my respite from drinking or drugging is temporary.*

☞ Willpower is the death grip of what those in recovery call "white-knuckle sobriety."

> *I "set my mind" to stay away from the first drink. I hold myself in a rigidly guarded posture when any painful emotion arises*

within. I won't "let it bother me." How? By refusing to consider it, by dismissing it as "minor — no big deal," or by "thinking positive." When it tries to push through and effect me, I tighten my grip physically, throughout my whole body. I don't seem to notice my knuckles turning white on the armchair. Then, just when I think I have it licked, a quiet inner tickle starts itching for a drink. But I have "set my mind" and I "push it away," wherever that is. Ask me tomorrow if I had any urges to drink and I will have forgotten or I will deny it. To me, my ability to push it away means it wasn't a "real" urge — it doesn't count. Didn't I hear you ask if I had a "serious" urge? Wait until I have a serious urge - then I will admit it to the group. Of course, if my mind is really set, I can block feelings and urges before even I know they are there. I may even boast, "last night I went to a party and the Jacuzzi was full of champagne. Sure, I got in. But I didn't drink and it didn't phase me a bit."

Why did I go to the party and/or dive into that Jacuzzi?

"Because I wanted to prove I am strong. I control alcohol. It doesn't control me."

The fallacy of white-knuckle willpower is that I "set my mind" against something outside me. I am still missing the most basic point: the problem is not out there. It resides inside the mind, behind all the barriers and blocks I have set up. What isn't in my unconscious mind lies inside the biochemistry of my physical brain — the very circuits with which I perceive, think, feel, and decide.

A body of water may not "cause" waves, but it is pretty hard for waves to form without one. And if the water is frozen, the waves can only vibrate rigidly until the ice shatters or melts. The white-knuckle mind is frozen. The waves of truth — thought, fact, or feeling, — can hardly break through to awareness. The result is rigid decisions, choices made in the dark.

What a "dry" alcoholic/addict doesn't let him/herself know is exactly what can hurt the person the most. Out of (conscious) sight is not out of (subconscious) mind.

> *The very feelings and desires I have "set my mind" against build in pressure and tension. The longer I shut them out, the more powerful they become. The more rigid and desperate becomes my grip on self. One day, my white knuckles go critical — white turns to red. Something has to give or something will burst. Suddenly, the knuckles loose their grip and the fingers relax. Palms open to the sky as they seem to ask that helpless question, "What's the use?" And then they pick up that first drink I swore I would never take, as my lips say "F--- it."*
>
> *I have just had a white-knuckle relapse.*

To increase understanding of the above section, complete Recovery Exercise #2 at the end of the chapter.

☞ The Third Pill — "Power of Alcohol Equals Need for Help"

> *I may drink for a day, a week, months, even years. The dam has burst and I need relief from all the problems and cravings I have been denying. And, sooner or later, I will begin to realize that my willpower has failed. Knowing "It's the first one — so just don't take it," wasn't enough. Something got me to take the first drink again anyway. Even after my tremendous breakthrough and ferocious determination, not to mention my proud boasting and self-control. I really wanted to quit this time and didn't. Just wanting wasn't enough — my "self" wasn't enough. So I keep drinking until I can't drink any more or something outside interferes. And sooner or later, I face "a moment of truth."*

The third "pill" to be swallowed has two sides. They are as closely related to each other as supply and demand in economics, as inseparable as pressure and volume in the behavior of gasses.

When I experience both sides and how they dictate to each other, I have swallowed the third pill. I am ready to work at recovery.

To feel this truth about self is more important in the beginning than putting it in words. For the most part, those who have lived through the experience will recognize it in the form of words soon enough. One dry verbal formula that seems to summarize the emotional truth is:

"The power of alcohol/drugs over me dictates the amount of help I need to survive."
"There," our humbled EveryPerson admits.
"I don't control alcohol. The drug controls me."
"Okay."
"I can't lick this by myself. I need help, a lot of help, for a long time."
"Yes."
"My life is a mess and if I want to clean it up I have to find a way to live without the drug, something I have completely failed to do on my own."
"Where did you say those meetings were?"

As mentioned elsewhere, "realization" describes an experience in which something was real all along, only I didn't "get it." Now I do, and it is real to me in a way that I can almost taste or feel. This changes me, not the "reality" that I have finally appreciated. And what changes is my reaction to the reality I now see.

This acceptance is recognizable by a humility that can only come from being humbled.

I am "sweetly reasonable" because I now see the gun at my head and my own spastic finger on the trigger. And I don't want to die.

What have I accepted in facing the power of alcohol over myself? I am now saying, "I don't want to be like that, but I am." And in facing this I stop wanting to be different from what I actually am.

This is the very essence of self-acceptance.

"I don't want to be so out of control I can't even hide it, but I am."

So I stop wanting to be something I am not.

"I don't want to have a problem so big it will ruin me and so big I can't solve it all by myself."

But I do, and I stop wanting it to be other than it is.

"I don't want to admit that I have tried to impose my beliefs on reality. That I routinely brushed off any facts contradicting my ideas about myself and about life."

But I did that, and I stop wanting to be able to do that again. In fact, I want all the help I can get to keep my believing grounded in reality, with a capital "R." I want to remember, not forget.

And, oh, most shameful and repulsive of all, "I wanted to be 'captain of my own ship.' I would have settled for being able to 'paddle my own canoe.' But now I have to admit that I need help from others, just to be able to handle daily life without alcohol or drugs."

"All my life I have tried to stand alone, be tough, not use crutches. Now I see that the whole time I leaned on my bottled crutch I was using it to pretend I needed nothing of the sort. Galling, bitter pill, cruel truth, too painful to bear. Yet bear it I must and will."

"Asking for help was a 'taboo' for me, of the same or even greater magnitude than the incest taboo for most people. Bet-

ter I give in to secret lust for my sister or brother and have the whole world know. Yes, better that, than to telephone someone—stone, cold, sober—and ask for (gag, choke) help! I would almost rather die than to admit to another and to the world that I have a problem beyond my wisdom or my strength." But only "almost."

"More than anything, I wanted to be strong, and alcohol/ ☞ drugs made me feel strong. As I depended on the bottle, I did not have to depend on people. But now I must face that I am "weak" and I was weak all along. I hate the fact I needed alcohol, but no more than I despair that I must now admit I need people. If only I were not too fond of breathing to commit suicide — oxygen itself seems to be addicting. The gun is pointed at my head: get help or die."

I probably won't say all of this to my helper, but feelings this powerful are not hard to see. And I may drop little bits and pieces that hint that the rest of the third pill is going down ☞ hard. Empathy and respectful silence may be the most any professional can give me. My fellow alcoholic may share his or her own "dark night of the soul." When I am ready, I may find the following distinctions helpful and comforting.

☞ *A note on being "tough" versus being "strong"*

"Strong" and "weak" are two black-and-white labels that block many alcoholics and addicts in their struggle for acceptance and life.

1. Who is stronger, the person who admits having a problem with alcohol/drugs and with living? The one who faces that painful reality, gets the needed help, and learns to live without alcohol or drugs? Or the person who continues to be "strong," admits nothing, asks for nothing, and dies of the problem they never admitted having?

2. Being "tough" is like a baseball player being hit by a ninety-

mile-an-hour fastball and refusing to rub the throbbing arm. I pretend to not be hurt when I am. Why? For the effect on someone watching and for the ability to keep going when hurt. Being "tough" is a good thing, when it's time to be tough. Many of us learned to be tough in our abusive, shaming families. Why? Because of the "someones" who were watching and in order to keep going when we were hurt. But we did not learn to be truly "strong." The "strong" person stops to face and feel the pain of a problem. When I am strong, I let myself be important enough to consider that the audience just may be irrelevant. I can consider that maybe the "performance" is less important than my well-being. And I look directly into my pain to see what it is about, Serenity Prayer in one hand and my telephone in the other. I am "strong" enough to admit I have limits and ask for help.

☞   Being "tough" means pretending I am not hurt to protect myself from you and keep going, no matter what it takes.

☞   Being "strong" means facing the pain of my problem and dealing with it, no matter what you think or what it takes.

Something to Say Instead of "F--- it": "HELP!"

Imagine walking along a cliff above the ocean one day, relishing the air and the view. Suddenly, your footing gives way and you lurch into space. The awesome power of gravity seizes you and you scream for help, even as it pulls you to the rocks below. Crying for help is the natural reaction of the survival instinct threatened by mortal danger. How far an alcoholic/addict falls is determined by how long s/he delays the moment of realizing his or her peril. The good news is that the fall can be arrested at almost any point above impact.

☞   "You can't scare an alcoholic" is a tribute to the power of denial. In truth, alcoholic/addicts will die of their disease unless they develop and nourish a healthy fear. It may be more accurate to say "you can seldom scare an alcoholic the first time. And some you can never scare at all, the ones who must die — the ones who are too tough."

> *The alcoholic/addict who has swallowed the third pill is ready to work. I will now talk about what bothers me. Even how much I hate being addicted and/or needing help. My inner world becomes more accessible to me and to others. Long forgotten drinking escapades, many painful to recall, spontaneously reenter consciousness. This seems like an "intervention" by the one witness who literally knows all, the unconscious mind. Urges to drink are felt and recognized as such. "I never realized how often I felt like drinking when I was sober before."*
>
> *When I was white-knuckling I wanted to "keep it out of my mind." Now I seek and welcome reminders of my disease. I know this awareness is something valuable and do not want to lose it. Where I used to complain about how "boring" and "repetitive" AA was, I now become a cheerful AA bore myself!*

Such a person is a joy to the would-be professional helper, and also quite rare.

Most people in early treatment need help fully grasping the power of the disease, especially how it operates during abstinence. Written drinking histories, shared and processed, can be a powerful tool. And so can experiential tools such as the "Relapse Post-Mortem," illustrated in the chapter of that name. Another powerful role-play casts the alcoholic/addict as one of the "Significant Others" — spouse, child, boss. Group and therapist then interview this "eyewitness" from that point of view. Gestalt therapy techniques can be very effective at triggering awareness, making things real. Having the person "be" the damaged liver or even the disease itself, are just two examples. Cognitive therapy offers many tools for helping people look at their problem, the cost, the distorted thinking, and the part they themselves have played. And don't rule out an actual "intervention" after entering treatment.

☞   The goal of treatment is to trigger an experience that illuminates drinking/drugging experience. To connect thought and feeling, feeling and action, action and consequence.

☞   Whatever else we do as helpers, we must practice what we preach. If we do not live acceptance in our work and lives, how can we recognize or cultivate it in others? This sometimes includes the paradoxical acceptance that our own acceptance may never be perfect!

This is just as true for the issue of accepting help, so loathsome
☞   to so many alcoholic/addicts. One place to start is to make sure every person we would help knows going in that we need his or her help. We must acknowledge frankly our dependence on the patient, that we can accomplish nothing without the client's participation. In this sense, there is no such thing as "involuntary" treatment. Partnership can start from a mutual understanding of "One
☞   won't hurt" and "F--- it." Once that is established, we can address the "anti-help taboo" (often called "counterdependency") even more directly:

"What don't you like about asking for help? What sort of thoughts or feelings does it give you to even think about it?

"Picture yourself sharing in group or in a meeting. What happens inside?

"What do you think will happen if you don't learn to ask for help next time you are overwhelmed? Are you willing to make this a goal of treatment?

"Would you try some small, safe asking-for-help tasks and report back?

"How about using other recovery tools to prepare yourself to use this one?"

☞   The first clinical principle the author ever learned was "Start where the person is." You can try to directly force someone to pick up a proven tool. But it usually works better to get this particular addict/alcoholic actively engaged in exploring his/her own blocks to using it. Why spin our wheels or those of our patient/

partner? Instead, let's offer a shovel, gravel, weights, anything
☞ that might give the partnership some traction. If we try all the
tools in our toolbox and we are still stuck, there are still two options remaining. One is to accept it. The other? Ask for outside
help!

*To increase understanding of the above section, complete Recov-
ery Exercise #3 at the end of the chapter.*

References

[1] DuWors, G. "Three Tough Pills to Swallow". Alcoholism, The
National Magazine, February, 1982.
[2] Johnson, Vernon E. *Intervention, How to Help Someone Who
Doesn't Want Help*. Minneapolis: Johnson Institute Books, 1986.
[3] Storti, Ed. *Crisis Intervention — Acting Against Addiction*.
New York: Crown Publishing, 1988.
[4] Anonymous. *Alcoholics Anonymous*. New York: Alcoholics
Anonymous World Services, Inc., 1955.

Recovery Exercises

1. When did it first occur to you that you might have a problem
    with drugs/alcohol? What did you say to yourself about it?
    What did you say to others, or what would you have said if
    asked? What were some of your early ideas of what you might
    need to do about the problem as you saw it? Each time alco-
    hol/drugs caused some real-life problem, what did you say to
    yourself at this stage. Share and discuss, giving real examples.

2. The second "pill": Describe your realization, if you have had
    one, that it really is the "first one." What led up to it? How
    many times had you tried to control your drinking? Over how

many years? The very first time you "got it" that you could not drink or drug at all, what did you think you needed to do to prevent yourself from taking the first drink/drug? Did it work? If not, what do you make of that now?

3. The third "pill": How much help do you think you need to stay clean and sober? For how long? What is your track record for asking for help when upset, when craving? If you have relapsed, try to see what reasons you have given yourself on each occasion in the past for not going to meetings, for not telephoning someone, for not asking for help with real problems in treatment. What do you say to yourself about turning for help to a "higher power" when stressed or craving? What do your answers, past and present, tell you about what stands between you and lasting sobriety? Write, share, discuss.

6

The Relapse PostMortem — Links Over Time

The Concept

One day I decide to quit drinking/drugging and I stay quit long enough to show that I mean business. Another day, I say to myself, "One won't hurt" or "F--- it," and I take that first drink/drug of physical relapse.

One very practical question haunts the relapser, counselors and families. *What changed (or didn't?) — between the point where I quit and the moment I started again — what changed?* If we can answer this, we may be in a position to answer the payoff question. *What (tools) would prevent this from happening again?"*

After a suicide, a staff of investigators sifts through the facts of the death. They explore and connect memories and observations of survivors, any clues left behind. The goal is to understand and learn, to anticipate and prevent similar suicides in the future. Whatever is learned will not benefit the deceased. But after an addictive relapse, many of the same psychological questions apply. The same sources of information may be tapped, but the victim may both contribute and benefit personally from the exploration.

Terry Gorski [2, 3] has developed a system for looking at relapse that seems to have this goal. The method described here uses the name "Relapse PostMortem (RPM)" [1]. That is how the author originally conceptualized and published it. Beck (1993) uses the term "postmortem" in describing "cognitive therapy of substance abuse." In fact, Gorski and anyone else who goes back over how a relapse happened is doing a postmortem. The method presented here is simple in concept, relatively easy to learn, and consistently productive. It may not prevent the next relapse, but it will shed light on the last. Used regularly, it will educate the attentive helper and/or group member about the realities of relapse in a way that no book or lecture can.

The principle of a relapse postmortem (RPM) is the same as that of good fiction writing: "Show, don't tell." We are trying to show alcoholics and addicts their relapse process in a way that hits home, out of their own experience.

The requirements of the therapist are the same as for the "lost keys" tool described in Chapter 2. S/he needs a willingness to learn together, a grasp of "what-and-how" questioning, and an ability to keep things focused in the here-and-now. The difference is that now we are looking at *several* points in time between decision-to-abstain and moment-of-relapse. A fictionalized sample goes like this:

Barry's Relapse

A recent relapse victim often volunteers when the purpose of the exercise is described. Sometimes, it will be a matter of taking people in turn as they enter group. The RPM can also be used in individual sessions. Simply offer it to the client troubled by relapse, as a way to learn from it.

In group this particular fictitious day, "Barry" has expressed remorse and discouragement.

"I just don't know why I drank again," he says.

Therapist says, "Sounds like you are beating yourself up with that question 'why.'" After a pause, "Would you like to try looking

at what happened, so that you and the group might learn something we can all use?"

"Sure. I have to break this."

"Okay," says the therapist. "What I'd like you to do is come sit
in this Invisible Time Machine" (pointing to an empty chair).

"In this chair, we pick a date and you become yourself on that
date, as if today were that day. Understand?"

"Like the day I drank?"

"That could be one of the days. But we are going to start a bit
farther back. Did you go to a treatment program when you got
sober last time?"

"Yeah, I went to the a drunk driving school for two years, for
two-time offenders. And AA, too."

"What was the school like?"

"It was okay. The counselors were sincere and some of the
films really shake you up."

"How about group?"

"Sometimes it is good, if someone would work, but most of
the students don't think they have a problem."

"Do you?"

"Oh, yeah! My DUI was in a blackout and I rolled my car.
Plus, the cops don't know, but I had two priors in Colorado."

"So this is actually your fourth?"

"And worst. And I swore after the third I would never drink
and drive again. I thought that was all you had to do. That's
where most of the people in my group still are — just don't
drink and drive. None of them go to AA except for the required
meetings."

"How many do you go to?"

"When?"

Early Abstinence

"Let's say this is your first month of abstinence. How many are you going to?"

"That's easy. I'm still waiting to go to court and I go every night. Get a slip signed, too, in case I need it."

"Are you going for your legal case or because you think you need it?"

"Do you want to know what I think now?"

"Not yet. Try to answer as honestly as you would have at the time, which is now!"

"Okay — I think I'm really seeing the light. You can't do this by yourself and it isn't enough to just drink and not drive. If you're an alcie like me, you'll drive after you drink! So, I'm definitely going to give this AA thing a real shot."

"You think you are an alcoholic."

"Yeah, I thought so before, but I thought I could just not drive and still get away with it. My drinking has been out of control for years, but I could always work."

"What does it mean to you to be an alcoholic? Try to explain it as you would to someone who had never heard the word."

"Well, an alcie is someone that if he takes a drink, he's going to get drunk. You don't just drink socially or have one and quit. So you can't drink at all."

"Barry, are you telling me you can never have another drink, as long as you live?"

"Well, I just try to not drink one day at a time."

"As you begin your first month of sobriety, what do you think will happen if you have a drink a year from now."

"I just don't think about it. I'm trying to live one day at a time."

"But what do you believe would happen if you had one drink in a year?"

"That's negative, I don't want to dwell on it. (This is what I would have said then.)"

"This question seems to bother you ..."

"Yes, I don't like it."

"At this early point in your sobriety, can you tell me why?"

"Probably not. It just seems so negative to be thinking about it and I'm trying with all my might to not think of drinking. And it seems so hard just to get thirty days. A year seems like forever."

"Okay, how are you liking AA?"

"It's great. Everyone's very friendly and they give me phone numbers. And some of the speakers are stand-up comics. Can't believe all the women!"

"Are you using the phone numbers in this first month?"

"Nah. I never think about drinking and I go to meetings every day, so I don't need to."

"Any thought yet of getting a sponsor?"

"I heard one guy speak who said God was his sponsor. I kind of like that."

"You want your orders straight from the top?"

He grins.

"Do you participate in meetings at this point?"

"Mostly I go to speaker meetings and I share sometimes in small meetings."

"Book or step study?"

"Nah, don't even know what that is!"

"What do you think it will take for you to stay sober?"

"That's easy. Don't take the first drink and go to meetings."

"How long?"

"I haven't thought about that?"

"What's going on in the rest of your life? Single?"

"Very, girlfriend dumped me after the DUI. She had enough."

"So you are alone. Job?"

"Oh yeah, computer tech for XYZ."

"You like it?"

"I enjoy technical work. I wish I made more money."

"How about friends?"

"Mostly drinking buddies from the bar near my apartment (so I wouldn't have to drive) and a couple of drinking buddies from work."

"You still see them?"

"Yeah, I go down to the bar and drink cokes. But it's not the same."

"How so?"

"Drunks are stupid," he blurts.

The group laughs.

"But you still go?"

"Yeah sometimes, they're the only friends I've got and my family is back in Colorado."

"Aren't you taking a chance?"

"How?"

"By going in a bar."

"It doesn't drink me. I drink it. Besides, I want to test myself."

"Why?"

"To prove I'm strong."

"So, you've got a fourth DUI, a pretty good job, a lot of AA meetings, and your social life still depends somewhat on the bars. You know you're alcoholic, but you don't like the question about what happens if you take one drink a year from now. Staying sober means don't take the first drink and go to meetings. And a human sponsor doesn't appeal to you."

"You've about got it."

Midway in Abstinence

"Let's jump our Time Machine forward again. How long do you stay sober altogether?"

"About fifteen months."

"Let's go to about seven and a half months then. Do you remember this period?"

"Sure, after I took my six-month chip."

"How are things going?"

"Can't complain."

"Job about the same?"

"Oh yeah."

"Ever tempted to drink?"

"I don't let myself think about it."

"Ever have dreams about it?"

"How did you know? — sometimes it's so real I wake up with a hangover. And other times I dream someone is chasing me and I can't get away."

"Still going to AA?"

"Maybe not quite as much."

"How much?"

"Three or four times a week."

"Why the change?"

"I was OD'ing on meetings. Same stuff, night after night. And if I can go in the bars without being phased a bit, I figure I can go a whole day without a meeting."

"Sponsor?"

"Nah. I don't feel like I need one. You have to solve your own problems. I do have a good counselor at DUI school, though."

"What's good about this person?"

"Understands my problems and gets me talking about stuff that even surprises me."

"What do you make of that?"

"How do you mean?"

"Well, does it mean you might be able to use some help solving your own problems?"

"I never thought of that. I just like the counselor and feel understood."

"Do you tell your counselor you go in bars to see your old friends?"

"Yeah."

"What is the reaction?"

"Good way to have a slip."

"What do you think?"

"Hey, I was doing it three months before I said anything."

"Have you made any buddies in AA?"

"Nope."

"What happens?"

"What do you mean?"

"Well, you are going some place pretty regularly. You must see the same people and be getting to know them."

"Not really. I just go to the meetings when it starts and beat feet after the closing prayer."

"To go?"

"Mostly home, sometimes down to the tav to shoot a little pool."

"Anything happening with the opposite sex?"

"Nah, I tried to hit on a couple of AA women, but their sponsors told them they weren't ready and if they were, I wasn't."

"How do you take that?"

"Pisses me off!"

"What are you doing about sex?"

"Rosey Thumb and her four sisters."

Group laughs.

"Let me ask you something I asked seven-and-a-half months ago. If you drank a beer, a year from now, what do you think would happen?"

"Still sounds like a negative question to me."

"Still bothers you?"

"Not as much. I figure I might have one and get drunk that night, but I'd get right back on it the next day. That's about the worst. But nothing is going to get me to try it, either."

"Why not?"

"I have seven-and-a-half months I don't want to blow and I want to get my license back. Still on probation. And I would just sort of feel stupid, and like I let everyone down."

"Who would you let down?"

"Mostly AA and my counselor, and myself."

Barry's Moment of Relapse

"Let's jump forward — set the Time Machine for the day of your relapse now, Barry."

"Okay."

"Job?"

"Same job, but I've been made a supervisor about four months ago."

"How do you like that?"

"I like the money, but I never knew how lazy most people are. They just don't give a shit."

"How do you mean?"

"When I'm on a job, I don't quit until it's done. These guys beat feet the minute their eight hours are up, sooner if they can get away with it. And they give me a lot of shit."

"How?"

"Oh, everybody wants an extra day at long weekends and everyone thinks I'm unfair if they don't get what they want."

"You can't seem to please them?"

"I never thought of it that way."

"Do you talk in AA about these problems?"

"Tell the truth, I don't go too often anymore, maybe twice a week."

"How come?"

"I dunno. Since I finished the intensive part of drunk driving school and stayed dry a whole year, I can't see spending my whole life in meetings. And I want to spend more time with my girl."

"You have a girlfriend now?"

"Yeah."

"How did you meet?"

"She started drunk driving group just as I went to monthly."

"So she's had two DUIs?"

"Yeah."

"Is she alcoholic?"

"Nah, just got drunk at two different weddings."

"Does she drink?"

"Not when I'm around."

"Other drugs?"

"She smokes a little dope."

"You?"

"No, I hate weed."

"Do you talk to her about your frustration as a new supervisor?"

"No."

"How come?"

"I don't want to worry her I guess."

"Do you ever feel like drinking after dealing with your workers all day?"

"Yeah, it occurs to me sometimes."

"What do you do when that happens?"

"I just don't let myself think about it."

"Ever take any kind of action?"

"Like what?"

"Talk to someone, go to a meeting."

"I don't need a meeting to not drink. Once, I dropped by my old counselor, but other people were scheduled."

"Any sort of stress symptoms — headaches, diarrhea, etc.?"

"Yeah, I seem to get more headaches lately, and my blood pressure was up on my annual physical. The doc said it wasn't too bad, just relax."

"Have you followed up, had it tested again?"

"Nah."

"Any reason?"

"I just have to get used to it."

"So, you've got a promotion, a new girlfriend, and quite a bit of stress. You get occasional urges to drink and you handle them by not thinking about it. AA has less and less appeal. Still go to bars?"

"As a matter of fact, no, that just got too old. I don't fit there anymore. Rather go home and be with my girl."

"You live together?"

"Practically."

"Any talk of marriage?"

"Give me a break!"

"I take it you feel you've got enough to handle."

"Yeah, but sometimes I feel like I'm using her."

"Why?"

"I don't want to get married. I just can't handle that. But once I caught her crying and she wouldn't tell me why."

"So you've got problems you keep from her and she's keeping something from you?"

"That sounds pretty negative."

"Is it unfair?"

"No, I just didn't think of it that way."

"The day of your relapse, when did you first think of taking a drink?"

"That's easy. It's Saturday and I had to work overtime because one of my Saturday crew promised his kid to take him fishing. The customer carved me a new asshole for how the guy has been screwing up. Me, I'm feeling like a prime sap for having covered for him."

"You said 'Yes' when you wanted to say 'No?'"

"I'll say!"

"So what happens?"

"I get off about seven p.m. after a ten-hour day. My girlfriend is at her folks in Tucson. I'm tired, dirty, hungry, and pissed. All I can think of is one lousy beer. One lousy beer. Cold, in a frosted schooner, Miller's draught. One lousy beer. It's like a song I can't get out of my head. I'm a man. I've got a man's responsibility. I want a man's drink. One lousy beer. So I decide I'll just go to the nearest bar and have one."

"Any thoughts at all to the contrary?"

"If there were, they get drowned out by 'one lousy drink.'"

"Give yourself a minute, see if anything comes back, might be an image or feeling, not a full thought."

"You know, I think I saw myself in an AA meeting, maybe at the podium, just saying 'one lousy beer.' But it wasn't enough to stop me."

Barry and Group Debrief

At this point we want the group to share their own experience. Once this is done and the volunteer and his group seem ready, we can look at what we all learned.

Barry sees it this way. "Right from the beginning, I somehow stayed on the outside of AA, I didn't really get in."

Someone in the group says, "I did that. I was on the program, not in it."

Several others nod their heads.

"Any idea what held you back?"

"Well, I didn't want to get a sponsor or share my problems. That sure became very clear to me today. I shared more today than I ever have anywhere, anytime in the past."

"You shared a lot, and I think everyone here has benefited from it. How does it feel to share like this?"

"Kind of good, like I'm really doing something different this time and not just scratching the surface. But it's kind of scary, too."

"Worried about what we're all thinking of you?"

"That, and whether I'm not just fooling myself again."

Several group members share what they think of him for sharing as he has. Then we try to tackle the issue of "fooling myself."

"How do you think you were fooling yourself?"

"Telling myself I was strong, didn't need help, even when it was obvious I did. Deep down, I don't think I was really convinced I couldn't drink one drink ever."

The group can share and explore their own attitudes toward needing help and "being strong." They can rehash the denial that surfaced in his RPM, and share their own. Barry and the group can finish by identifying goals and tasks, things he can do differently to get different results this time around.

Barry has two primary needs if he is to survive and remain sober. One, to deepen and maintain his acceptance of the disease itself and, two, he must learn to cope with life without his drug. These are, of course, the two requirements for *anyone's* recovery from addiction. Tasks tailored to his personal experience may include:

1. Redo and share his drinking history in detail. It will be important to emphasize the effects of "the first drink" as behavior and "one won't hurt" as thought.

2. Get a sponsor and start seriously working the Steps. Tasks in preparation might include making telephone calls to others in recovery. In counseling, this should be followed by processing what it was like and ideas/feelings that may yet block him.

3. Give up supervisory responsibility until sponsor and/or counselor and he agree he is ready to try.

4. Share at least one thing that bothers him daily with a meeting or AA member. He may need to participate in a structured learning experience, one that develops and practices AA and other coping skills, such as cognitive behavioral or rational emotive techniques.

5. Potentially, use professional counseling and/or psychotherapy or couples therapy to explore the relationship with the girlfriend. Resolve whether he can keep her and sobriety.

6. When ready, use therapy to explore his need to please, fear of angering others, apparent low self-esteem. Here lie childhood

and unconscious "character defects" that may yet do him in. Once he is aware of them, he can bring all twelve AA steps to bear.

7. May need to use therapy to become more emotionally connected to self, to reduce attitude/blocks to routinely "thinking about (and feeling) it." This may be necessary before he can work the Steps for his "emotional sobriety."

The critical reader will undoubtedly spot other issues and strategies for preventing fictitious Barry's next relapse. What we can hopefully all see is the persistence of denial, of alcoholism itself. We see the common resistance to asking for help, even as the problems/feelings are building to relapse. Fiction or not, Barry is seen daily in every program in the country. In some ways, addressing the specific living problems is the easy part. The lifelong challenge is to recognize and interrupt the insidious, recurring denial. Denial of the disease itself and denial of the inability to cope.

References

[1] DuWors, G. "Relapse Post-Mortem." Professional Counselor Magazine, May/June, 1988.
[2] Gorski, Terrence T., Miller, Merlene. *Counseling for Relapse Prevention*. Independence, MO: Independence Press, 1982.
[3] Gorski, Terrence T. Keynote speech and workshop. ALMA-CA (now EAPA) Western Regional Conference, Palm Springs, CA, 1988.

Appendix to Chapter 6
The Learning From Relapse (LFR) Workbook

The LFR Workbook is included here for the reader to try. It is designed to explore one period of abstinence that ended in relapse, one, and only one. Of course, if you want to look at more than one relapse, you can work through the LFR Workbook for each one. Most people, most of the time, will use it to look at their most recent period of abstinence. Use it to learn for yourself and/or with others. If you don't have a problem with alcohol/drugs, try it with anything else you may do that is self-destructive. Think of something you have quit and then gone back to — when you get to the questions on surrender and use of support, try answering as if you will die if you relapse again. The author developed the LFR Workbook in response to a need for something quicker than the RPM role-play. The LFR Workbook can be given to a whole group and then processed collectively. Feel free to copy it for purposes of helping agency clients, not for sale, publication, or paid workshops.

You may wish to use only one question of the LFR Workbook at a time. The first is the "Addiction Conviction Scale" described in Chapter 1. It is designed specifically for the person who said "One won't hurt" at the moment of relapse. However, a lot of white-knucklers suffered a subtle erosion of their conviction without even being aware of it. The next two questions relate directly to stress and the white-knuckle relapse, the person who said "F--- it." Chapter 4 describes many of the issues in this relapse. Chapters 11 through 15 give actual tools for coping instead of saying "F--- it." The subsequent (4th) question about "will" carries with it the question of "Surrender." Use it when alcoholic stubbornness is an issue and the client seems ready to question this attitude in self. The last question tries to help the relapse victim who worked a strong program of recovery and then gradually faded. For these clients, this may be the only question you use. A detailed set of questions for processing each of the separate tracking questions of the LFR Workbook is included.

LEARNING FROM RELAPSE (LFR) WORKBOOK

(Copyright ©1996 George DuWors, MSW)

Before you start: The purpose of this workbook is to *understand* one specific period of not drinking/drugging and how it ended back in the first drink/drug. It is impossible to understand anyone, including yourself, while judging or condemning. The first step of the workbook, then, is to put down the invisible hammer with which you may have been beating yourself up. It is crucial to try to look at yourself and to think as a friend, a therapist, or loving Guru/Higher Power of the human being who lived through this process. Yourself.

Every relapse ends a "<u>P</u>eriod of <u>T</u>emporary <u>A</u>bstinence" ("PTA"). Every PTA has a *beginning* (the day we actually quit drinking/drugging), a *middle* (still clean and sober, about half way from the beginning to the end) and an *end* (still clean and sober, waking up the day we take the first drink or drug since quitting).

We can each look at our own PTA to see what changed (or didn't), between beginning and end. If we can answer that question, we can begin to see what needs to be done to prevent this from happening again. We are then ready to identify tools and to start using them.

PTA ("Period of Temporary Abstinence")

BEGINNING	MIDDLE	END
(Quit)	(Still abstaining)	(Waking up, day of first drink/drug since quitting)

WORK: Identify your PTA by filling in the blanks below. Choose the one you wish to understand better by using this workbook.

I want to learn from my period of not drinking/drugging that lasted _____ weeks/months/years. (Circle one)

1. The *beginning* of my PTA (the day I quit drinking/drugging) was _____ (Enter month and year if possible, or any other way you remember the time, i.e., "after my arrest.")

2. The *middle* (half way from beginning to end) of my PTA was _____ (Month and year, if possible, or any other way you remember the time.)

3. The end (the day I took my first drink or drug since the beginning above) of my PTA was _____ (month/year, if possible, as above.)

CONCEPT: We are going to try to *track* what changed during your PTA by measuring the same five things on each of the different days. It is like a doctor measuring your pulse or your blood sugar at different points in time. However, these are not "scientific" questions that you need answer precisely, only your best guesses. Nor are they legally binding. You can change your mind as we go along.

Each tracking question is merely a tool to look at your own experience as best you can recall. The important thing is to answer the questions as you would have if you had been asked at the BEGINNING, MIDDLE, and END, without judging or condemning yourself.

After each of the five tracking questions, there are a series of "Processing Questions" to spell out what did or did not change for you personally. The processing questions then connect to tools for preventing this from happening again.

TRACKING QUESTION #1

WORK: Picture yourself at the BEGINNING of the PTA you selected and rate yourself on the strength (from 1 to 10) of the following belief as you would have then. Once you have done this, picture yourself at the MIDDLE, then at the END and rate yourself as you would have then.

Belief: "I cannot take so much as one drink/drug without losing control."

Circle your choice for each point in time

Beginning: 1 2 3 4 5 6 7 8 9 10 ("10" is the strongest possible belief.)

Middle: 1 2 3 4 5 6 7 8 9 10

End: 1 2 3 4 5 6 7 8 9 10

Before processing your answers to the above question and/or those that follow, it is necessary to answer one more, right at the moment of the "red light" against drinking/drugging turning to "green." This is usually the moment of physical action to get or take the first drink/drug.

WORK: Try to go back to that moment, at the very final moment of the PTA you are looking at. Try to hear what is in your thoughts or feelings as you "go for it." Check below whether it seems closer to:

"One won't hurt"_____ or "F--- it!"_____ or Both_____

PROCESSING TRACKING QUESTION #1

> **WORK: Read and compare each of your three answers to Tracking Question #1 above. Select the "BELIEF PATTERN" (A, B, C or D) below that best describes how your numbers did or did not change. After you pick one of the patterns, do the "PROCESS" and "WORK" for that pattern, which will be found below, in alphabetical order.**

BELIEF PATTERN A ___ My belief scores started low (6 or less), stayed low.

BELIEF PATTERN B ___ My belief scores started high (8 or above) and stayed there.

BELIEF PATTERN C ___ My belief scores started high (8 or above) and dropped 3 or more.

BELIEF PATTERN D ___ Other.

PROCESS FOR BELIEF PATTERN A (ONLY): If this describes my scores, "what changed" for me was "nothing." I never did have enough belief in my addiction to stay clean and sober. If I am going to stay clean and sober this time, apparently I must develop a strong conviction that I really do have addiction, that it doesn't go away, that I will never be able to have "just one."

> **WORK for Belief Pattern A: Tools for accomplishing this that I can start using today are: (Complete this list using what you already know, books or other people's ideas. Then read and complete the "WORK" for Belief Pattern C on the next page.)**

____ Contract to not drink/drug ___ days while exploring this issue.

____ Complete and/or ____Review and/or ___Share my "Chemical History"

____ Attend ____ and Share ____ at ____ Step One Meetings.

____ Individual and/or ____ Group and/or ____ Family treatment with _____.

____ Prayer, for _____.

____ Reading, specifically, _____.

____ Other: _____.

PROCESS FOR BELIEF PATTERN B (My scores started high (8 or above), stayed high.)

WHAT CHANGED: If this describes my answers for Tracking Question #1, "what changed" for me was something other than my belief. I never lost my belief in the addiction, but must have relapsed for other reasons. If I am going to stay clean and sober this time, apparently I must look to other changes to understand my relapse, using the questions below.

WORK: If this was your pattern, go to "Tracking Question #2"!

Note: If I said "One won't hurt" or any of its variations at my moment of relapse, I did not keep a strong belief, regardless of my scores. I still need to complete Belief Pattern C, next processing question below.

PROCESS FOR BELIEF PATTERN C (My scores started high (8 or above) and dropped at least three points.)

WHAT CHANGED: If this describes my answers for Tracking Question #1, what changed was my strong belief in my own addiction and the lifelong impossibility of controlling use. My belief appears to have faded from a powerful conviction in the beginning to watery doubt and/or outright denial in the end. I must find a way to maintain my belief in my addiction, even when I have been clean and sober long enough to start feeling comfortable.

WORK FOR BELIEF PATTERN C: Tools for maintaining my belief that I cannot drink/drug without losing control are:

____ Twelve Step Meetings, ____ per week.
____ Daily Recovery reading of _____.
____ Working with Newcomers at _____.
____ Working Twelve Steps with _____.
____ Professional treatment _____.
____ Other: _____.

PROCESS FOR BELIEF PATTERN D ___ Other
(Specify): _____

WHAT CHANGED: If my scores do **not** follow the three common patterns, I may still use the questionnaire by following the next instruction.

> **WORK FOR BELIEF PATTERN D: Even though you did not follow Belief Patterns A, B, or C, if you scored 8 or above the day of relapse, check "Belief Pattern B" and go to "Tracking Question #2." If you ended at 7 or below on Tracking Question #1 the day of relapse, check "Belief Pattern C" and complete the "WORK" list for C.**

TRACKING QUESTION #2

> **WORK: Now go back in time and rate your level of stress/frustration at the BEGINNING, MIDDLE and END of the same PTA between "1" (minimal) and "10" (overwhelming). Circle your choices.**

Beginning: 1 2 3 4 5 6 7 8 9 10

Middle: 1 2 3 4 5 6 7 8 9 10

End: 1 2 3 4 5 6 7 8 9 10

PROCESSING TRACKING QUESTION #2: STRESS LEVELS

> **WORK: Comparing my stress/frustration levels at the BEGINNING, MIDDLE, and END, the change I notice is (check one that fits the best):**

STRESS PATTERN A: None. Started high (7–10) and stayed high.

STRESS PATTERN B: Started high, dropped at least three points in the middle, came back up <u>or</u> started low but ended high.

STRESS PATTERN C: Started high or low, but was low (below 5) the day of relapse, the day of my first drink/drug of this PTA.

> **WORK: Based on the change (or lack of change) in my stress/frustration level above, I apparently need to (pick the letter below that matches the STRESS PATTERN chosen above — If you chose Pattern B above, circle and read "B" below):**

A. Find ways to reduce and/or cope with my stress right from the beginning.

B. Use time when stress is reducing (heat of drinking/drug related problems is off) or is still low to prepare for new, <u>non</u> addiction-related problems that drive it back up.

C. See that I can relapse with little stress, probably out of complacency and/or euphoria and/or boredom. I probably said "One won't hurt," saw the first drink/drug as "no big deal."

   If so, my issues for this PTA were covered under Tracking Question #1.

Note: Tools for dealing with stress will be developed after the next question, which identifies what the stress was about.

TRACKING QUESTION #3: LIVING PROBLEMS

   CONCEPT: A "living problem" is a real situation that will persist for some period, even if we deal with it. Relationship problems, a difficult situation or condition at work, chronic pain, physical illness, financial problems, kids, etc. are all living problems.

> **WORK: List your three biggest living problems at the BEGINNING, the day of quitting drinking/drugging that started this PTA.**

1. _____

2. _____

3. _____

> **WORK:List your three biggest living problems in the MIDDLE, about half way through the period of abstinence.**

     1. _____

     2. _____

     3. _____

> **WORK: List your three biggest living problems at the END, on awakening the day of taking the first drink or drug (before taking it!)**

     1. _____

     2. _____

     3. _____

PROCESSING TRACKING QUESTION #3: LIVING PROBLEMS

CONCEPT: The questions to process "Living Problems" are based on at least the feeling of stress and (most likely) saying "F--- it!" at the moment of relapse. The most obvious thing about "F--- it" is that the two words mean nothing by themselves.

Below you are going to find one major translation (#1) and then a whole set, (#2), of what "F--- it" may really mean. Both types of meanings (#1, #2) often appear in the same relapse. (Tracking question #4 explores yet another level of meaning!)

> **WORK: Check any translation below that expresses your attitude at the moment of relapse which brought this PTA to an end. Pick as many as apply, and do the "WORK":**

TRANSLATION (of F--- it) #1: _____ "F--- it" often means "I've had it!" and is usually accompanied by a feeling of "snapping," reaching a limit.

Implication: "I've had it" means that I let so much emotional pressure build up that I burst. I need to reduce that pressure *before* it bursts by talking to someone who understands.

WORK FOR TRANSLATION #1: If I identify with "I've had it," I can develop a plan to increase my sharing by completing the following:

PEOPLE: Looking at my list of living problems as of the day of relapse, to whom was I talking about them? Check all that apply:
_____ Sponsor _____ Counselor/therapist _____ Friend
_____ Significant other _____ Other (specify) _____

FREQUENCY: How often did I talk about what was bothering me?
_____ Never _____ Daily _____ Weekly
_____ Monthly _____ Less than monthly

BLOCK: When I think about opening up to someone about what is in my heart, the strongest feeling that stops me is _____.

BLOCK: The reason I give myself for not sharing what bothers me the most is
_____.

PLAN: Three ways I can begin to decrease my blocks to sharing today are (own ideas, from books, or from others):
Practicing _____ times per week at/with_____
Counseling to understand/reduce it with _____
Prayer for _____ Other _____

TRANSLATION(s) (of F--- it) #2:

WORK: Review each of the meanings of "F--- it," (a), (b), (c), and (d) below. Check any that apply.

(a) _____ "I quit." or "I give up."
(b) _____ "What's the use?!" (Futility, discouragement, frustration, resignation.)

(c) _____ "F--- *you!*" (Anger, hurt, getting drunk at someone, can also mean "F--- *me!*")

(d) _____ "I don't care." or "Who cares?!"

If I relate to *any* of these translations, I need to look at my list of living problems (people, places and things) in Tracking Question #3. These are the things that I was stressing *about* in Tracking Question #2. These are usually the "it" in "F--- it." In effect, each of these translations means **"I cannot/will-not or should-not-have-to COPE!"**

Implication: If I am to stay sober, I must learn to cope. To "cope" means to face something that is not how I want it to be and to sort out what I must stop wanting (accept) from what I <u>may</u> be able to get (change). It is to <u>apply</u> the Serenity Prayer to real problems.

WORK TO COPE WITH MY LIVING PROBLEM(S):

Problem — The Wants: Look at your list of Living Problems at the END, the day of Relapse. Use the first two columns of the "Problem/Solution Worksheets" (next page) attached to spell out your frustrations. Write the things you wanted (in the "WANT" Column) versus what you actually got (in the "GOT" Column) for each living problem.

Solution — Accept vs. Change: Now go down your list of "What I got," item by item. For each one, place it in the "Accept" or "Change," columns of the worksheet. You know you must "accept" something if you have no control over it. You may be able to "change" something if there is an action under your control that might make it how you want it to be. If parts of an item could go in different columns, divide it. You have now defined and described your solution, everything you must work to accept or to change (see Chapter 14 for an example).

The Plan: Use the "SPARROW" planning sheet (page after next, described in detail in Chapter 12, example in Chapter 14) to spell out the tasks necessary and possible to bring about "Accept" or "Change." You now have a plan for coping with your problem. The only thing left is to carry it out.

Problem/Solution Worksheet

WHAT I WANTED	WHAT I GOT	MUST ACCEPT/ STOP WANTING (NO CONTROL)	MIGHT CHANGE/ GET WANT (MAY CONTROL)
	OBJECTIVE		
	(facts, situation)		
	Subjective		
	(thoughts,		
	feelings,		
	impulses)		

SPARROW WORKSHEET: COPING PLAN

I NEED TO ACCEPT/ CHANGE: I WILL USE THE FOLLOWING:	_____ (PART OF MY PROBLEM)
SHARE:	What _____ With Whom _____ Daily__Weekly__Monthly _____ Other _____
PRAY/MEDITATE:	Time _____ Place _____ Form or subject _____
ACTION	What _____ When _____ How I will prepare _____ _____ Report Progress to: _____
READ	Title _____ By _____ Discuss with _____
RETHINK	Method (i.e., Step 5, RET) _____ _____ Reality Check with _____ By _____
ONE DAY AT A TIME	Specific self-talk _____ _____ _____ How often (mimimum) _____ Any time I experience _____
WRITE	Method (12 Step, RET, Cognitive _____ Therapy, Journal) _____ Share with _____ Frequency (Minimum) _____ Any time I experience _____

© G. DuWors, 1999

TRACKING QUESTION #4

> **WORK: Using the ten point scale below, rate the strength of your belief at the BEGINNING of this PTA that the following statement applies to you:**

"I can (or should be able to) do anything I set my mind to."

Circle the most accurate number on the scale between "1" (just might be true) and "10" (totally and absolutely convinced). Then rate this belief at the MIDDLE and END.

Beginning: 1 2 3 4 5 6 7 8 9 10

Middle: 1 2 3 4 5 6 7 8 9 10

End: 1 2 3 4 5 6 7 8 9 10

IMPLICATIONS: If your belief was low in the beginning and went back up, your relapse process consisted of a subtle return of your belief in your own willpower. If your belief was high all along, that may be the problem. If it was low throughout, this may not be your problem.

PROCESSING TRACKING QUESTION #4: WILLPOWER VS SURRENDER

TRANSLATION #3 (Of "F--- it"): Yet another meaning of "F--- it" at the moment of relapse may be: "If Life (Reality, Sobriety, God) doesn't give me what I want, or gives me too much of what I *don't* want, I'm out of here (and I know just how to leave!)" In other words, "My way or the highway!"

Notice: *We are still sober when we say this!* There is no drug or alcohol in our brain yet.

> **WORK: _____ Check this line and complete this section if you identify with "F--- it" as expressing this attitude.**

Implication: This is the voice of an attitude in the chemical-free self called "self-will run riot," a deep part of the *sober* personality called "Ego." The usual name of the change from this lethal and self-defeating attitude to one of realism and humility (and serenity!) is "surrender."

> **WORK: Complete the following three sentences:**

My strongest negative feeling about the very idea of "surrender" is

_____.

The whole idea of "surrender" goes against my belief that

_____.

If I continue to approach life with my old attitudes, I can probably expect

_____.

> **WORK: Tasks to reduce ego / self-will.**
> **Next to the following tools of surrender, I will list specific things (what, when, where, with whom) I can start doing today to be free of my self-will, or at least reduce it.**

MEETINGS_____

STEPS _____

SPONSOR _____

PRAYER/MEDITATION_____

PROFESSIONAL HELP _____

OTHER _____

TRACKING QUESTION #5

The below scale rates your recovery activity from "2" (intentions) to "10" (consistent and coordinated action). It tries to measure what you were actually doing at the time to recover and remain sober.

   2 - Willpower
   4 - Any sort of support group (AA, church, etc.), 2 or 3 weekly
   6 - Support group; 4 or more per week,
   8 - Support group, 4 or more per week, at least 2 in AA, contact with sponsor at least weekly.
10 - 4 groups a week as above, sponsor contact weekly, working steps, daily prayer/meditation.
___ - Other, you assign score based on how hard, long and often you were willing to work.

> **WORK: As you have before, go back to BEGINNING, MIDDLE and END of your PTA and score your recovery activity with the above scale. Choose the number which best describes what you were doing to remain abstinent. Circle the number you have chosen for each point in time below.**

Beginning: 1 2 3 4 5 6 7 8 9 10

Middle: 1 2 3 4 5 6 7 8 9 10

End: 1 2 3 4 5 6 7 8 9 10

PROCESSING TRACKING QUESTION #5

The below processing questions are designed primarily for those who had a strong commitment to active Twelve Step Recovery and lost all or most of it. For this kind of relapse, the words at the moment of relapse are less important than the earlier loss of internal commitment and external recovery program.

Dropping out of, or reducing, a recovery program is a decision, more likely a whole series of them. It is especially important to put the personal hammer down as we look at these decisions, ever seeking to *understand* rather than to punish ourselves. We are looking for the elements of our decisions of which we were *not* fully aware at the time — motives, attitudes, assumptions, feelings, even "craving," etc. Healing as these awarenesses may be, they can also be initially more painful than our imaginary hammer. It is best to complete this series with support nearby. Do *not* complete while full of self-hate and/or suicidal!

WORK FOR TRACKING QUESTION #5 RECOVERY ACTIVITY: Complete the sentences below as honestly as you can. Discuss with others as indicated:

---

1. The apparent crisis or major change in my life before deciding I did not "need" (so many) meetings was:_____.

2. The biggest stress/frustration in my life before my relapse was:

_____

3. At the point at which I (started to) cut back attendance, being in the groups left me feeling_____.

4. Looking back now, I can see this feeling meant that

_____.

5. If I have this feeling about meetings again I will

_____.

6. At the point at which I (started to) cut back my attendance, to skip meetings, I told myself_____.

7. Using 20/20 hindsight, the real reason I was deciding not to go appears to have been _____.

8. If I start thinking this way again, I will_____.

9. Looking at the whole process, from decisions to cut back meetings to the "decision" to take the first drink/drug of the physical relapse, I can now see that the attitudes/motives that seem to have been controlling me were

_____

_____.

10. I will discuss this set of questions in depth with _____ to check and increase my understanding.

11. Once I am as clear as I can be about these attitudes, known as "character defects" in 12 Step Recovery I will:

a. Work Steps 4 through 9 with _____.

b. If they appear to involve reactions and life experiences beyond the "living problems" addressed by Self-Help recovery, begin counseling or therapy with
_____.

c. Both _____.

SYLVAIN 91

7

The Link(s) We Call Denial — A Wall and a Will

The relapse postmortem (RPM) is a tool that will enlighten the therapist even when it does not "cure" the person. Used regularly, over a period of time RPM will reveal endless variations of denial: the sometimes subtle and often glaring gaps in acceptance that undercut recovery efforts and whittle away at sobriety.

This chapter and the two that follow explore and further describe the fatal role of denial in relapse. This is done with an eye for using practical understanding to help the alcoholic/addict (gambling, food-addicted, etc.) person. This particular chapter ambitiously aims to spell out what denial is, a wall and a will. The following chapter looks at denial as concrete mental behavior. Chapter 9 then focuses on the Dr. Jekyll-Mr. Hyde split as a particularly insidious form of denial, one that is intimately involved in the first drink and often over-looked by the treatment field. This paves the way for two more chapters (in addition to Chapter 5) on acceptance.

When Does Denial Exist?

I have an objectively observable condition.
An objective observer observes it.
I do not observe my condition as such, denying its very existence.

The objective observer observes my lack *of observation of my own condition.*

The observer correctly concludes that I am "in denial."

☞   I am "in denial" when you can see my "problem" *and* my inability to see it myself.

Sometimes denial exists and no one else knows it, because the problem is so well hidden. Denial exists as I lift the toilet tank to get my hidden vodka, whether anyone else sees me or not. Denial exists if an objective observer would see a problem, if allowed to see *all* the facts. Philosophers might titillate themselves whether this is a tree falling in the forest with no one to hear. Those of us who would help the secret drinker (eater, gambler, addict) have no such luxury. We know that his/her very life depends on recognizing the problem that exists outside awareness.

☞   Notice that denial is something that happens between people. In its purest forms, it cannot even be recognized without the consciousness of a second person. And the importance of the other person is not limited to merely recognizing denial. To some degree other people, real or imaginary are the very reason to "not admit."

"Not admitting" I have a problem is something I do for an audience, real or "imaginary" (real only to me!). To admit has all sorts of implications for our relationship. First, you may think less of me for having a defect. You may also think less of me for the very act of admitting — the interpersonal equivalent of crying "uncle." Now I am less than you in status — the Japanese, who have a horrendous alcohol problem, have no monopoly on the concept of "face." More than one AA speaker has said, "I couldn't save my face and my ass at the same time."

The biggest question of all still remains:

What do we do now that I have admitted this problem? Will you fire, arrest, divorce, or reject me? Will I crumble in humiliation and commit suicide? Or will I go to treatment and have my life exposed to others, possibly run by them? How will

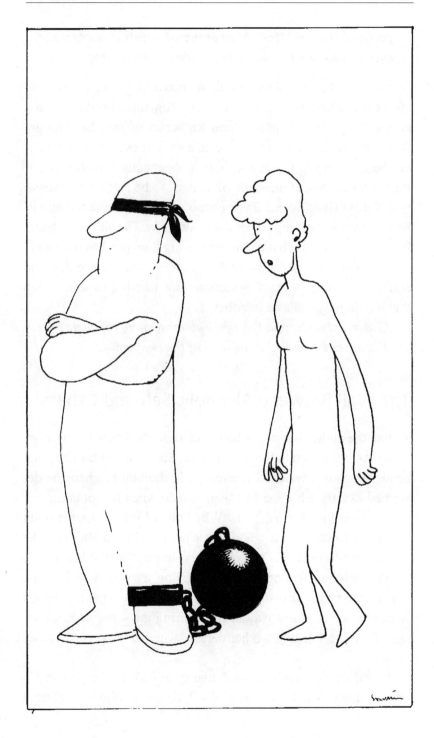

you feel? How will I feel? Most of these fearful questions occur even if "you" are my counselor, loving and recovering.

☞ Clients who complain that their recovering counselors have "forgotten where they came from" are sometimes right. It is too easy to forget how long and hard we ourselves may have fought facing the problem. Once you scale a wall or even a mountain, it ☞ can be very easy to forget how high it once seemed. Non-recovering professionals, at the same time, need to be particularly sensitive. You will help no one if you cannot grasp the shame and humiliation you are "helping" a person to swallow. The shame of being in a category to which the non-recovering therapist has not had to admit belonging. Many in early recovery contemplate AA and suffer the Groucho Marx syndrome: not wanting to join a club that would have me as a member.

To increase understanding of the above section, complete Recovery Exercises #1 and #2 at the end of the chapter.

The Wall Between Alcoholic Self and Others

A man the author has never forgotten described how his wife secretly followed him to the liquor store. She watched him buy and drink his vodka, watched where he hid the bottle. Then she described exactly what she had seen him do when he got home.

He denied it. When asked, "Why bother? What possible point was there to denying it when you were caught red-handed?" he did not miss a beat. His response was simple, "It shut her up."

The helpless feeling others, including us would-be helpers, experience facing this sort of "wall" is precisely what the person in denial needs. It is a way of transferring the sense of helplessness from the self to the other person, whether done consciously or not.

Is this cynical and manipulative lying? Does the person "in denial" know what they are doing? To ask a slightly different question, do they have a choice? If we can begin to answer even some of these questions, we may become more comfortable and effective in helping this person. The recovering reader may lose some of that shame and gain insight.

Adult children of alcoholics may look back to childhood and ask what they would have asked then. That is, if questions had been permitted. "Didn't Mom or Dad know what they were doing when they spoke so abusively? Didn't they realize they were conveying such an unmistakable wish I did not exist at all? How could they not see how that felt to me — how it *still* feels?! Don't they know they are hurting us when they beat, molest, ridicule, criticize, reject, or abandon us? How can they not know?" This last question is the practical focus of this chapter and the two that follow.

A trivial but revealing example involves an alcoholic father who also smoked. He would not allow his kids to roll the car windows down when he lit up. They asked him to, coughed theatrically, and made continuous cracks. To permit them to lower the windows would be to admit something. He would be conceding they had a valid need for relief caused by his smoking. But if he admits he is poisoning and suffocating his own children, how can he live with himself and still smoke? Denial of their suffering, however, gives carte blanche to "just one" cigarette. And if one does not hurt, why not "just one" more? We have to understand the bind this smoker is in. If we can, we may be able to gently help him look at his own feelings when his kids object to his smoking. We can try to help him connect with even a small dose of his own guilt or empathy. We *may* be able to help him see that there is really only one way out of the dilemma. This is, of course, precisely what the denial avoided in the first place.

> *Denial protects my craving by blinding me both to my dependence and to the price paid by self and others.*

An AA speaker, a businessman sober four years, pitched from the podium. He was sharing the fruits of working his program for that long. "You know," he said, "this past year other people have become real to me. I can feel their presence."

Wow!

What is he saying about the nature of his alcoholism and his denial? Is this pure biochemistry? If other people were real to him from the beginning, would his disease have run such a devastating course? And does this lack of empathy not qualify as a "disease" every bit as much as any genetic factor? The difference is that empathy can be developed, that people can grow emotionally and socially. Genetic engineering is not yet able to turn pickles back into cucumbers. Until it is, we helpers have our work cut out for us. The author can well picture such an alcoholic, "dry" by some genetic therapy of the future. He has no doubt that such a man or woman will still need AA and/or some other human therapy. Our job may be more clearly necessary than before, precisely because the drug itself will no longer be a distracting issue.

Harry Tiebout [1] worked with early AA members and wrote of his experience as their psychiatrist. He was one of the first to describe the "wall" many alcoholic/addicts feel between themselves and others before "surrendering." The author still hears people describe this experience of self in just such language, "a wall."

"Denial" appears to be one name for this wall.

It seems to consist of a block to allowing myself to imagine your feelings. I am particularly blind to those painful feelings in you resulting from decisions and actions by me.

The person hiding behind the wall seems unable to perform the simple act that makes all human relatedness possible: taking the role of the other.

Meanwhile, this mysterious barrier protects my right and need to keep drinking/drugging.

Given the chance to empathize, a powerful "whirr-click" of defense seems to activate in the mind of the practicing addict/

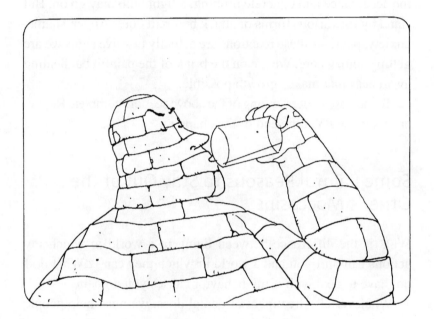

alcoholic. It often has such force and power the alcoholic does not even seem to know what has happened, not till later, like the speaker above. What the person may be aware of is a feeling of threat, anger, or of the "wall" itself. A helper may be able to open this up, to get the person looking at it and wondering about it. With genuine acceptance and concrete probing, a light bulb may go on. But stand by for various forms of attack before it does! Anger, shame, anxiety, panic — these reactions are actually positive signs we are getting somewhere. We are on the brink of the painful but healing awareness that makes growth possible.

To increase understanding of the above section, complete Recovery Exercise #3 at the end of the chapter.

Some Painful Reasons to Stay Out of the Other's Moccasins

What is the difference between living in a world in which my actions can hurt you and a world in which they can't? What do I not have to deal with if my behavior causes you no pain?

Whatever else treatment of denial does, we must help people live in a world in which they can hurt and be hurt. People may remain "dry" without this recognition. But such abstinence depends on clinging fiercely to the wall between self and others. This is a lonely and tense way to go, white-knuckling it, to be sure.

Apparently, there is a price for coming out from behind my wall. My choices are now influenced by their impact on a world with other people in it. To mix metaphors, a rolling stone suddenly gathers a whole load of "moss." I may still "want what I want when I want it." But I am no longer willing to hurt you to get it. I even want you to be happy! And I know that my behavior does affect you, as yours affects me.

But the person still in denial rebuffs any external influence.

> *As a matter of (subconscious) principle, I will not allow the other to affect my experience. Still less will I permit them to control my behavior. Neither my behavior nor my beliefs will allow outside input — self must control self at all costs. I am a fortress, barricaded by the stone wall of denial and surrounded by the moat of alcohol. No one will tell me what to do with myself or what to believe about myself. No one will make me feel what I don't want to feel. Having cut self off from emotional contact, I spiral down the course of my disease.*
>
> *The question of awareness remains. Do I know what I am doing? Do I have a choice?*

☞   The frustrating answers for would-be helper and would-be recovering addict/alcoholic seem to be "Yes," "No," "It varies." Many people can talk about their denial and even their conscious lying. Others can't. Many beat themselves up for what they do or say — they assume they are acting out of choice (more later). What seems to be true is that we humans can know what we are physically doing. We can even claim to be acting exactly as we intended, getting results we expected. Yet we can at the very same moment be oblivious to the craving that drives us. Not only that, we may not have the slightest grasp of the true meaning and impact of what we do. At this point, the psychology of denial encounters the foundation for forgiveness. We confront the plea of Jesus for the human race: "Forgive them, for they know not what they do."

> *Am I aware of the physical and emotional cravings, aided by the unconscious defenses, that made me do what I did? That robbed me of rational options even as I "rationalized?" Am I aware of the power of physical addiction and the presence of unconscious feelings, fears, attitudes that compel me with such power? Do I see the true impact of my actions on others or even on myself? Do I know I have just chipped another flake*

off my self-esteem? Can I recognize the rock of guilt I have just added to my sack? Do I see the scars I have just carved in my children, my spouse or, perhaps, my career?

This is why the first step of AA is so important.

To admit and experience "I am powerless over alcohol and my life is unmanageable" is to recognize that a force other than conscious, rational will controls my behavior. How galling. I didn't want other people to control my actions or beliefs. Now I have to admit I was controlled by a drug. What I may never admit is that this could not have happened without participation of my unconscious thoughts, feelings, and attitudes. At this level, character is involved in the disease and it will have to be involved in the recovery.

Recognizing the power of the unconscious is the last barrier of denial to fall. Some alcoholics remain abstinent for life without clearing it, oblivious to their other compulsions and self-defeating reactions.

Denial of hurting others, also protects the drinker from "looking in the mirror of self" [2]. It delays "pitiful and incomprehensible demoralization"[3] and "hitting bottom" or "surrender." In other words, denial protects alcoholics from the painful awakening that launches recovery. What makes this truly a "disease" (even without neurochemistry), is that an alcoholic/addict treats the self the same as others.

If I can't recognize emotional pain in myself — of course, "One won't hurt." If I can't admit what I care about so much that it hurts — I refuse to empathize with my own feelings, too — it is only natural to say "F--- it" and drink or drug instead.

To increase understanding of the above section, complete Recovery Exercises #4 and #5 at the end of the chapter.

The Wall Between Alcoholic and Self

Students of behavior modification have quantified this principle: the more quickly consequence follows behavior, the greater the impact on learning. They are not entirely wrong in the case of addiction — drugs that are smoked reach the brain the most quickly. And drugs that are smoked are the most addictive. But there is no room in traditional behaviorism for a "rat" who disconnects behavior from consequence altogether, an "organism" that forgets painful events as quickly as it produces them. Picture a research animal that can dance on an electrified grid while making no connection to pulling the lever that turns on the juice. This is a "rat" unable to learn indeed, more surely than the hamster spinning endlessly in its exercise wheel. In a lab animal, it would take neurosurgery to produce this condition. In a human being, our neurochemistry apparently gives us the dubious privilege of blocking the feedback without which we are doomed. The good news is that whenever we are able to stop doing that, our brain is intact.

☞   It takes more than pain to get an alcoholic or addict sober. Otherwise, no one would last on skid row or in jail or in the misery of a toxic family. It takes an emotional connection between the pain "I" suffer and the action "I" took. This is what I must *realize*. Without at least this much, voluntary recovery does not have a chance.

> *To let myself see how much I hurt you by my drinking, is to feel the guilt and shame of all that I have done. This includes my humiliating inability to face it up until now. I see myself as "selfish" and "wrong," a "fool," blinded. But this is not all — I also see myself compelled by the need and/or desire for alcohol. This addiction/compulsion is not just shameful, it is frightening. I don't understand it, but if I see it at all, I see myself blind and driven for years. And there is no visible guarantee that I will be able to regain control of myself just because the blinders are off. I may*

not be able to live with alcohol now that I see what it does to me and to others, but that in no way assures that I can live without it. No wonder I have avoided this moment for so long! No wonder I will rebuild the wall if I possibly can.

Educating and convincing me that I have a disease may help me swallow this bitter pill. It definitely gives me a solid reason to not take "just one." It is another matter to tell me my emotions are not involved in this disease. Especially when my denial has blocked the emotional experience that makes recovery possible.

For some, this seems to set up a pattern of sober denial that can facilitate short-term (one to two years) recovery and long-term relapse. For others it creates chronic white-knuckling, a dry drunk without end. Is there a hereditary link in the chain reaction of alcoholism? Unquestionably, for some people. Do alcoholics have "underlying" emotional problems? Frankly, no. The emotional problem is right there on the surface. You have a glimpse of it every time he or she uses any drug to change a feeling. Denial of this emotional reality is the seed of most "F--- it" relapses and many wishful ones. And this denial is so often shared by the most sincere of would-be helpers.

Lorie Dwinell and Jane Middelton-Moz in their book, *After the Tears, Reclaiming the Personal Losses of Childhood* [4], spell out how self-help books often set up the "adult child" for failure. Such books often paint ideal pictures of how we should function. The treatment field still sometimes tells people that, if they just work their AA program, they will be "weller than well." The good news is that AA does work. The bad news is that it does not necessarily work *by itself* for all problems for all people. One of the great gifts of the ACA movement has been to reassure so many dry alcoholics who lack "emotional sobriety " [6]. To explain why they are not "crazy" or "failures" just because they may still be struggling, after working all Twelve Steps. Claudia Black's (1990) book *Double Duty* [5] brings this point poignantly home. The good news is that most of these "other problems" are treatable and that treatment seems to work best *with* self-help. They seem to "potentiate" each other, like two drugs!

To increase understanding of the above section, complete Recovery Exercise #6 at the end of the chapter.

The Will Behind the Wall

Denial feels and acts like a "wall" to those on both sides of the barrier. To those on the outside, it also looks like blindness and deafness. However, it does not seem to be quite the innocent disability of the physically blind and deaf. This wall of addictive denial is not passive, nor is the energy behind it.

The repeated biblical admonition, "let them who have ears to hear, hear," seems to have been directed at people *not* in denial. It seems to be excluding those who have mentally cut off both ears and covered both eyes. The resulting deafness and blindness responds to the light of threatening truth as ancient kings rewarded messengers bearing bad news. "Off with their heads!" Likewise, the Old Testament prophets complained repeatedly about the refusal of the "stiff-necked people" to face their shame. They could have been lamenting the intransigence of so many of our twentieth century alcoholic/addicts. These biblical references address a central psychological fact about denial — it is a will, regardless of whether it is conscious or unconscious. Nor does it matter whether the object of my denial is physical (cancer, spinal chord injury, alcoholism, etc.) or mental (grief, divorce, inadequacy, alcoholism, etc.). A mind in denial is a mind fiercely determined not to admit the reality it denies. And, above all, not to feel the pain it will feel if reality gets through.

William James' [7] definition of "will" emphasized the mental effort to pay attention to an idea in the face of distraction. His own example of inability to hold fast to an idea? The alcoholic who is unable to sustain his image of self as "drunkard." James quotes such a person saying, "This time will be different" and taking the first drink. This is a variation of "One won't hurt" still in common use today. In fact, James' list of alcoholic excuses to take the first drink rival those of the Big Book.

What James did not seem to consider is that another, more powerful will may be fueling the distractions. Denial itself may be seen as a will of iron vigor, a ferocious determination not to be distracted by real facts or inner warning signals. As we have seen, it blocks out past experience, or any amount of pain to self or others. It holds fast to the image of self as "normal," tunes out any messages that would jeopardize the inalienable right to drink/drug. Once recognized, the will of alcoholic denial is awesome to behold. This is so whether it arises in the unconscious mind, the intellect, brain chemistry, or all three. One thing is certain. If the phenomenon of "surrender" has any reality at all, it is the will in alcoholic denial that must "admit defeat." There is no evidence that neurochemistry of addiction changes with surrender. In fact, a large part of surrender is that the physical disease *won't* change, that "this time" will *never* be different.

But what is the force of this will and where does it come from? First and foremost, it is a will to use the drug and to experience its effects *without* challenge from others. It is the will to experience the chemical illusion of omnipotence at worst; of relief, at least. It is a fierce determination to protect, apparently guarding both the immediate right to drink and a precious picture of self as "normal." Which craving is more powerful? — the physical desire for the drug itself? — the more illusive desire for psychological relief? — or the relentless inner pressure to maintain a certain image of self? We underestimate *any* of them at the peril of recovery.

Let us not forget that denial is also a philosophy — a way of approaching reality and life. The philosophy of denial posits that reality is what I define it to be. As a result, contradicting facts are not only threats to my drinking and/or self-image, they undermine my sense of reality. This would make any of us nervous.

The person in denial seems to be a philosophical idealist (one who posits that reality is what my mind creates it to be). I am not open to painful intrusions from a reality that I have not dictated and I am a true believer in "constructivism." This is the theory that my reality is created entirely by the words with which I "construct" it. My simple mistake is to misunderstand what words really do. As Anthony Demello [8] points out so eloquently, words "point." They "carve out" pieces of reality, abstracting from it, even adding to the whole by so doing.

But reality was there first. If not, all "prophesies" would be self-fulfilling. "One won't hurt" would be an accurate prediction, if words of prediction control and create reality. It is both a fact and a spiritual principle that reality comes whole. No word can capture all of it, any more than one ice ax can chop off a whole glacier. Spirituality itself becomes direct, wordless contact with reality. This is not possible if I am busy pasting words on it, like a blind person pinning tails on a donkey that won't stand still. This is the trap that ensnares both the theologian and the "fundamentalist." Both worship "the letter" and remain blind to the spirit. Both will cut your physical or moral throat in the name of a spirituality which forbade any such thing.

Demello points out another frustrating fact about reality — it never stands still, least of all, in the here-and-now. To be in "conscious contact" is to be in motion, while to say "F--- it" and drink/drug is to try to "stop the world and get off." If reality weren't real, nothing would happen when I try to "escape." My mental departure would have no more effect than crossing an invisible and nonexistent boundary line. I could believe whatever I *wish,* and there would be no such thing as denial.

To increase understanding of the above section, complete Recovery Exercise #7 at the end of the chapter.

References

[1] Tiebout, Harry. "Conversion as a Psychological Phenomenon". Paper read before the New York Psychiatric Society, April 4, 1944.

[2] Martin, Father Joseph. Film, "Guidelines for Helping the Alcoholic". Carpentaria, CA: FMS, 1976.

[3] Anonymous. *Alcoholics Anonymous*. New York: Alcoholics Anonymous World Services, 1955.

[4] Dwinell, Lorie and Middelton-Moz, Jane. *After the Tears, Reclaiming the Personal Losses of Childhood*. Pompano Beach, Florida: Health Communications, Inc., 1986.

[5] Bill W. "The Next Frontier: Emotional Sobriety" in *The Language of the Heart, Bill W's Grapevine Writings*. New York: The AA Grapevine, Inc. 1988.

[6] Black, Claudia. *Double Duty*. New York: Random House, 1990.

[7] James, William. *The Principles of Psychology*, (2 Volumes). New York: Henry Holt & Company.

[8] deMello, Anthony, (Edited by Stroud, Francis J.). *Awareness, The Perils and Opportunities of Reality*. New York, London, etc.: Image Doubleday, 1992.

Recovery Exercises

1. Write a list of things people told you about yourself when you were in denial that you could not see or believe. What did they see that you could not? How did it feel when you did see? Are you better off?

2. Pick something people are telling you about yourself that you do not believe. Imagine that this thing is true. How do you feel? How do you think others will look at you if it really is true? How do you feel about that possibility? Share and discuss with counselor/group.

3. Write a list of three specific ways you hurt someone you cared about while drinking/drugging. Try to put into words what you said to yourself about it at the time. If there were no words, try to describe how you did or did not look at their pain and the fact it resulted from your drinking/drugging. If any passages in this chapter fit, find and quote them.

4. Make a list of five to ten ways you personally refused to be controlled by anything or anybody while drinking/drugging. For each example, try to spell out how you wound up losing control anyway. Try to identify what did control you.

5. Pick at least one good example of irrational, self-defeating behavior on your part. Try to spell out what you were aware of as you reacted in this way — conscious observations, intentions, decisions and feelings. Then try to identify other wants, feelings or attitudes that may have controlled you at the time. Do not be afraid to ask group and/or counselor for their impressions.

6. Have you felt a "wall" between yourself and others? If so, imagine *being* that wall. Then let this wall-self read and answer these questions:
What are you protecting me from?
What do you think will happen if someone else "gets through?"
How willing are you to allow a gate to be built, one that I will control?

7. Read this chapter and underline the three passages that you react most strongly to. Write/share what you think your reactions mean — what do they tell you about your problem and about your recovery?

Denial —
Four Ways to Catch It in the Act

Relapse Prevention as Denial Reduction

As we have seen, "One won't hurt" denies the loss of control that defines addiction. In order to believe this falsehood, I must somehow bury the evidence, at least enough that *I* can't see it. "F--- it" denies caring, choice, possibility, while seeming to assume a "fix" is still a solution of some sort. Saying either of these things is a "defense" in itself, but my ability to say them depends on other defenses (links) that make these two possible. This chapter describes four of these other mental actions, all of which strip my awareness, my access to truth or reality. If "... twisted thinking is the major *cause* of your suffering" [1] and "the truth will set you free" [2], these links are bars of the prison. They are not the only ones. In Chapter 9, we will look at the Dr. Jekyll/Mr. Hyde split, and there are others. The ones described here make sense to the relapsers with whom the author works. Each sheds some further light on "One won't hurt" and "F--- it."

The role of continuing denial in repeated relapse seems clear, making "denial reduction" synonymous with "relapse prevention." The concrete observations of this chapter are shared to give both helper and relapser renewed energy. It is hoped they may help to maintain perspective for engaging the common enemy, denial. Millions in research money fund the quest for the missing genetic link.

But helpers and addict/alcoholics are pretty much left on our own to tackle the problem of denial as such. No one seems to pay to study "acceptance" or "realization" as such. To be fair, "Project Match" evaluated outcome for three therapies focused on these phenomena, even if they do not use the same vocabulary. Cognitive behavioral therapy directly addresses the issue of the addictive belief system. Remotivational therapy might be legitimately called re-acceptance therapy — the cycles of change are all too recognizable as cycles of denial and acceptance. The Twelve Step counseling of Project Match, of course, hammered away at acceptance, aka "Step One." But the research questions took these seemingly different approaches as givens while it pursued the question of which one worked best for whom. Project Match did not, to this consumer's understanding, attempt to define or measure denial and acceptance. Nor did it try to identify how one becomes the other and what the helper/client team might do to make that happen.

A Patient's Definition

 "Denial is when you say what is, isn't."

A newly recovering alcoholic came up with this descriptive definition in group years ago and the author would be hard put to improve on it. We might be a little more technical and say that denial consists of not believing a painful truth, thereby avoiding the painful feelings and choices that would follow. That is the apparent motivation — but how does the mind *do* it?

Denial as Prejudice

An analogy with prejudice gives us a glimpse of the mind dispensing with irritating facts that threaten belief. For example, a male chauvinist might believe that a woman cannot do the work he does. Unfortunately for him, a woman joins his department or job site. Not only does she do this particular job, she does it measurably better than him!

Does he alter his ideas? No, not our male supremacist.

"She's getting breaks from the boss, the customers, probably sleeps with them," he alibis.

"Beginner's luck," he concludes.

By a few well-chosen explanations, he dismisses the facts that threaten his precious belief. And if he can't explain the facts away, he can fall back on an even more primitive and complete way of ridding himself of the troublesome facts: he forgets them! In these ways, prejudice protects itself from reality.

Denial works in a similar way. I can explain away the facts that threaten my cherished belief that I am a "social drinker," that I am "okay," "in control of myself," "normal." Or, I can just forget them.

We cling passionately and stubbornly to our beliefs about other people or groups. How much more vehemently do we defend our most cherished beliefs about ourselves! Seeing denial as prejudice also reminds us that every *dis*belief hides a belief — every denial is the flip side of an affirmation! Empathy for what denial protects may soften it, while relentless battering of the wall only seems to make it thicker.

> *What prejudice about self is protected by "One won't hurt?"*
> *I'm "normal." I'm "strong." I'm okay and I'm in control of myself — and I would never knowingly do something that would hurt myself or anyone else. Why, that would be "crazy" or "cruel," and I am, I believe, "nice." Like the spouse-beater who says, "I couldn't have caused her black eye because I'm not that kind of person!" Prejudice: clinging to mental categories and labels in the face of facts that contradict them.*

What about "F--- it?"

> *Maybe the prejudice is negative. When "I quit" is what these words mean, perhaps, I protect the negative image of myself as a*

"loser." Or as "inadequate," a child, really, — you can't expect me to continue to cope. Then again, maybe I believe I'm a "victim."

And if my prejudice about myself is "positive?" The very fact I say a resentful "F--- it" avoids facing the fact I'm quitting. If I think of myself as a "winner," how can I admit I'm quitting? I may also avoid saying "I don't care" by using "F--- it." Of course, I'm a "caring person!" — just ask me. The spirit of "F--- it" is blame, that something else is not how it "should" be, justifying my relapse. I only do what I do for "good" reasons, when someone else is "bad." Whatever else recovery requires, it is going to entail facing what I have really been doing. I must give up my rigid and out-dated ideas of who I am. "Cleaning house," they call it.

To increase understanding of the above section, complete Recovery Exercises #1 and #2 at the end of the chapter.

Denial as "Not-Thinking-About-It"

Ask a recovering person who feels badly now about something done while drinking. "What did you feel about this incident then?" The answer will so often be, "I didn't think about it."

"Not-thinking-about-it," is the essence of denial.

How do we think? By spontaneous mental associations — ideas, memories, images, even words and phrases that "pop into our minds" as we contemplate something. And by questions, asking ourselves what this or that means — how does it work and what should I do? So how do we "not think?" First, by avoidance, by not looking at whatever would trigger our associations and questions. Second, by refusing to pay attention to spontaneous inner signals, "pushing them out of my mind." It usually helps to stay very busy and never sit still. How do we stop questions? All of the above, and getting angry if someone else has the audacity to ask the question we blocked in our own mind.

To spell out the role of questions in problem solving:

- I notice my car needs gas and fill it up, vaguely troubled. In response to this vague inner signal, I ask myself how recently I was last at the pumps and question my log.
- I see it has been less time or fewer miles than usual and check the mileage, asking myself and the numbers if it has dropped.
- I see the mileage has dropped and ask myself what is wrong.
- I wonder if I am losing fuel and raise the hood.
- Everywhere I look — carburetor, fuel lines, gas filter, I look with questions. Does it look as it should? Do I see or smell a leak? When I find my leak, I have answered the question "what is wrong?" and, very likely, "what needs to be done?"

The inside of human experience is not a machine. But we still think in questions to face our personal problems, if we let ourselves think at all.

- "What's bothering me?" (How specifically do I feel? What are my feelings about? What do I want? What are my choices? What is the best thing to do? God, what made me do that again?)
- "When did it start?"
- "What can or should I do about it?"

The addict/alcoholic thinking "One won't hurt" is already cut off from inner signals.

We saw in Chapter 2 I am in touch with neither wants nor feelings, nor with the pain that "just one" painkiller will nowhere near relieve. And the last thing I want to do at this moment is think. Like, gee, is that really true? What happened last time I said this? Did I get "hurt?" Just how many times have I said this and acted on it? What is making me say it again now? Is there something I want to escape from? Am I an addict/al-

coholic or not? If I have changed my mind about being addicti-
ve, how come? What did they say in meetings and/or in treat-
ment to do when this thought comes back? Where are my pho-
ne numbers? Where are my reminder cards? So much to think
about — I'm getting a headache. I know what would take care
of these annoying questions and thoughts — "just one!"

"F--- it" avoids thinking much more directly, precisely be-
cause the two words are so meaningless. I do the most mean-
ingful negative thing I can do about my addiction — pick up
the first drink/drug of relapse — while saying to myself two
words that are devoid of meaning. But one of the "it"s in "F---
it" is clearly the effort of recovery. Some of this work is mental
and requires deliberate thought. What am I so upset about?
What might I have to accept about it? What change? If I resent
this, what was my part in it? What makes me think my frustra-
tion justifies my drinking? Do I have the disease or not? Keep in
mind, "white-knuckle sobriety" is based on "not thinking about
it." Not thinking about drinking or about what made me drink,
about feelings and problems and my inability to cope. The need
to grow? F--- it!

Curiosity about my own behavior is one of the greatest assets I
can bring to any form of therapy or self-help. Denial snuffs out
curiosity, as surely as an elephant stomping a mouse, in person
and helper alike. Therapy can awaken and support curiosity by
asking questions once blocked in the person, especially if the helper
is prepared to deal with the anger and/or anxiety they trigger. Show
this writer a person who refuses to look at questions about how
they got into this mess. He will show you someone who is in denial
and will get into the mess again.

To increase understanding of the above section, complete Recov-
ery Exercises #3 and #4 at the end of the chapter.

Denial as "Isolation-of-the-Connected"

Much has been written about the importance of the human capacity for forming or recognizing patterns. A number of years ago, the author heard a scientist from the Rockwell "Think Tank" discuss robotics. One difficulty these scientists were has stuck to his clinical ribs ever since. At that time, they had not yet been able to create a robot that could discern patterns. They just wanted one to work in a relatively simple production-line environment. Yet a human eye connected to a human mind was still needed to discern which widgets were assembled backwards. This capability seems to have separated man from machine at the time. Its level of development may still separate us from animals. This would seem most clearly true in "perceiving" patterns made up of elements that are not physically present at the same time. A hawk may be able to spot a "pattern" representing a mouse on the ground, much as the sailor waits for his eye to form the pattern of whatever appears on the horizon. But it takes a human mind to see a pattern of truancy, a tendency to exaggerate, or a weakness for the letter-high fastball.

Understanding two things about pattern formation shed light on how we blind ourselves. First, the process of perception involves a passive phase. It is something that we "allow" our minds to do, much as we allow our stomachs to digest food. We may strain to see, only to have our best efforts rewarded when we stop consciously trying. If we become mentally receptive, somewhat passive, the mind will form patterns about what it encounters. This is its nature, to organize experience. This is why meditation can work so powerfully, or "letting go and letting God." Second, this process depends much on my willingness to let it happen. I cannot force a pattern to form, but I can surely block it.

- "A man convinced against his will is of the same opinion still."

- "There are none so blind as those who will not see."
- "Let them that have ears to hear, hear."

These folkways capture a truth about the nature of all important human realization, the process of coming to see what was not previously seen. We must be willing, but we cannot force ourselves to see. And we must let the truth come to us, if we are to know it at all.

☞ "Alcoholism," any addiction, can be known by the "addict" and anyone else only as a pattern. To not see alcoholism is to not see the forest for the trees. Alcoholism is a forest that emerges out of a number of discreet events, all tied together by one common denominator ... every tree gives off the odor of alcohol, whether from roots or branches.

"Isolation" is that perverse and subtle response that blocks my mind from forming the pattern. I see the trees, each one. I even smell the alcohol, though I may place blame elsewhere. But I don't connect the trees into a pattern that outlines my problem: alcoholism. My problem/life is like a dot-to-dot drawing and I seem unable to connect the dots. The facts start to add up to something and some part of me must see where they are going. And that part of me blocks the picture before it can form in my conscious mind. The Gestalt won't close. The "aha!" won't come. How do I stop it? I don't know. I don't even know I am doing it, though I get pretty huffy if someone tries to close the Gestalt for me.

One way isolation shows up is in the honest answers to the questions of an assessment interview. Asked directly, many alcoholics/addicts will admit to their DUIs, missing work, hitting family members, etc. The counselor is getting excited about the clear forest that is emerging (to the counselor.) But the client so often
☞ still sees only trees. The counselor may be surprised, even stunned, that the person does not see this obvious problem. Didn't the facts

come out of your own mouth? The addict/alcoholic may be just as surprised that the counselor seems to think there is a serious problem. Treatment for what? Who's sick? The would-be helper asks how the the person could *not* see the need for help now. Answer: isolation.

This assessment coin has a flip side. A surprising number of people share how the assessment interview itself "opened my eyes." How? Precisely by putting so many discrete facts of a lifetime together, all at once. For some, it is a powerful "intervention" in itself. It apparently connects facts that had been in the person's mind all along. The interview simply brings them all together in one time and place for one apparently receptive mind.

It is painfully clear that "One won't hurt" isolates that particular drink, the one I am about to take. By so doing, it disconnects the fatal decision from all the hurtful drinks that will follow. The wishful relapse also isolates this moment from a pattern of having done this before. One of the DSM [3] diagnostic criteria for the disease of "substance dependence" reads "...the substance is often taken in larger amounts or over a longer period than was intended." "One won't hurt" is the voice of that "intention." Another DSM criterion includes "...unsuccessful efforts to cut down or control substance use." "One won't hurt" is the voice of those "unsuccessful efforts."

> *If I face that voice and all the times "it" has spoken and I have listened, I face two of my very own "criteria," criteria that are so personal and so universal at the same time. On the other hand, if I use "This time will be different" or "I can handle it now," I imply all those times when it was not different and I did not "handle it." Yes, there were some dots of trouble with my drug of choice, but this dot does not really connect to those. In fact, it is not really a dot, because time has changed me. How — what are you asking me to think about?! Sooner or later, my survival requires that I connect one of the biggest*

dot/patterns of all. The one for repeatedly disconnecting the other dots, whether I used "One won't hurt" or "This time will be different" or "No one will know." This repeated self-decep- tion is a "criterion" (a dot!) for addiction. It is what the AA Big Book calls "that strange mental twist," a form of denial which is here called "isolation."

How does "F--- it" isolate the numerous interconnected expe- riences of addiction and relapse? White-knuckle sobriety begins with the separation of drinking/drugging from coping with prob- lems.

It starts by denying that the problem lies with my sober self. I just "set my mind" to stay clean and sober. When some- thing bothers me, I "stuff" the feelings. Each upset becomes another "rock" in my proverbial "gunnysack." By the time "I've had it," the accumulated "dots" I did not resolve or connect are what I let fly. I did not look at each upset. I did not look at the pattern of repeating this cycle. Each of the upset/dots is part of this cycle. Each cycle is a "big dot" in a long-term pattern of big dots. If I can allow them to connect, they all add up to one thing — my pattern of addiction.

Let's not forget the most fundamental disconnect of all. When "F--- it" means "My way or the highway," I *must* have what I want, or else! Life itself is a series of frustration dots for all hu- man beings. And the striking thing about all these rebuffs by re- ality is this: Life goes on.

Every time I thought I had to have something and did not get it, life went on! What would that tell me, were I to connect those "dots?" That my urgent "needs" were just wants after all, that I got along without them. Most of all, that it is con- ceivable to take "no" for an answer from life, without having to say "F--- it" and drinking or drugging.

"Hitting bottom" or "surrender" seems to involve seeing the forest created by so many painful trees. As mentioned above, the author is usually encouraged when an alcoholic in early recovery reports spontaneous memories. These are revealing and painful drinking episodes that were dismissed at the time they occurred. Every drinker in denial has a collection of such memories, like an unopened photo record of the disease as it unfolded. The day that album falls open is the day the person gives up isolation-of-the-connected — the "Gestalt" of the addiction can now close. Aha!

To increase understanding of the above section, complete Recovery Exercises #5, #6, and #7 at the end of the chapter.

Pseudo-responsibility: "Beating Myself Up" as Denial

After a recurrence of any form of self-defeating behavior, many people will beat themselves up with words.

> *"Asshole."*
> *"Dummy."*
> *"Stupid."*
> *"I'm such a fool."*
> *"I can't believe I did that (again). I'll never forgive myself."*
> *"I'm so ashamed I'd like to crawl in a hole."*
> *"If I could slug myself, I would."*

Such is the language with which we "beat ourselves up," alcoholic/addicts included.

This does not sound, on the surface, like someone "in denial" of a problem. Not until you've heard it over and over again, from the same person, someone who has been doing and saying the same thing, for the same reason, time after seemingly endless time. Over and over again.

It turns out that "beating myself up" almost always is part of the problem, not part of the solution. Geneen Roth [4] spells this out poignantly for overeaters in *Feeding the Hungry Heart.* Show this author a person beating himself up for something he or she did or didn't do — he will show you a person who is going to do or not do that very same thing again.

Why is this so? How come self-punishment does not correct behavior? Worse, how does it seem to perpetuate the very behavior it punishes? The answer to these questions lies in the denial on which self-punishment is based.

First, consider when we punish people. An infant soils its diapers and causes inconvenience, distasteful odors, perhaps, disgust. Do we punish the infant? Yet the same child, three or four years later, steals a cookie he was expressly told not to eat. Why do we punish him or her? Simply because we think she or he is old enough to at least begin learning to exercise choice and control.

     The key here is the assumption that the perpetrator has control.

> *This is no less true when the perpetrator is my Self. When I punish myself for what I did or did not do, I assume and affirm my own self-control. I cling to my power of choice, punishing myself for not using willpower and willfully ordering myself not to let it happen again.*
>
> *What is the First Step of all Twelve Step programs?—to admit I am "powerless" over the very behavior for which I have been punishing myself. In other words, the very fact I am punishing myself reveals that I am denying my powerlessness! I haven't seen enough of my problem to admit I have lost control. I do not really believe that one important AA shoe fits me — that I "have lost the power of choice in drink." No wonder I can't solve what I can't yet see.*

And this is just the first level of denial.

A gory metaphor describes the profound denial of a deeper problem that controls problem behavior: compulsive, addictive, repetitive, impulsive, nonassertive, aggressive, self-defeating be-

havior of virtually all types. Anything we beat ourselves up over
— each can be viewed as blood oozing from a wound. Why?
Because virtually all such behavior appears to be triggered by painful feelings. Pain is the wound, out of which the behavior flows.
This can be true even if the pain originates in biochemistry, or
even if such pain would not trigger craving in someone without
addictive disease.

> But, what do I accomplish when I beat myself up? It seems
> to go something like this: Some "blood" appears in the form of
> some "stupid" behavior. Annoyed, I wipe it off. A few moments
> later, I look down and notice the blood oozing from my person
> again. "Stop that, you jerk" I command, once again wiping
> myself off. Does "it" stop? Hardly. Now I'm really getting an-
> noyed. I may even smack myself in the bloody mess, furiously
> ordering myself to never, never do that again. Am I getting the
> idea yet? Hardly. More, I am not even looking for my wound.
> Not only that, but don't let someone else try to tell me there is
> a wound under all this blood. They may risk getting a wound
> for themselves! I am not looking and I don't want to look. No,
> far better to beat myself up for what I "chose" to do. Yes, better
> that than to admit I have lost my power of choice.
>
> Fear and shame guard the gates to consciousness of my per-
> sonal wound(s). After all, it is frightening to look down and see
> a bullet hole, a knife, a decubitus ulcer, or a malignant tumor.
> How bad is it, doc? Do I really want to know? And it may feel
> even worse to touch my sense that a parent did not love me, to
> connect with my feeling of unworthiness, guilt about Vietnam,
> shame about incest, etc. These things may not "cause" addic-
> tion without biochemical predisposition, but they certainly
> contribute to many a relapse. In effect, the "bio" part of my
> disease points the gun at my "psychosocial" head. It commands,
> "Learn to deal with the emotional part of this disease, or I pull
> the trigger!"

Is a wound something to be proud of? Do I look forward to beach weather, so I can show it off? Yes, I may have been completely innocent when wounded, but part of the reason I hide this sucker away is the shame I feel about it. Once I get past the fear and shame, then we get to the core of the problem. Wounds are painful. If I don't look at and don't see it, I can virtually disconnect my awareness from the pain. Hey, if some "bleeding" occurs, far better to distract myself with self-flagellation and righteous anger. It almost works, almost all the time. Do I know I am doing this? Sometimes, sometimes not.

When I say "One won't hurt," I deny pain, both what I may be trying to relieve and what I am about to cause. When I beat myself up afterwards, I create pain to distract myself from whatever is left. I also distract myself from facing my compulsion, my loss of control, and, above all, from the terrifying necessity to give up my "pain-killer." I avoid the mere fact I was controlled by something other than reason or reality when I said "one won't hurt."

When I say "F--- it," I say that staying in reality is not worth it. Use of my drug for relief is worth it. Afterwards, I beat myself up instead of looking at what happened. I don't go back and look at what I was upset about in the first place, how I coped. I do not seek out the tools I did not use and what stopped me from doing so. "Beating myself up" is a "fix" in its own right.

 Professional helpers and relapsing addict/alcoholics need to work together for three things:

1. To understand that beating self up for relapse is a good way to get ready for the next one.
2. To face and feel the primary fact avoided by self-punishment: being under the control of *something,* addiction, physical and/ or mental.
3. To gently explore and work with deeper emotional pain that may have been involved.

AA and sponsors have traditionally started with "power-lessness" and the "disease concept." Members are encouraged to set the hammer of self-hate aside — "Let us love you until you can love yourself." Some degree of self-acceptance settles in. When there seems to be enough, the hammer is gone and a shovel takes its place. It is called Step Four, a "searching and fearless moral inventory." Most people find this process includes facing the pain that was there all along. This is a delicate point at which sponsor and therapist may work together. Our target is the pain that sometimes said "One won't hurt" or more often "F--- it." With or without professional help, Steps Four through Nine work to heal the pain. Steps Ten through Twelve work to keep it from coming back. All this work is what I can do instead of my old behavior, saying "One won't hurt" and then beating myself up because it hurt so very much. That, or saying "F--- it"/"I can't cope" and then beating myself up instead of learning how.

To increase understanding of the above section, complete Recovery Exercise #8 at the end of the chapter.

References

[1] Burns, David. *Feeling Good, the New Mood Therapy.* New York: Signet, 1981.

[2] *New American Standard Bible.* La Habra, CA: The Lockman Foundation, 1960.

[3] American Psychiatric Association. *Diagnostic and Statistical Manual of Mental Disorders (Fourth Edition).*Washington, D.C.: American Psychiatric Association, 1994.

[4] Roth, Geneen. *Feeding the Hungry Heart, the Experience of Compulsive Eating*, New York: Signet, 1982.

Recovery Exercises

1. Write down three of the most positive things you have always
    believed about yourself. See if you can spell out in what ways
    and how often they ceased to be true when you drank/drugged.
    Be sure to share how you feel about what this shows you and
    don't beat yourself up.

2. If you have relapsed, were those positive things true about
    you right at the moments when you were saying "One won't
    hurt" and/or "F--- it?"

3. Make a list of 2 (5, 10) painful things that were caused by
    your drinking before you admitted you are really an addict/
    alcoholic. What did you think or say to yourself about them at
    the time? How are your thoughts different now? Your feel-
    ings?

4. If you don't think you are really an alcoholic or addict, write
    down 2 (5, 10) of the most painful things caused by your use.
    What did/do you tell yourself about them? Share with coun-
    selor and/or group and ask for feedback. If someone you cared
    about said the same things you do, what would you say to
    them?

5. Write down any moments you have realised something about
    your disease. Share how it felt and how it changed you.

6. Read Chapter 1 of the AA Big Book. Highlight each "aha"
    that Bill W. has about the disease and/or recovery. He does
    not call them that, but he makes it clear there were numerous
    times something about the disease became more real to him.
    Share your reaction to each one and any similar moments you
    have had, including those in treatment and/or in AA.

7. Complete and/or review your own chemical history. See if you can identify "dots" that it connected for you when you did it, and even now, when you reread it. Be sure to share these with someone. If you share in AA, CA, NA, try to communicate this experience to at least one new-comer.

8. If you are someone who beats him/herself up over relapse, picture a time when you were actually doing that. Imagine someone telling you you were denying your problem as you savagely beat yourself for it. Write and share what you think your first reaction would have been. Now ask how that very same self , the one doing all the beating, would have rated you on these two scales. Pick a number from "1" (low belief) to "10" (rock solid belief) *at that moment*:

    1. I have lost the power of choice over drink/drug and desperately need help to stay away from it/both.
       1 2 3 4 5 6 7 8 9 10   (Circle one)
    2. I don't know how to cope with life and desperately need help to learn how.
       1 2 3 4 5 6 7 8 9 10   (Circle one)

    What do your answers tell you about yourself and about "beating myself up?" Share and discuss. Reread the section in this chapter on "pseudo-responsibility" until you can spell out how it applies to you.

Dr. Jekyll and Mr. Hyde — The Devilish Links of Disownership

Dr. Jekyll, Meet Mr. Hyde — An Exercise[1]

The first question of the author's favorite group exercise is always the same:

"How many of you have been told you are a 'Jekyll-and-Hyde' when you drink?"

The answer today is typical.

Twelve of the sixteen alcoholic inpatients raise their hands.

"How many have at least been told you are a different person when you drink?"

All the hands go up.

"Okay, what I'm going to do is divide the blackboard in half. I want each person here to share one example of what you are like sober. And how it changes when you drink."

Several hands go up immediately:

"I'm polite when I'm sober and belligerent when I drink. Nobody can tell me anything."

"I never miss a day of work sober."

"I'm shy sober — when I drink, I'll ask anyone to dance."

The examples flow freely and the counselor's job is to keep them as specific as possible.

---

[1] This exercise was first published as "Dr. Jekyll Meet Mr Hyde" in *Professional Counselor Magazine*, January-February, 1988.

One man offers, "I lie a lot when I'm drinking."

"Could anyone in the group give me some examples of the lies you tell?"

Again, they come through with their personal cover-ups and excuses. But one of them looks a little puzzled and embarrassed. "When I'm drunk," he shares, "I'm likely to tell any damn story. Hero in the war. Test pilot. Private eye."

"Anyone else like that?"

There are a few sheepish grins around the room and some nods.

It seems helpful to clarify that alcoholism generates two kinds of deception. The "survival lie" to get booze or to escape consequences of drinking it. And the seemingly harmless "fantasy lie" to appear larger than one really is.

Both sides of the board are full now, so it is time to start looking at the meaning of the facts we have laid out.

"If most drinkers experience similar kinds of personality change when they drink, what does this tell you about the problem? How does it help?"

A slim, young black man voices a reasonable and frequent conclusion. "The Mr. Hyde side of the board gives you a lot of reasons to not drink."

"*Dis*-incentives — good reasons *not* to?"

There are usually murmurs of agreement.

"That makes sense — but see if this does. How many years have each of you known about your personality change? How many years ago did you first hear about it?"

We add up their answers, one by one. The total for the group of sixteen is over one hundred fifty years.

It's time to take off the kid gloves.

"It would be reasonable to think Mr. Hyde's self-destructive behavior is a strong reason not to drink. Yet the group has continued to drink for almost ten years, on an average, being aware of it. How do we make sense out of this?"

The room is very still. It is as if each alcoholic/addict there stopped breathing or moving at the same instant. However, a tougher question remains.

"Try thinking of it this way. The goal of all chemical dependency treatment is to help you *not* do one thing. Take that first drink or drug. Have you ever asked yourself, who takes that drink, the 'dry' Dr. Jekyll or the 'wet' Mr. Hyde?"

Several of them mutter, "Dr. Jekyll" shifting in their seats.

The air has left the room again and people need to catch their breath, to let it sink in. At this point, it is important to have a question we can work with.

"Dr. Jekyll, without a drop of alcohol in his brain, picks up the first drink and changes himself back into the monstrous Mr. Hyde. There must be *something* about being Mr. Hyde that he prefers — what is it?"

The group comes back to life.

Dr. Jekyll "gets bored", "can't relax", "gets fed up with being a people-pleaser."

Mr. Hyde "has all the fun," "gets the sex," "never worries."

Now, we can circle back to the most important question of all.

"How might your answers help?"

One of the more verbal members of the group articulates it perfectly: "It tells you what Dr. Jekyll has to work on, sober."

At this point, the war hero/test pilot/private eye puts up his hand.

"Think it's gonna be kinda dull around here if I just gotta be me all the time," he comments.

"You fear you will miss the fantasies?"

He nods.

"Let me put it another way. You are not just saying good-bye to a liquid chemical, ethyl alcohol. What Dr. Jekyll loves most about living in Mr. Hyde's fantasy world is the "powerful illusion of power" [1], power to recreate your self and universe at will. This is, of course, the power of God. Anybody here remember Step One of the AA Twelve Steps?"

One of them sees the connection.

"Admitted we were powerless!"

Sometimes the beginning is just the right place to end.

To increase understanding of the above section, complete Recovery Exercises #1, #2, #3, and #4 at the end of the chapter.

This exercise works at the beginning of treatment with virtually any group of alcoholics. But with primary alcoholics, the results are consistent and the identification is built-in.

A caution: Cocaine addicts who do not identify as alcoholics may complicate it, either because they feel powerful all the time, or because their paranoid personality changes go so far beyond the loss of reality experienced by an alcoholic Mr. Hyde. Heroin addicts may identify with the radical change in behavior when using, not so much with the personality shift. The author has only tried the exercise once in an inpatient dual-diagnosis program. Never again!

The most consistent group reaction is dismay at the realization that "the good guy" takes the first drink, that moment of silence. The goal of the exercise is to help newly sober alcoholics see and feel — to "realize" — what so many have never really grasped, to think about what it means when the *sober* person takes the first drink/drug of relapse. The separation of the "good guy" from the act of taking the first drink turns out to be crucial. Without understanding how this works, you will never fully understand what makes continued drinking possible. The distancing of the "good self" from the actions of the "bad self" robs the real self of an internal reason to change.

☞ Exploring the emotional reactions to this truth can be productive and healing, even though shame and guilt often surface first. But if they are faced, it becomes possible to face how the disease controls the sober mind, and to do the work that will prevent the diseased control from coming back. This is true "relapse prevention."

The mental separation between self and action we see here creates an illusion for the person. It may actually feel like a "demon" somehow took over, that something other than the self is in control. But this experience is a direct result of the mental separation. In exploring further, we may call it:

The Devil of Disownership

A hard-drinking man gets bored one night and drops by his favorite beer joint. He sits down beside a pretty woman but feels too self-conscious to speak. Drinking more and more beer, he finally loses his shyness. The man feels so different that it seems as if he has actually become another person. Smiling, he starts to flirt with the woman and she is delighted. Sound familiar?

Kris Kristofferson [1] evoked this familiar scene much more colorfully in his song "The Silver-Tongued Devil and I:"

> *I took myself down to the Tally-Ho Tavern*
> *To buy me a bottle of beer.*
> *And I sat me down by a tender young maiden*
> *Whose eyes were as dark as her hair.*
> *And as I was searching from bottle to bottle*
> *For something unfoolish to say,*
> *That silver-tongued devil just slipped from the shadows*
> *And smilin' he stole her away.*

It is no secret that people drink alcohol to release inhibitions, to become more outgoing, and to get what they want from the opposite sex. But the drinker's illusion of becoming another person can evade the most observant eye. Kristofferson not only spells out the illusion. His tongue-in-cheek chorus captures the fatal conviction that this "other person" is responsible for all alcoholic shenanigans:

You know, he's a devil, he's everything that I ain't,
Hidin' intentions of evil, under the smile of a saint.
All he's good for is gettin' in trouble
And shiftin' his share of the blame
And some people swear he's my double,
And some even say we're the same.

The attitude, my actions are not really mine because I'm not really me when I'm drunk, is called "disownership." This becomes a way of looking at self that enables the person to live with sick and destructive behavior.

In effect, "It's not really me that's doing all those horrible things. Why should I change?"

The alcoholic/addict may be the last to become aware of this subtle attitude. A largely subconscious defense, disownership accounts for much of what is "cunning and baffling" about addiction. It also accounts for the fact that so much treatment "bounces off." Sure, the client believes what we are saying in our groups and classes, but without even being aware, he or she assumes we are talking about that "other." You know, the one who drinks and does all that crazy stuff, not the good soul sitting here in treatment, a model citizen.

Kristofferson's "I" begins sliding off the hook in the first three lines of the song. He describes his "self" as a separate being he "takes" to the bar. His "me" is someone for whom he buys a beer or pulls out a chair. This use of language effectively separates the doer and the deed.

In treatment, people often attempt to separate themselves from their behavior. Perhaps the most common way is to talk about what "you" do when drinking, not what "I" do.

"'You' get loose and say anything and don't go to work," says one.

"'You' just don't give a damn when you drink."

"'You' get more opinionated, won't listen," says another.

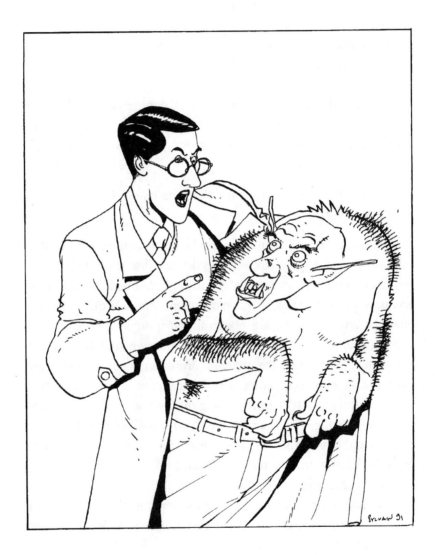

In this way, "you" may avoid talking about what "I" actually do. The silver tongue slithers away from the truth on a string of casually misplaced pronouns. AA speakers and stories certainly do not share what "you" were like, what happened, and what "you" are like now. Can there be any real acceptance as long as the person subtly displaces the alcoholic behavior away from self?

As we saw above, another way a person may disown alcoholism is by claiming to be a "Jekyll-and-Hyde." This implies being a "saint" when sober — that evil Mr. Hyde is the "devil" who causes all the trouble! A man convicted of killing several people while driving under the influence, shares his story. He looks the audience in the eye and says, "I wouldn't hurt a fly."

If he didn't, who did?

If there is any real "devil" here, it is the mental twist by which the person holds his or her real behavior apart from what they consider to be their real self. In a word, "disownership."

Even the disease concept of alcoholism can be distorted as a way of disowning behavior. "I can't help it — I'm sick." Or, "My disease made me do it — it wasn't really me." To be sure, the drinking personality is not "the real me." What comes out under the influence is a part of the personality that is inhibited without alcohol. To be inhibited means an impulse is stopped by something else inside yourself, usually something rigid, automatic, self-conscious. Apparently, the part of the person that does the stopping disappears with alcohol, put to sleep by the drug. But who took the drug and knocked the "inhibitor" out?

> *Who took the real drug into my real body and put Mr. Hyde in control of my real behavior?*

Something behind the wall of sober inhibition may have reached out and said "One won't hurt," or "F--- it." That something may well be neurochemical. It may be neurotic, unconscious, or some "bio-psycho-social" brew. But that mysterious something belongs to the sober self who lives behind the wall.

I "own" it. And until I digest this emotional and physical reality, I have no "motivation" to do anything about it.

☞   Father Joseph Martin [2], in his classic film *Guidelines*, made a powerful and relevant statement. "Pain," he says, "is the greatest gift God can give an alcoholic. The pain of looking in the mirror of self and wanting to throw up."

Here is the picture: the silver-tongued devil stares back from the mirror in silence, mask off, eyes wide with horror and grief. "Saint" and "devil" meet for the first and last time. Neither survives, but the person who remains will take one of two forms. A real human being with one self and a powerful thirst for life and growth. Or a corpse.

To increase understanding of the above section, complete Recovery Exercise #5 at the end of the chapter.

For the Reader in Early Recovery

The aim of "Dr. Jekyll and Mr. Hyde", of most chemical dependency treatment, is to facilitate "God's greatest gift." The exercise works best in a sober, protected environment or support group. But some readers of this book are struggling on their own to recover, to stop saying "One won't hurt" or "F--- it." You are urged to share any strong reactions to this chapter with others — sponsor, counselor, minister, or priest. A friend in recovery, perhaps. When you are ready, the material below and the following two chapters may help you better understand and grow from the experience.

Two Cultural Supports for this Dualism

Western culture routinely makes two separations which feed alcoholic disownership. First, we separate ourselves from some of our behavior or from our bodies; and second, we separate real behavior and consequences from "intention."

I. The Spirit Versus the Flesh

The mind/body separation may have roots in our Judeo-Christian traditions. "The flesh" is an enemy — the self exists apart from the body through which it thinks, feels, and acts. Our culture excuses much in the name of physical disease, and excuse-seekers learn to trade on that "compassion." Addiction is a disease. If I have it, the disease is part of who I am, just as surely as Shaquile O'Neal's height is part of who he is. The person is more than the body, but not less. And without the body, the person ceases to exist in any practical way.

☞   Heredity may help determine who gets the disease, but it must not be made an excuse. It is just a partial explanation of the kind of person I am. It determines some of the raw materials I have to work with, like my eye color, gender, or baldness. What I do with them is on me.

To separate my "true self" from my physical body is both a trap and an alibi. And this includes separating my true self from the physical acts of my body. It is, after all, the only one I have, and nobody directs or controls its muscles but me. If the muscles of the hand on my body hit you, my true self hit you. If I do not accept that, my true self is giving his blessing to the last time I hit you, and to the next. I will do it again, precisely because I don't believe "I" did it in the first place!

A disturbing example of just how destructively this can work comes from William Satoran, MSW. The author's fieldwork instructor in graduate school (1976-1977), Bill now specializes in treatment of child molesters in Seattle, Washington. Many of his patients are also alcoholic. Not infrequently, Bill encounters a "perpetrator" who claims that he's "not really a child molester." Why?

Because "I only do it when I'm drinking." Bill, then and there, contracts with the man to give up drinking and seek treatment for alcoholism. Some months later, Bill may learn the person is drink-
☞ ing again. He is forced to point out, "If you know what happens when you drink, then aren't you choosing to let it 'happen' again?"
☞ Is this not true for *any* Jekyll-Hyde alcoholic?

Imagine an epileptic who knows he has seizures without his medication. Picture this person deciding to stop the meds. Now picture them getting behind the wheel and having a seizure. There is a tragic accident and someone you love is killed. Would *you* accept having the disease as a defense?

Rebuttal: The epilepsy analogy breaks down at the point of decision to stop meds. There is nothing in the disease of epilepsy itself pushing toward that fatal decision to terminate a treatment that prevents "relapse." Part of what makes addiction so deadly and insidious is the process by which it takes over the drug-free mind before physical relapse. The "decisions" to stop treatment and/or take that first drink/drug are themselves symptoms. Symptoms apparently produced by craving that is very much part of the disease itself. In terms of the epilepsy analogy, the first "seemingly irrelevant decision" may be seen as the first small "seizure" for the disease of addiction.

Clarification: If saying "One won't hurt" or "F--- it" is a "grand mal seizure" for an addiction, what is the preventing medication? Is it not the heartfelt realization of the person that *this is true for me.* Followed by *doing whatever it takes* to head off these two thoughts.

> *What else would get me to take an anti-craving drug or go to an anti-craving meeting, make an anti-craving phone call? Or "surrender" to an anti-craving God?*

What about society? Does this mean alcoholics should never be punished? No, it just means that rational punishment will be designed to protect both society and alcoholic/addict from craving.

Moral judgment evolves into "What do we seek to accomplish and what works." "Punishment with love!"

The most chilling and extreme example of disownership in the author's collection comes from the *Seattle Times*. It does not involve alcoholism or drug addiction directly. Serial killer Ted Bundy apparently spoke of the self who took over at the time of his murders in the *third* person. "'He' wanted me to do it." Is there any question this was a sick human being? No. Is there a possibility Ted Bundy was the victim of inherited biochemistry? Yes. But if he were to have a chance to recover, would he not have to give up this strange detachment called "disownership?" If he even could? Would he not have to become real to himself, even before his victims could become real to him? Ted Bundy did not recover, but many alcoholics and addicts do. And one thing they almost all seem to have in common is this realization: literally, it becomes real to the person him- or herself that "I" do what I *do*. It was true all along. But my "getting it," my realization of it as a fact that I experience, *that* is what seems to change everything.

To increase understanding of the above section, complete Recovery Exercise #9 at the end of the chapter.

II. Pavement for the Road to Hell

The separation of purpose from behavior appears early in the Old Testament. Like the original Hawaiians, the Chosen People had "cities of refuge." An accidental murderer might be protected while facts were established and blood relatives of the victim cooled off. Every child learns early on that there is a difference between hurting on purpose or "by accident." Some children learn by precept and example that being drunk is an excuse, too. Mom says "Daddy didn't mean it" when he was (drunk and) cursing you out. Apparently, he did not mean it a few years later when he beat and/ or molested and/or left you.

*The "Dr. Jekyll" alcoholic hides behind the respectability of
"dry" behavior. I take no responsibility for "intending" to do
anything that happened when I drank (and when I will drink
again). Yes, I hit my wife, but I did not plan or intend to. Yes, I
forgot the kid's ball game, but those things just happen when
I drink — I don't mean to. Miss work? The calendar shows I was
planning to meet Mr. Flugelhorn at nine a.m. "Judge me by my
intentions, not my actions," I plead. "(I do)."*

More scientific excuse-makers would argue that the *whole* process is biochemical. The "person" does not participate, does not really exist, not in a way that makes a difference:

*My behavior is "output," fundamentally caused by biology.
I am a robot genetically programmed to respond as I do. "It
just happens." "Realizing" that I am a robot would change nothing. "Waking up" to the reality of my strings would not stop
me from being a puppet.*

Bill W. learned early on that he had a "disease." He was very excited at this "self-knowledge," and then he got drunk again. Bill was making a point in telling his own story of relapse in the Big Book. Using himself as an illustration of what did not work, he was preparing the skeptical reader for the dire necessity for "spiritual experience." And at least one significant spiritual writer has defined "love," "awareness," and "spirituality" as different words for the same thing. Anthony deMello observes that each requires/enables us to "see reality clearly and make the appropriate response." Like Solomon with the two mothers and one baby, or Jesus with the woman taken in adultery. I may see my biochemistry controlling my behavior, destroying me, destroying my family. But I will not become able to make the "appropriate response" until I see one more thing: *I* am the one doing the doing. The fact I cannot control myself is no longer an excuse — it is an appalling and intolerable personal reality. Fully "owned," it opens me to anything that might help.

Dr. Jekyll and the Wishful Relapse

"One won't hurt" bluntly denies my alcoholism. But do the words "disown" it? Yes. And it is precisely by asserting the *intention* to have just one, or to ensure "this time will be different." The patent nonsense of intending to control use sets up the alibi — I didn't *mean* to lose control. Gee, sorry about your car, face, money, etc. One of the bitterest pills to swallow is adult responsibility — realizing we play in a game in which we and others suffer for what we do, not the child's game of good and innocent intentions. "That's nice, dear. You tried," just won't cut it.

As we have seen before, it is essential for my recovery that I realize my relapsing mind was drug-free. That when I say "I'll just have one," there is no chemical in my brain. Dr. Jekyll, the pillar of society, is the one who says, "No one will know, etc." We might even make the plausible argument "Mr. Hyde" reappears *before* the first drink, that "he" takes it.

What matters most is that I see the physical fact that no drug clouds "our" brain when "he" takes over my mind.

The wishful relapse often involves disownership in at least two other ways.

One, I may have disowned other problems and upsets, so much that I no longer know they control me or drive my wish to escape. Two, I am usually disconnected from any emotional pain, from my craving, from my actual experience. I am in a dissociative state. "One won't hurt" is just one symptom of my disconnectedness.

To increase understanding of the above section, complete Recovery Exercise #6 at the end of the chapter.

Dr. Jekyll and the White-Knuckle Relapse

"F--- it" implies both some sort of awareness and some sort of consequences. "I know bad things will happen if I drink/use but ...." the use of these two meaningless words, "F--- it," already puts distance between me and what I am doing. Imagine a healthy, honest person saying, "I know I may kill an innocent person in my car if I drink, but my personal suffering makes the risk to others worth it. I choose whatever may happen, but take no responsibility for it. It is the best and wisest thing to do." No, far more comfortable and distant to say a meaningless, evasive expletive. And if I do hurt or kill someone, "My God! I never meant for that to happen." Like "One won't hurt," "F--- it" sidesteps the decision I make and the fact I am making it.

Even more than the wishful relapse, the white-knuckle relapse consistently involves disownership *before* the moment. "White-knuckle sobriety" is based on disownership of my emotional and coping problems. I may "own" what happens after I drink/drug, but there ain't nothing wrong with the sober me. Then I disown feelings and problems as they arise, white-knuckling my way through them. But they don't "disown" me. They accumulate, building up to that moment I say "F--- it" again, disowning what I am doing and all the disownership that has led up to it. What does AA have me do? Take an "inventory" of what I own! And it counters my blaming of others with one galling, empowering question — What was *my* part in the problem?

To increase understanding of the above section, complete Recovery Exercise #7 at the end of the chapter.

References

[1] Kristofferson, Kris. "The Silver Tongued Devil." Resaca Music Publishing, © 1971.
[2] Martin, Father Joseph. "Guidelines for Helping the Alcoholic." Carpenteria, CA: FMS, 1976.
[3] Anonymous. *Alcoholics Anonymous.* New York: Alcoholics Anonymous World Services, 1955.
[4] DeMello, Anthony, S.J. (Edited by Stroud, Francis). Awareness, the Perils and Opportunitiers of Reality. New York, London, etc: Image Doubleday, 1992.

Recovery Exercises

1. Make your own personal list of how your personality changes between being sober and drinking. What does your "Dr. Jekyll" like the least about your sober existence? What will you have to work hardest on so that he does not change back to "Mr. Hyde?"

2. What did you like best about being "Mr. Hyde?" Can you see any healthy ways to achieve this? If not, ask your sponsor, counselor, or others.

3. Write down your reactions to reading the exercise the first time. In particular, how did you feel as you read about "Dr. Jekyll" being the one who takes the first drink? Read it again, if it helps. What do your reactions tell you about yourself and your recovery needs? Did you see anything you have not realized before? Can you spell out how this might help you avoid future relapse? Write and share.

4. Write down three fantasies you have had while drinking. What wish do they appear to fulfill? What does this tell you about what you may want? Is there a way to get what you want in reality, without drinking? Ask group for feedback.

5. Write down three things you used to say to yourself about your drinking/drug problem, before you admitted to it. How did the words create or imply separation between you and "the problem?" Share with group.

6. Think of a time you said "One won't hurt" and relapsed. What life problems were you disowning? With hindsight, how big was the craving — would "just one" have ever satisfied it?

7. Think of a time you said "F--- it" and relapsed. What life problems were you not owning up to? What did you care about so much that you could not stand it?

8. Think of a time you started to drink, saying either "One won't hurt", or "F--- it." List all of the painful consequences of that relapse to yourself and to everyone else effected. If you had been asked at the moment of relapse, would you have taken responsibility for what your drinking would cause? What about now? Share with group. Do they think you are accepting responsibility for preventing this from happening again? Ask them.

9. What is your reaction to being compared with child molesters and/or Ted Bundy? What upsets you the most about it? In what ways is the comparison true? Share and discuss.

10

The Iron Law of Ownership[1] — The Link that Sets Us Free

Disownership is a living reaction, an active link that blinds alcoholics/addicts from seeing their own role in the addiction. Disownership prevents seeing any reason to do something about the problem, from realizing the very fact it is *"mine."* For recovery to be possible, the links of this reaction have to be dismantled and replaced. The logical and psychological opposite of disownership is a link and an experience called "ownership."

The term "ownership" is used far more often than it is defined or described. Yet ownership is the true starting point for all recoveries from all self-defeating behavior. Why? Because if I do not recognize a problem as mine, why would I do anything about it? Emotionally, it would make no sense. Do we go to the dentist for someone else's toothache? This is what often makes the codependent so much harder to treat than the chemically dependent. The defining attitude of codependency is obsession with the other person's problem (usually as an escape from my own). To participate in treatment, attend AA, deny myself alcohol, all require work. Why would anyone do all of that for someone else's problem? True, a codependent appears to do an exceptional amount of work on someone else's problem. (Addicts and alcoholics do a heroic amount of work for their escapes, too!) But a closer look shows

---

[1] Expanded from "Alcoholism: the Responsibility of Ownership," in *Alcoholism, the National Magazine,* December, 1981

that all this work serves at least one unconscious function. To distract the "co" from having to experience his or her own problem, much less do the work of recovering from it.

☞   *For recovery to occur, the most important fact about an addiction is not what caused it, but who has it.*

Knowing the "cause," such as heredity, does not yet help us much to treat the active alcoholic. Realizing, mentally and emotionally that "I" *have* an addiction is altogether a different story. The person who knows this is "my problem" and "my life" is ready for (my!) recovery. Many will need little further treatment at this point and those who do will embrace it willingly. Why? "Because I'm doing it for myself."

☞   If they are going to be of any genuine help, helpers need to have a working concept of acceptance as ownership, ownership at a level that alters the person's reactions. For those trying to recover, the concept of ownership is far less important than the experience. In this chapter, both the helper and the recovering reader are offered the author's understanding to date: what ownership is and how it interrupts both the "wishful" and the "white-knuckle" relapse.

The Iron Law of Ownership

We start at birth, with one piece of property, a piece of property that is ours until the day we die. In fact, the only way it can truly be taken away from us is death itself. No other person can enjoy the use of this possession, yet no deed of title or "registration" is required. Ownership of this property is based on physical fact, not the cultural fictions of "laws." The property with which we are all born is, of course, the mobile kingdom enclosed within our skin. Our body! It goes where we go and we go where it goes. Unlike "me and my shadow," it even follows me into the darkness, or do I follow it?

My body is mine and no one else's. Everything within my body is mine and no one else's. This includes not just my organs and blood; but also my feelings, my awareness, memory, and perception, and, whether I like it or believe it, my consciousness and my unconscious mind. This is no less true when I am being beaten, molested, raped, or when I am drunk.

This leads us to an obvious and self-evident fact that most people ignore most of the time. We may call it the "Iron Law of Ownership":

Anything that happens within the skin happens to the person who lives inside that skin.

Someone in the room has a toothache. There is a dentist, but he needs to know who has the toothache. If the person with the toothache does not admit he has it, the dentist can do nothing. Equally important, if the pain is in my mouth, I am the one who feels it, and I am the one who will suffer all the effects and complications of the rotting tooth.

Hopefully, this is all self-evident and some readers may well be asking "So what?" There are three ways to answer that very reasonable request for relevance:

"So What" Number One — Ignorance Is No Excuse

This "Iron Law" is easy enough to understand in the case of a toothache. But what if the "event" occurs and I don't know it? The simple truth is that most of what happens within us is outside our awareness. Much of it is irretrievably outside, some of it, willfully out there.

Suppose I have cancer growing in my bowel but don't feel it and don't know it. Detected, it could be removed with relatively minor surgery but I don't go for check-ups. Six months from now, I have stomach pain. I see blood in my stool, I have a "clinical" symptom.

So I go to the doctor and he says, "It's too late. We can slow it down some, but you are going to die. No more than a year."

"Wait, Doc, I didn't know it was there! I would have come in six months ago if I knew. You must save me. It's not fair!"

The doctor tries to soothe my upset as he silently wonders what kind of nut I am. It turns out I'm a very common one.

It's not "fair" that some people get alcoholism and some get cancer and some get perfect health. What is relentlessly consistent for all is: *whatever happens inside my body happens to me and whatever happens inside your body happens to you.* And the fact we do not know what is happening in there does not protect either of us. Ignorance is equally impartial in not protecting us from cancer or from acid indigestion. In fact, the one thing that might save us both is just the opposite of ignorance — awareness. This is just as true whether the inner condition is cancer or rage or inferiority or guilt.

The plot thickens. We also "own" the feelings and motives inside us, whether or not we are aware of them. We have to realize that the *effects* of buried feelings are not confined within our skin. They alter our perceptions, which affects what we decide, shaping our behavior. Our actions, in turn, create external consequences. Sooner or later, these "fruits" return within us as more "experience."

"What goes around, comes around."

"The chickens come home to roost."

The consequence/event may occur far from me, whatever my behavior contributed to it, but I "experience" it within my skin. That is where I "know" about it and "feel" it. If nothing happens in there, I have had no experience. One of the most terrifying things about facing my addiction is to look back at a lifetime of feelings suppressed and/or anesthetized, a life of non-experience. Much of the healing from "facing" my past may be this. I allow myself to look at my disowned deeds and allow myself to feel now what I did not feel then. Painful and bittersweet as it may be, I am now reclaiming my life as something I lived.

☞   Many people do not realize we own our behavior for just the same reason we own our feelings and our bodies. Behavior, too, happens inside us! The pen that wrote the first draft of this manuscript was controlled by the fingers of the author's right hand. The fingers of his right hand were controlled by a complicated sequence of expanding and contracting muscles, each controlled by the firing of thousands of neurons in sequence. And this "chain" starts with an order from his brain. The physical behavior is muscular action in response to neurological signals, regardless of outward effects. Notice that this all happens inside the writer's skin, as surely as daydreams or digestion.

My brain may control my behavior in such a way that I do things that I regret or you object to. It is still *my* behavior, precisely because it happened inside me and no one else. This is just as true whether my brain is operating in full awareness or whether it is under control of biochemical or unconscious forces. Under the Iron Law of Ownership, I escape neither the internal nor external consequences of my actions. In this sense, no one ever "gets away with" anything.

☞   My "purpose" or "intention" is irrelevant under the "Iron Law" itself. I will suffer the natural inner and outer consequences of my behavior, regardless of what I "meant" or planned. Others will suffer real consequences of my real actions, whatever I intended. "Purpose" itself is an inner event that may or may not control my action. I may well be controlled by something other than purpose or reason, but these other inner events (biochemical, unconscious, etc.) are also "mine" under the Iron Law.

Ignorance is still no "excuse" from the consequences of any resulting behavior.

The question of purpose *is* relevant to premeditated human punishment. Mother Nature does not forgive — drop a brick on your foot and gravity will not ask whether you meant to! Human beings sometimes do forgive. The question of what the alcoholic does or does not do "on purpose" is still very much alive. Many alcoholics/addicts live comfortably with the idea that anything done under the influence is not done "on purpose." As a result, they will not punish themselves with guilt or shame, nor will they make the effort necessary to prevent the next "accident." Many sick families raise their children to live with abuse. How? By teaching them the parental abuser didn't "mean it." Such children are custom-trained, often marrying and staying married to abusers who see no reason to (learn how to) control behavior that is never "on purpose."

Ignorance may result from simple lack of information:

I didn't know alcoholism was hereditary, that I shouldn't drink at all. I didn't know my remarkable capacity to drink everyone under the table was a symptom. Wow! That's first- stage alcoholism?! I did not know that some people can never drink with "control."

If this is truly innocent ignorance (and I am not already addicted!), I will respond immediately when told the truth. I will correct my behavior in accordance with the new facts.

But there is another kind of ignorance, one that results directly from ignoring facts that were ready at hand:

I didn't know because I didn't want to know. I did not see because I refused to look. Worse, my will was so strong and/or unconscious I couldn't see.

Q: "What did you think when you had that blackout?"
A: "I just didn't think about it."
Q: "What did you think when your best friend said he thought you had a problem?"
A: "I pushed it out of my mind."
Q: "What did you do with all these facts we've just put together? You evidently have known them all along."
A: "I forgot them as fast as I could. I wouldn't dwell on them. Why live in the past?"

Years ago, a real patient (here) named "Tom" taught the author a powerful lesson:

Epitaph for a Sober Alcoholic

"Tom" had been sober and attending group for over two years when he came in for an individual session. He had been struggling for several months with feelings of listlessness and fatigue. Now he had let the group know he had almost accepted the offer of a beer.

We began the session by going over Tom's group record. Oddly enough, complaints of physical fatigue first appeared during the time he quit smoking, about a year after he sold his business and retired.

"Why did you try to quit smoking when you did?" asked the author.

"This cough I got — it kept getting worse."

"Did it get better when you were off cigarettes?"

"Yes."

"What happened when you started smoking again?"

"It came back."

"But the fatigue began while you stopped smoking and has not let up since you started again?"

"That's right," he grimaced.

Fatigue, cough, and smoking were evidently connected. Tom's personal physician was treating him for anemia with iron pills, but they were not helping. If the connection were psychological, there had to be a link in Tom's own thinking. This was what we began to look for.

"Tom, the problem you were trying to solve six months ago was a cough. So why quit smoking?"

"I thought smoking was causing it."

"Did you ask your doctor?"

"No."

Strange.

"What did the cough mean to you?"

"I might have bronchitis or emphysema."

Hmmm, he omitted lung cancer. So the author asked if he had worried about it.

"I didn't think about it too much." Eyes downcast, lowered voice.

"I don't think about it" is so often an alcoholic's way of saying, "My head is buried in the sand of denial." It would be simple enough to find out if Tom were playing ostrich.

"Tom, in all the times you went to your doctor for the fatigue, did you ever tell him about this cough?"

"No."

That seemed to clinch it.

"What do you suppose he might have done if you had?"

Tom started grinning sheepishly, as if caught with his hand in the proverbial cookie jar.

"Given me a chest X-ray."

"Sounds like you weren't too eager to find out what it might show."

He never did admit that. But he did go in for an X-ray the following day.

Tom did not have emphysema or bronchitis or lung cancer, nor was he suffering from post-retirement depression. The cough was caused by the pressure of his enlarged heart pushing on the lung. The fatigue came from the same diseased and overtaxed muscle. Tom was admitted to the hospital immediately, but it was already too late. He went into cardiac arrest and died within two weeks.

A possible epitaph?

"What I didn't (want to) know hurt me."

      You want to test me for willful ignorance? Just present me a few of the facts I have been avoiding (and duck!) Watch for my anger, anxiety, shame, counterattack. Or try persistent, probing questions, concrete and nonjudgmental, especially questions about my thoughts and feelings at the moment of the first drink/drug. You are focusing my attention on "Dr. Jekyll's" participation in the "decision." I may actually have to look at my childlike wishful thinking, or at my white-knuckle willingness to let others pay the price for my drinking. I may suddenly wonder whether you are an alcoholic. If not, let's fight about whether you can "understand" me. If you are, let's fight about your "holier-than-thou" attitude. Let's not keep looking at my mind in the act of deciding to take the first drink!

But just as the ignorance may be willful, it may also be subconscious. The average human being is driven by ferocious wills of which they do not have a clue. Why should alcoholic/addicts be any different?

Ignorance does protect me from one thing and one thing only: the temporary, healing pain I will feel when I face the truth. My unconscious has some inkling of what the real truth is. In fact, that is the source of much of the pain of facing up at last, to see how long I have been deluding myself.

      Here helper and relapser have to do a balancing act, humbly recognizing the lifelong power of and lack of control over the unconscious mind. Yet keeping the person open to further revelations:

If I beat myself up for years of denial, I am probably still in it. Why? I still think I "should" control the power of the unconscious. Humility and acceptance come when I see how blind I was. And realize how blind I probably still am. How else would it be possible for "more to be revealed?"

"So What Number One" and the Moment of Relapse: "One won't hurt" is an ignorant statement when made by an addict/ alcoholic at the moment of relapse.

The one thing guaranteed when I relapse is that there will be plenty of "hurt." Obviously, believing I will only have one does not stop me from having twenty. It does not protect me from any or all of the consequences of my loss of control. Clearly, "ignorance is no excuse" in the case of the wishful relapse.

What about the white-knuckle relapse?

My ignorance of what the act of relapse really means does not change the meaning, whether it is "I quit," "I don't care," "F--- you" or "I've had it." My ignorance of what was bothering me beforehand did not make the pain go away. In fact, it robbed me of the opportunity to cope. Ignorance of my own emotional being is precisely how things built up to that snapping point, to saying "I've had it" or some other version of "F--- it." The emotional self-ignorance directly "caused" my relapse, far from protecting me. Nor does it protect me from all the consequences to which I say, "F--- it." An attitude of "Damn the torpedoes! Full speed ahead!" does not defuse the torpedoes released by relapse. As they blow up all around me, my ignorance does not "excuse" my white-knuckle relapse, either.

To increase understanding of the above section, complete Recovery Exercises #1 and #2 at the end the of chapter.

"So What" Number Two — Ownership is a Fact, Not a Should

"Shoulds" are weak motivation.

I "should" quit smoking, lose weight, spend more time with my kids, get an advanced degree, change jobs, etc. We all live with a head full of shoulds that never get done. "Shoulds" from other people are even weaker, since those are just opinions. After all, what do they know about me? And who are they to say?

☞ *Ownership of a disease is a cold, dry fact about a warm, flesh and blood person.*

Whatever is eroding me from within will continue to erode my life until I become aware of it. And not just intellectually aware, I have to have the kind of realization of truth about myself that I can "taste" and "touch." Only then can my (links of) will for survival and/or self-respect be energized to wrestle with the problem. For some forms of cancer, this recognition may occur in time. For others, it may come too late to save my life, if at all. The overwhelming majority of alcoholics and addicts can save their physical and psychological lives, if they can overcome the barriers to seeing and feeling the problem within.

"Should" I face my problem? This question is irrelevant. We do not choose to "turn off" our mental defenses, like throwing a switch.

"Should" I do something to save my life if I have a life-threatening problem? That question is irrelevant, too. If I want to live, I will act. If I truly don't care or seek death, opinions will make no difference.

The fact is that most people want to live, and to be able to live with themselves. Once I genuinely see what I have got and what it is doing to me, I will generally act. No one has to say "you should."

A doctor may tell a diabetic "you should" quit eating sugar. But the "should" is really based on two assumptions: that the person believes this particular problem exists, and that the diabetic person does not want to die. The more precise authority of the doctor is this:

"Using all technology at my command, I have looked inside the organism bounded by your skin. I have found that you have the condition known as diabetes in there. One of the consequences of this disease is that your body is unable to break down sugar. Should you eat sugar, you may well go into a coma and die. I assume you do not want to suffer this consequence of your problem. One action you can take is to refrain from sugar."

- This is your problem, within your skin.
- Here is what it will do to you, inside you.
- Here is what you can do about it, *if you want to.*
- It's truly up to you.
- No "should."
- Only the cold, dry fact about a warm, flesh and blood person. "Me."

☞ The more serious and relevant debate is how much the rest of us "should" do. How much effort "should" we make to help an alcoholic wake up to what is going on. The evolution of the field is one of more and more action — we call it "intervention."

☞ *The Second "So What" and the Moment of Relapse:* "One won't hurt" is an assertion of fact that happens to be dead wrong.

Whether there is a disease of any kind inside my skin is a question of fact. Whether I "should" take that one drink/drug is a matter of opinion. My spouse, employer or judge may think not. But why "should" I listen to them? What I need to listen to, if I am to find any real motivation of my own, are the facts about what happens when I do drink. The facts of my own experience, including the reactions of spouse, boss, and judge.

Do I drink/drug more than I intended? Do I betray my values? Do I become a Jekyll/Hyde? Do I hurt myself or others? How much of the suffering in my life would never have come to be if I never did take "just one?" How many times have I quit? Tried controlled drinking? Promised myself to have "just one?" And what do I care about? What do I stand to lose? These are all questions of fact about me. Not "shoulds."

"Should" I cope instead of saying "F--- it?" "Should" I care when I say I don't? "Should" I have faced the problems that built up to the breaking point? "Should" I have prayed, called my sponsor , gone to counseling? Who knows and who is to say? The fact is I said "F--- it" (again) and relapsed.

The fact is I was (or wasn't) upset. And the upset was inside me. Right where the drug went — imagine that! the fact is I did or did not use new tools for coping before relapsing.

"Should" I have?

Who is to say? The fact is I do or don't see myself needing to quit. I do or don't see myself needing to learn a new way to cope with life. I will or won't try something different.

Again, no "shoulds." Just those cold facts about that warm soul. Me.

"So What" Number Three — Two Things Only the "Owner" Can Provide

The third "so what" for the Iron Law is the most positive and practical:

"There are two things that only I can provide for the solution of my problem: one, my physical presence for whatever help is available. Two, the effort to do whatever specific parts of the job can only be done by me, precisely because the problem is inside my body."

I have a toothache.

The dentist is in his office.

I don't go.

He can't help.

AA says "bring the body and the mind will follow." A mind that will accept that is already halfway there, and the people who stick in AA are those for whom the advice was true. The people for whom the advice did not eventually work are not sticking around to complain. Either way, if AA helps, it only helps those who bring their bodies, and this is no less true for all other forms of treatment. Court programs and Employee Assistance Programs (E.A.P.'s) contribute at least this much to the solution — they get an awful lot of bodies to treatment who would not have gone on their own.

Whether treatment then works depends on whether the person becomes actively involved in doing "my part of the job."

I go to the dentist (my wife made me).

He says, "Open wide."

"Uh-uh."

"Bite."

"Bite my shorts."

"Spit."

I swallow.

The dentist can no more help me than if I had not showed up at all, unless it is to talk to me about the "problem" as I see it. He will probably have to start with my feelings about being there — my "resistance!" And the "talking" needs to be about ninety percent listening.

Basketball superstar "Magic" Johnson once had knee surgery that kept him out of action for much of a season. The doctor did the cutting and patching and then sent Magic for "rehabilitation."

Magic did not reach into his wallet for a couple of bills and say to one of his loyal fans, "You go on down to Dr. Sweatbacks rehab and do my routine for me. I have to make a 7-Up commercial."

As much money as this superstar made, no one else could do his work. Only Magic's body could exert the energy to "rehab" a problem within Magic's body.

The highly personal experience of ownership ("waking up," "hitting bottom," "surrendering," etc.) must match the ice-cold Iron Law. This "so what" defines my choices and leads to action. A person who has not experienced some form of realization seems emotionally incapable of embracing recovery. A person who has experienced it, seems incapable of leaving recovery footwork un-done. That is just how much the reactions will change. "Surren-der" may be nothing more than heartfelt submission of the will to this Iron Law. With its three humble "so what's," formation of this "ownership" link of acceptance is critical to active recovery, re-covery that continues to nourish itself. This is recovery that "owns" the task of maintaining "ownership" itself.

No one could go to treatment for Betty Ford.

No one could go to treatment for big league pitcher Bob Welch.

No one went to treatment for Elvis, Bill Holden, or Richard Burton, Jim Morrison, Jimi Hendrix, Janis Joplin.

No one went to aftercare for "Beachboy" Dennis Wilson, John Belucci.

The Third "So What" and the Moment of Relapse: We have been calling "One won't hurt" the "wishful relapse."

> *If I realize it has been* my *relapse, where can I take my body and mind for help to not do that again? In Chapter Three, we saw that forgetting plays a large part in the wishful relapse. Where can I go to get my memory jogged? Who helps with wishful thinking? If physical craving is involved, where can I go for help with that? What can I do? What are the tasks only this mind/body can do to sustain its own memory of the hurt "just one" always leads to? To recognize fantasy for what it is and to reduce craving? Am I willing to go to meetings? To therapy that concretely addresses these things? To read daily remin-*

ders? To give memory a "booster shot" by helping other alco-holics/addicts? Would I take antabuse or anti-craving drugs? Quit a toxic job or relationship? And if I don't do these things for my recovery, what will become of me? Of my life?

Because "F--- it" usually involves being upset, the first question is given.

Where can I go and what might I do to maintain aware-ness at all times of just how stressed I may be? And then, where can I go for help when I am upset? Not just when it has built to craving, any time I am upset. And even if others can help, what are the tasks only my mind and body can do for an upset that is within? But do I even have to wait till I am upset? Is there footwork only I can do for me now, footwork that changes some "links" in my reactions so I get less upset, less often? Footwork, perhaps, that reduces some of my blocks to asking for help? Or, can I do something to progressively increase my "serenity." What if craving continues to be a problem? Where can my crav-ing body take itself for help with that, and what is my part of the job?

Ownership Versus Blame: a Parable

One of the biggest reasons I do not accept what I "own" is my fear of being "to blame." A simple, if somewhat gory, parable separates the responsibility of blame (being "the cause") from the responsibility of ownership. Many people have found it helpful over the years.

EveryPerson (EP) was walking down the street one day, a blameless Soul who had never done anything wrong in his or her entire life. The next thing EP knew, s/he was lying on the sidewalk. His/her wallet had mysteriously disappeared. And the handle of a large hunting knife had mysteriously grown from EP's navel. It seemed to be attached to a blade.

EP fought going into shock as a pool of blood began to form. Within moments, a crowd had gathered and sirens wailed. As the paramedics began to ease EP onto a stretcher, EP's head cleared. S/he knew exactly how to get out of this one. EP had a method that had never failed.

"Wait!" EveryPerson cried. "Don't take me to the hospital for surgery and long, painful convalescence. You've got the wrong person. Go find SomePerson who did this. It's their fault. I'm not to blame at all. Why should I have to go through rehabilitation and do all that work?"

In the same scenario, the omnipotent self-blamer cries, *"Wait! What makes you think I need a hospital? I made this happen by going for a walk and/or by cheating on my income tax. Or maybe by being a bad son/daughter, I surely caused the problem by willing and/or deserving it. And I can cause the solution by using the same control that got me into this mess. Take your ambulance and transfusion and pound sand!"*

Father Martin [1] has been quoted earlier as saying "the greatest gift God can give an alcoholic is pain, the pain of looking in the mirror of self and wanting to throw up." But what is this "looking in the mirror of self?"

> *Obviously, it is some kind of awareness of what myself has become, a realization that I feel. The feeling is apparently shame — I see my own "leprosy" and I wish it removed at all costs. Father Martin clearly implies that some sort of shame may be necessary for recovery!*
>
> *Logic and experience both tell us what is different about the shame I feel looking in Father Martin's "mirror." I now feel it is mine. I feel ashamed of me. It is no longer "just your opinion," "your problem," or "Mr. Hyde's problem." I may be so pained by what I see of myself that I do not even consider how I look to you. Nor is it something that can wait until tomorrow*

or until I'm "ready". It is no longer just "a problem." It is the problem and I've got it today. I can barely live with myself as long as it remains this way.

The greater mystery is why more do not commit suicide. Perhaps, it is because, by this time, there has been enough said. Or heard on TV, remembered from childhood Sunday School, that the price of any solution is *obvious.* Quit drinking. Most already know about AA, the not-so-isolated leper colony for alcoholics, one from which there is daily return to normal society. But these "surrenders" have been happening since long before AA was founded, the "religious experiences" described by William James [2] at the turn of the century, for instance. Most sound like AA testimonies by "drunkards" who have overcome "demon rum."

No, there seems to be something in the experience itself that is healing, something that generates hope. What is happening? A self that has shunned truth about itself for years has finally been able to look and to see. This alone takes courage, however involuntary, and this simple act inevitably increases self-esteem.

 I don't like what I see, but I can be proud that I no longer look away. Not only this, but the truth has been crying all along to be let out, for just as long as the walls of denial have kept it shut in. As painful as the experience may be, the part of self that knows and seeks truth is triumphant at last. The "defeat" of denial is a *victory* for the self that hungers for reality and wholeness. And the healthiest part of us knows that truth really is the source of whatever freedom or healing we may have. This is one principle on which psychotherapy and spirituality seem to agree. Here lies hope. And the truth that lays the foundation for freedom is the truth about me, about what I have.

Ownership.

To increase understanding of the above section, complete Recovery Exercise #3 at the end of the chapter.

References

[1] Martin, Father Joseph. "Guidelines for Helping the Alcoholic." Carpentaria, CA: FMS, 1976.

[2] James, William. *The Varieties of Religious Experience.* New York: Longmans, Green & Company, 1902.

Recovery Exercises

1. Review "So What #1." Write down any reactions you have/had as you read this. Have you used ignorance as an excuse? If so, write and share what you told self or others when you did so. How does it feel to do this now? Do you think your chances for recovery go up, down, or remain the same when you do this?

2. Think of a time when you really believed you were not an addict/alcoholic or "not that bad," ie., that you could handle it yourself.
   → Write down three negative consequences of your continuing to drink/use back when you were "ignorant."
   → Although "Life" did not protect you from these consequences, can you forgive yourself now for what you did not see then? If you even hesitate, be sure to share about this. Ask for help!
   → Did anyone try to tell you you had a bigger problem? That you needed help? How did you react?

3. List three ways in which life has wounded you.
   → Do you see your responsibility for your wounds?
   → Does your group/helper think you do? What makes them question it, if they do?
   → Prior to your last relapse, where were you going for help

with these wounds? What part of the job of healing them were you doing or not doing?

→ Where will you go and or what will you do differently this time to take care of your wounds? What does your group/helper think of your plan?

11

Acceptance: Why We Need It

The Moment of Relapse as a Moment of Rejection

The wishful relapse brazenly rejects the idea there is anything hazardous about taking "just one." An unmedicated diabetic, munching jelly beans by the fistful, could not be less accepting of the disease in question.

> To prevent this kind of relapse, I have to accept the reality of my own addictive reactions. A process in itself, my acceptance needs to become a link in my reactions to any future possibility of taking "just one." And the new link, in turn, may need "maintenance."

The white-knuckle relapse also rejects rather than accepts:

> In the beginning of my abstinence, I reject the need to learn how to cope, trusting in my willpower. When this breaks down and I say "F--- it", I reject the primary fact about addiction: whatever I am [not] coping with, relapse will make it worse. I reject all other coping alternatives and I reject responsibility for consequences that I seem to know may follow. But most of all, I vehemently reject "it," whatever person, place or thing that contradicts my will.

☞   In sum, "One won't hurt" and its siblings ("This time will be different," "No one will know," etc.) reject the disease. "F--- it" merely rejects reality.

☞   No wonder the Big Book (p. 449) says "Acceptance is the answer to all of my problems." It is certainly the largest part of the answer to relapse, <u>if</u> it can become the most powerful link in my reactions to life. This chapter attempts to explore what acceptance is. As such, it is mostly a progress report on the author's own twenty-five year study of the subject.

When Do We Need Acceptance?

It seems that acceptance becomes an issue only when something is bothering us.

> Since "One won't hurt" permits an alcoholic/addict to drink/ drug without being troubled by guilt or fear, it only takes a little logic and common sense to see that having the disease must bother me. So much that I have to use denial — of the truth that one will hurt, will always hurt — to make that bother go away. In white-knuckle sobriety, I refuse to admit how much life bothers me. Right up to the point where it bothers me so much I say "F--- it" and drink or drug!

☞   The most important thing may not be *what* this thing called "bother" is, but *where* it is, inside me, the person that's bothered. I may be a NASA scientist fretting at my console about a dopey little robot hung up on a rock on Mars. Me sitting here on Earth — how many millions of miles away? But the fretting is inside me, right down here on the fourth rock from the sun. I may be pining for Juliet up in her tower, but the pining is down here and inside me. I may drink or drug (or gamble or binge eat) over a broken heart or a broken shoelace. Whatever the pain, including the pain of physical craving, it is inside me. And that is just where the booze or drugs (or twinkies, etc.) go.

Almost anyone can understand this intellectually. Rare is the person who appreciates what it means and lives accordingly. Most of us bog down in obsessing about how to fix the robot or the fair maiden, therapists, addicts/alcoholics, and "normies," included. When we take or do something to comfort our pain, we are actually aiming at the right target: the "bother" inside us. Unfortunately, we shoot with guns that jam, explode, or ricochet back at us. We try to make our bothers go away without looking at them, endlessly baffled by a target we cannot or will not see.

One of the most important statements in this book is this:

☞ *All of the things that bother a human being have one other thing in common — they are not how that human being* wants *them to be. In short, all "bothers" are frustrations.*

Loneliness wants company and boredom wants entertainment. Anger wants revenge or apology or whatever it is mad about. Fear wants an outcome that may not happen or doesn't want one that may. Take any of the negative emotions, — knock out the desire and you have nothing left to be upset about.

If I deny what bothers me, I am denying my frustration.

If I deny my negative emotions, I deny the frustration without which they could not exist.

I also deny how frustrated I am to have the emotion itself. Otherwise, why deny it in the first place!

If I drink or drug or eat over what bothers me, I am "fixing" the pain of my frustration, without dealing with the frustration itself.

If I am going to stay clean and sober, I am going to deal with frustration, without saying "One won't hurt" or "F--- it,"

*for the rest of my life. And there is no healthy way to do this
without learning to* accept *things that frustrate me.*

☞   *A frustration is a condition in which I don't get what I do want
or I do get what I don't want.*

Without the wanting, there would be no problem. It turns out
there are a number of problems with the problem of wanting. Do
not assume that the author has thought of them all!

To increase understanding of the above section, complete Recovery Exercise #1 at the end the of chapter.

Powerless — The Problem of Where Wanting Comes From

☞ What most of us seldom recognize or consider is that we do not
create or schedule our own "wanting." Where does "wanting" come
from? What makes one person want to be President and another
want a job as an assembly worker? What makes one person want
to sleep with the opposite sex and another to sleep with the same?
What makes one person want alcohol and another want gambling?
What makes me want to sleep for escape and someone else want
to eat chocolate?

The simple fact we do not control the wants that come to us is
what keeps psychotherapists and clergy in business. Marketing
and sales people, too, and let's not leave out cops, judges and
prison guards. Our wanting arises in us, like our questions and
feelings. Who can say now what he or she will be wanting in five
minutes or five years? Even the person with enough self-awareness to predict with reasonable accuracy, does only that. We may
predict —we do not control.

But wait a minute! Hold on! Aren't most of my so-called choices
based on what I *want*? And if those are fed into me by my genet-

ics or my conditioning or my unconscious, what does that make me?

It gets worse.

☞ Most of us have picked up some idea of what we "should" want. In other words, we want to be the kind of person who wants "good" things and not "bad" things. We want desperately to want some things and not to want others. And we don't have much say about where these special kinds of wants — our "shoulds"— came from, either. Mostly from being shamed.

☞ Now here is the very worst part. There is a crucial mechanism that is utterly lacking from the machinery of human desire: an "off" switch!

Powerless — The Problem of Turning Off Unwanted Wanting

As if being "chosen" by our wants were not humiliating enough! Once a "wanting" has arisen in us, we do not dictate how or when it will stop. We have no direct way to kill it. All wants are, in this sense, like demons that possess us, until they lose their fire. This is everybody, not just addicts and alcoholics.

☞ Only two healthy things seem to put out the fire of wanting — the satisfaction of getting what you want, or the inner "realization" that fulfillment is absolutely or relatively impossible. An alcoholic who still thinks he or she can drink and get away with it, is going to. An alcoholic who truly realizes "I cannot drink," cannot drink. The psychology of temptation is largely the tasting of possibility.

"Relative impossibility" is the recognition that the price of fulfillment is too high, that it is impossible to "have my cake and eat it, too."

Sure, I am still physically capable of picking up a drink —
just let me swing the IV out of the way. But it is beginning to

dawn on me that if I do it will permanently cure my favorite addiction at all. Breathing. In other words, I want something else [relatively] more than I want alcohol or drugs. What it takes to stop wanting the relatively impossible is to recognize it as such. Where "willpower" seemed to fail, "realization" of a truth that was there all along seems to succeed. It changes how I react because it has changed me, my internal links. I realize I cannot drink without losing control — it is impossible [and I don't want to lose control]. If the thought of "just one" pops in my mind, I wince and I may even chuckle, or I do what Bill Wilson did that fateful day in 1935. I pick up the phone.

Alternatively, I may reach the place where I can't drink [eat, gamble, snort] without despising myself. And I don't want to despise myself. This makes "F--- it" no longer an option. I do care and I do know it, not just with my head, but in my heart. When I know I cannot drink without paying an emotional price that is too high for me, I am able to lose enough wanting to be able to stop. Even that is often not enough by itself, not if I want to stay stopped. I may need to also know that, left to myself, I will once again become convinced I "can" drink. Realizing that my acceptance tends to fade, I may at last be able to make loyal and effective use of a maintenance program. One that constantly reminds me "you can't," "don't take the first one," or simply, "keep coming back!"

Wanting presents us with yet another complication. It is mostly a result of the glitch mentioned above, the fact that many wants are not "okay." What our mental machinery *does* come with is a built-in monkey wrench. If a "bad" want is trying to make itself known, we hit it over the head with this, almost literally. Literally enough that our "head," our conscious mind doesn't have a clue. The "nasty" desire goes underground where it can control our actions without our conscious choice. This is just as true whether my "demon" wanting is neurochemical or neurotic, physiological craving or emotional.

There are all sorts of tools for reducing frustration, alternatives to the relief I get from alcohol/drugs. But the tools will lie unused unless the route to alcohol or other drugs is blocked by my conviction, "No! I can't." And it is in the face of that solid wall — "No! I can't" — that the want must fizzle and grow dim, like a flame without oxygen. Behaviorists call it an "extinction schedule."

To increase understanding of the above section, complete Recovery Exercises #2 and #3 at the end of the chapter.

Spiritual Note

A word on spirituality and wanting. "Turning my will over" to God does not give me control of my wanting. In fact the implicit plea is for God to stimulate me with better wants, desires, and impulses. How does "surrendering" the outcome before it arrives help in a situation I fear may not go my way? In effect, it tells my desire that something better than itself is possible. Let's say the author wants an agency in London to hire him on a contract. To surrender is to accept in advance that a Higher Power may have a better gig in mind. Paris, Berlin, Cleveland. This takes off the intolerable pressure that says I *must* have what I want, when I want it. Whatever "God" is, this act of surrender relaxes me. It makes me receptive to something other than the exclusive object of my desire. If my surrender is real, it creates both acceptance and detachment.

Looking at surrender of will from another perspective, the desires of God Himself are not predictable. There is always an open-ended, ongoing problem, what does "He" want, here-and-now? And most spiritual teachers seem to agree that the answer lies within us, here-and-now. We look in the same place whether we look for what "I" want or for what "He" wants. And we are equally at the mercy of what we find. Several million sober alcoholics attest that "His" wants work out with considerably more mercy than the ones "I" started out with. Their wanting has been "restored to sanity."

To increase understanding of the above section, complete Recovery Exercise #4 at the end of the chapter.

Acceptance: What Is It?

Some Descriptive Definitions

What is this thing called acceptance?

I. After talking so much about "frustration," it makes sense to start this list with a definition based on the direct, literal connection between frustration and acceptance:

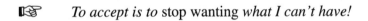   *To accept is to* stop wanting *what I can't have!*

As mentioned above, there are only two *healthy* ways to stop being frustrated. And one of them is to accept something the way it is, to stop wanting, willing or wishing it to be different. Not because it's "right," but because I don't control it. Not because I "like" it, but because that's the way it is. And because I'm tired of wasting my life energy, my very self, in a grim battle I cannot win.

> *I no longer wish to be a social drinker because I'm not.*
> *If something upsets me, I stop wanting the part I can't have and relax. I don't need a drink or a drug or an excuse to take one. I am free of my frustration, not by willpower but by realization of truth.*

II. A second way of looking at acceptance is based on how you know when you've got it:

☞ *The problem is still there but it does not bother you any more.* Don't take the author's word for this one. Check it out against your own experience and observation. Have you heard yourself or someone else say through gritted teeth that they "accept" someone or something. That is what acceptance is *not*! If I am still anxious, angry, depressed, — if I still have a negative emotion about something — I have not accepted it. But who has not faced ☞ some painful truth or fact and felt relief, a burden lifted? *That* is acceptance. If you are a reader who has not experienced this, you have much to look forward to. That relief is the equipment Mother Nature gave us for dealing with hopeless frustration. It does not come as fast as "chemical acceptance," but it lasts a lot longer and won't get you arrested.

(A bonus definition: Spirituality is the cultivation of acceptance.)

III. Our third view of acceptance explores one common metaphor for it: acceptance as "letting go."

What does *that* mean?
Let go of what?
Who was hanging on? And how? Isn't this just a "figure of speech?" A platitude inflicted on the afflicted by the unaffected?

Well, not entirely. If I need to "let go" I must be "hanging on" in some way. I am "attached" and need to "detach." The late Anthony deMello [2], a native of India, a Jesuit priest, and an American-trained psychotherapist gives us a definition he borrows from ☞ Buddhism. An "attachment" is an emotional state of clinging caused by the *belief* I must have something to be happy, or by the belief I must have it just to keep breathing.

What is one major reason I cling to the belief that "One won't hurt?" Is it not my conviction that I cannot be happy without my drug of choice? It may even be that this is my actual experience, that the only thing that ever made me feel normal or happy was the drug that is now killing me. I go back to that drug when there is no physical craving present, when things are good, when it makes no sense to me or anyone else — until we look at the idea and experience of "happiness" to which I cling. Happiness. Fun. Being "OK." Whatever "it" is, if I think life is over when I abstain from alcohol/drugs, I will hang on till the bitter end or until my thinking changes. *If my belief/attachment remains the same, I will drink/drug until it either kills me or has made me so miserable that I am willing to live without whatever I thought "happiness" was.* Then *I may be ready to learn that there is a different kind of happiness, one that happens to be real.*

What is one major reason I say "F--- it" and pick up that first drink/dose? Loss. If I believe I have to have that relationship, job, car , physical faculty, etc. to be happy, how can I "let go?" How can I tolerate life without my "fix-of-choice?" You'd say "F--- it, too!" At least, until you came to see happiness is possible without that relationship, job, car, etc..

This is where hope comes in. The kind of hope that makes it possible to consider a different way of dealing with disappointment of the most powerful desires. That it is not just a theory to say I can be happy without whatever I have lost, drug included. At this point, "detachment" and "surrender" appear to be virtually the same thing. Detachment steps back and allows no person, place or thing to be a condition for my being happy. Not through willpower but through understanding. Surrender steps forward and says, "Sure, I'd love to have him/her/it my way. But You're 'the boss' — I will accept whatever You give me *without conditions.*"

> *Whether, I surrender or detach, I am relieved of any reason or need to say "F--- it" and/or drink.*

IV. Acceptance as stopping the head-banging

Everyone has heard the phrase "Stop banging your head against a stone wall." We've pretty much all had the experience, too — the banging if not the stopping.

Now just exactly what does that mean?

We did not stand there banging our actual heads against a physical wall. Some of us have wound up in a cast because we beat our fists into something harder than we are. But not our "heads," not literally. What we *do* do is continue to will a disobedient fact in or out of existence. We will reality to work other than how it works, to act other than how she/he/it acts. Wishing. Longing. Worrying. Pining. Fantasizing. Ruing. Resenting. Possibly even grieving. These are some of the words we use to describe an inner reaction that clashes with reality. And that is the stone wall that bruises our stubborn will — whatever reality I am gnashing my teeth about!

> *In the wishful relapse I clash with the reality of my disease. In the white-knuckle relapse I clash with some other fact or truth that is not to my liking. In "acceptance," I find a way to stop wasting my precious life energy on a futile battle. This adversarial link in my reaction to the disease or to life is either gone or contained.*

V. Oh no, not that! (The most loathsome definition)

To accept something is to take "no" for an answer from life, a.k.a. "reality."

As children, we threw temper tantrums. Those of you who grew up stopped doing that and those of us who did not still suffer some form of this reaction. It is often called "relapse," especially of the "F--- it" variety.

We have already seen how "instant regression" may be one of the key reactions at the moment of relapse. This is not a metaphor — we actually experience ourselves as emotional children in this state. And emotional children may not be emotionally capable of taking "no" for an answer. This is where the concepts of Harry Tiebout discussed earlier still ring true.

Some AA's will say "I have to grow up or die."

Others will say, "God answers all requests. Sometimes the answer is 'no.'"

Most people in early abstinence have some insight about not being real good at taking "no" for an answer. Much of Twelve Step recovery seems clearly designed to increase that ability. This chapter has tried to describe the problem of frustration and relapse, as well as one possible solution, acceptance. The next describes an organized way to go about the work of accepting the seemingly unacceptable.

To increase understanding of the above section, complete Recovery Exercises #5, #6, #7, #8, and #9 at the end of the chapter.

References

[1] Anonymous. *Alcoholics Anonymous.* New York: Alcoholics Anonymous World Services, Inc., 1955.
[2] deMello, Anthony, [Edited by Stroud, Francis J.]. *Awareness, The Perils and Opportunities of Reality.* New York, London,etc.: Image Doubleday, 1992.

Recovery Exercises

1. List any three problems you ever drank or drugged over. Write down what it was that you wanted but were not getting each time.

2. If you can, write down three things you have wanted that you felt you "shouldn't." Which wants have been the hardest for you to admit? Can you remember who or what in your life told you each want was "bad?"

3. List three things you care most about that you will lose if you continue to drink/drug. Describe how you would feel to lose them. Rate your conviction from "1"[weak] to "10" [strong] that one drink/drug will cost you these things. Ask your peers to rate your conviction and to tell you why they rate you as they do.

4. List one to three things so precious you might drink/drug if you lost them. How willing are you to "turn them over," i.e., let a "Higher Power" take them or not? What does your answer tell you about how committed you are to living "life on life's terms?" What do your peers think? If you reject spiritual concepts, how would you handle such loss?

5. List three things that once bothered you and no longer do. How long did it take you to get over each? Did you do anything to bring this about? Was there a moment when you felt the "burden" lift?

6. List three things you believe you cannot be happy without. Have you ever lost one of them? Did you ever drink/drug for fear of losing one, only to have your drinking/drugging cause the loss?

7. List five things that have given you the feeling of "banging your head against a stone wall." Did you drink/drug over them? What things in your life now give you that feeling? What are you doing to stop your head-banging?

8. Picture one of your moments of relapse, if you have had one. Ask yourself how old you felt *emotionally* at that moment? If you have had more than one, try this several times. What seems to trigger the feeling? What can you do now when it happens?

9. Which words below have you or others used to describe your personality? For at least three of them, describe one situation where the word fit you. Try to spell out the want for which you wouldn't/couldn't take no for an answer.

Stubborn	_____	Demanding	_____
Persistent	_____	Controlling	_____
Rigid	_____	Intense	_____
Fearful	_____	Anxious	_____
Insecure	_____	Manipulative	_____

12

Acceptance: How to do it

The "SPARROW" Method

Okay, so I have to accept something and I know it.. I know I will suffer until I do and that I may relapse if I don't. I only have one little question for you.

How?

How do I get from point "A," where I know that I must accept, to point "B," where "the problem is still there but it doesn't bother me any more." What are the tools?

The author spent several years refining a practical list, one that identifies the toolboxes real people actually reach into when challenged to accept something. He did not create any of the toolboxes. They have all been around for years, though some of them have been constantly growing. Every reader has probably used tools from each toolbox, often without even thinking of it as a way to "accept." An enthusiastic scrabble player, it was probably inevitable the author would notice the list could form *some* word. Think of "SPARROW" like a computer menu, and inside each menu there are many submenus with many dropdowns. It is guaranteed that there will be readers of this book who know and/or use tools about which the author does not have a clue. What "SPARROW" does do is organize them.

"S" Is for "Share"

That's right. If the delusion that "one won't hurt" has popped back in your mind, *share* it. If something has you so upset you are thinking of saying "F--- it" and using a fix, *share* it. If someone you are trying to help not relapse does not bring up whatever is on their mind, ask them to share it.

☞   The word "share" is an interesting verbal pointer. It sounds like it points to something "I" do – but it is really always something "we" do. "I" may share, but if some "other" does not receive my sharing, I might as well be "the sound of one hand clapping." "To receive" implies understanding and acceptance, which always precludes judgment and usually at least delays advice. So the verb, "to share," says a lot about what someone other than the "one" sharing must be doing.

Sharing is probably the number one tool that the human race has used to accept the unacceptable since Cain slew Able. (If only Cain had talked about his feelings!) Perhaps, the last wartime crime against the Vietnam vet was this: to be in a rice paddy holding a buddy as he lay dying one day, to be walking around downtown Oakland in civvies three days later. No time to share. The worst crime against many abused kids is the "no talk" rule. Specialists in the field tell us that many kids do heal, almost without scars, *if* they can talk about it at the time. Not thirty years and four treatment centers later, in some therapist's office.

☞   The most important single reason to mention this (Sharing) toolbox is because of the great difficulty so many addict/alcoholics have reaching into it.

> One reason I turn to booze, drugs, food, work, sex instead of turning to people is I don't trust them. And probably for good reason. The parents who raised me may have compounded their abuse with that shaming "no talk" rule.

Claudia Black spells out this particular intergenerational cycle in her classic, *It Will Never Happen to Me* [1]. For many people, reading her book will be an important tool inside the "Read" toolbox below.

☞   Whether I am a helper and/or in recovery, I need to know one thing. *The most important menu in the "Sharing" toolbox is unquestionably the one for overcoming blocks to sharing.* Everything from traditional psychotherapy to small sharing tasks, spelled out, carried out, and processed. From sharing about sharing to the use of the other six toolboxes to prepare to share. Once I am able to share, it is only a question of planning with whom, about what, and how often.

To increase understanding of the above section, complete Recovery Exercises #1, #2, #3, and #4 at the end of the chapter.

"P" Is for Prayer (and Meditation)

Some form of prayer and/or meditation has helped humanity to accept what must be accepted since reality first defied desire. The secular therapist may not be comfortable talking about prayer. But

☞   if you work with people who are (or need to be) working a spiritual program, the subject is likely to come up. If you are genuinely interested in the problem of acceptance, it will be hard to ignore the self-reports of those who have used this tool to such effect. Talk to anyone who has actually said a heartfelt Serenity Prayer when upset. Talk to those who have kneeled and said the Third Step Prayer [2] when the chips were down. Observe for yourself those who practice meditation on a regular basis. God forbid, you might even try it yourself.

Science can tell us exactly what we do or do not control and why our particular frustration may be hopeless. But it stops right there. Science leaves the suffering human being to find acceptance by other means. Prayer and meditation, on the other hand,

☞   are tools designed for just that search. Science is about understanding and manipulating reality. Prayer and meditation are about being able to live *in* it, whether we understand it or not. At their best, these disciplines help the human fish to live in the water called reality.

☞   One way of understanding the experience of prayer is as a subjective, interactive relationship with reality. Part of what makes humans human is the ability to intuit the experience of another, to "take the role of the other," as we were taught in Sociology 101. But this ability does not appear limited to human relatedness. We use it with animals, whether they reciprocate or not. We are all potential "horse whisperers." Almost any artist or craftsman or musician gets into a subjective relationship with the work. "It" guides the artist. The author has an image of a safecracker listening to the tumblers and saying, "Talk to me, baby." A famous baseball pitcher would talk to the ball. In prayer, we appear to bring this human way of knowing and experiencing to bear on reality, on life. One fruit of this seems to be behavior that is based more on reality and less on desire. This is why it can be so helpful to anyone who is a slave of desire, an addict.

The Twelve Step prayer "menu" features the "Serenity Prayer," the "Third Step Prayer," and the "Prayer of St. Francis," as well as the "Lord's Prayer." Prayers for "willingness" are mentioned throughout the Big Book instructions on the steps, and there is a Step Seven Prayer. Recovering readers and their sponsors may well "prescribe" any of these to deal with particular frustrations. AA has its own official meditation book and unofficial ones abound. The secular therapist may not wish to discuss prayer the

☞   way a minister would, with suggestions as to ritual or content. However, exploration of the person's prayer experience can be more relevant than exploration of their sex life. Identifying barriers — "resistance" — to the use of this tool may be profoundly helpful. In discussing meditation, Bill Wilson explicitly urges the recovering reader of the Big Book to find the *other* excellent books available on the subject. It hardly seems likely that he considered

☞ himself the last word on prayer either. A therapist who has a few handy references on the subject may see some clients progress more rapidly, and relapse less frequently.

To increase understanding of the above section, complete Recovery Exercises #5, #6, and #7 at the end of the chapter.

"A" Is for Action

What do you mean "action?!" The whole point is that we are accepting things we don't control and can't fix. That's why we are frustrated in the first place. So how can action have anything to do with it — don't be ridiculous!

Au contraire, mon frere.

Picture this: I am a diabetic, calmly explaining how I "know" my Isles of Langerhans are kaput. "Yep, got this here diabetes and it's a kicker. Eat sugar and I could go into a coma and die. You betcha, I accept it. Just ask me. But don't ask me about the Hershey bar I munch on as I explain all this."

Who in their right mind would agree that I have accepted my
☞ diabetes? Common sense says that if I accept a fact I then act accordingly. In a sense, I now obey the very fact I have accepted. I do what it says instead of what I initially wanted. Think about it – the very fact my problem won't change creates the very strong likelihood that *I* will have to. I change internally so I am no longer bothered or upset, and I change externally so my behavior is "realistic." My reaction is now "controlled" by reality and not by my initial, frustrated desire.

After all, why do we fight acceptance so hard?

Is it not in part because we know we will have to change when we do accept. As long as I tell myself "One won't hurt," I avoid accepting my disease. I also avoid the behavior change dictated by a disease that guarantees one will hurt. And I may have to accept my mysterious inability to remember it is the first drink/drug. Only then can I be "motivated" to actively seek external reminders. On the other hand, I may respond to frustration by saying "F--- it" and drinking. I avoid accepting whatever part of the frustration was not going to go away. Is not the "it" that I "F---" at least partly the work I would have had to do? The effort required to change my own behavior or feeling?

So what is the "tool" exactly?

It is to identify how my behavior will be different when I am at peace with this reality I don't control. Hopefully, I can find some part of that action I am ready to take now.

A counselor or sponsor may be able to help me identify small tasks here, while some of the other tools may be able to help me get the job done. Any new action that is based on the new reality in my life moves me toward full acceptance. This is poignantly true when I must accept the loss of a loved one. To remove just one of the person's photos or personal belongings may trigger the flood of grief, which is the process of healing and accepting. *To avoid such actions is to avoid grieving and to remain stuck. If I have an addiction, my disease will easily convert my buried grief into craving, an impulse that seems to come "out of the blue."*

To increase understanding of the above section, complete Recovery Exercises #8, #9, and #10 at the end the of chapter.

"R" Is for "Read"

My heart is breaking and you tell me I have to accept she doesn't love me any more and I don't control that. And, and — *go read a book?!*

Well, actually, uh, yes. Maybe not right away – you probably need to do some sharing and use some other tools first. Maybe after the tears are down to a gallon a minute or so, then there are a number of ways to use reading to help accept and be at peace. We did hear you say you want to be at peace?

☞ One way to use the reading toolbox is to read about the problem in an objective way. In effect, we let science tell us precisely why we have to use these unscientific tools, what it is we don't control and how it works. I can study my diabetes or my cancer or my addiction and tailor my acceptance work on the most accurate possible picture of the problem. I can also research my child's ADHD or other learning disability. Books like Dr. Milam's *Under the Influence* [3] can be helpful to any alcoholic. *Uppers, Downers, All Arounders* [4] covers all the drugs, as does *The High Road* [5].

☞ The second way to use reading as a tool for helping myself accept the unacceptable is to read accounts by other people who coped with a similar experience. Christopher Reeves has written about his experience, as did Roy Campanella before him. As did Helen Keller and Victor Frankl. The Big Book of AA is designed to be read for shared experience. Narcotics Anonymous now has its own hardcover book, as does Overeaters Anonymous. Whatever your suffering, someone else has written about dealing with it. If not, your opportunity beckons. Of course that is the *last* tool in the acronym — "W" is for writing!

☞ The third way to use reading as a tool for acceptance is to read books about acceptance itself and how to do it. *Good Grief* [6] and *When Bad Things Happen to Good People* [7] are just two books that have helped many people to accept the seemingly unacceptable.

Don't take the "R" here too literally. If it did not mess up the acronym, the author would make it "I" for "Information gathering." But they won't allow "SPAIROW" in scrabble, and spell-check won't tolerate it either. Speaking of computers, the internet is now one of the primary places to get information. But so is your local video store — everything from "Days of Wine and Roses" to "My name is Bill W." If not, try the library or go back to the Net. Last but not least, it does sometimes help to talk to an expert. ☞ Try to find someone who has written a book.

To increase understanding of the above section, complete Recovery Exercises #11 and #12 at the end of the chapter.

The Other "R" Is for "Rethinking"

This "toolbox" is like one of those innocent little submenus in a computer. By linkage, it is connected to ("contains") some real ☞ monsters. How about all of the Twelve Steps, the slogans, sponsorship and all of the other toolboxes above and below? How about all forms of psychotherapy? Of spirituality? Religion?

Why is this?

It is because the cognitive therapists are at least half right. If something "bothers" me it usually has some kind of meaning to me. There is some sort of reason in my head or brain that makes me want it to be different. Mental meaning seems to be based on experience (memories) and interpretation. Physiological "meaning" seems to be based on the sense that something is "good" or "bad" for survival. Cravings feel like needs (and sometimes actually are.)

☞   Shakespeare said, "Nothing is good or bad but thinking makes it so." "Thinking," in this sense, appears to be a big enough bucket to hold the unconscious and its memories. And also to hold thoughts (images and fantasies) that seem to be generated by physiological craving. Shakespeare was in the ballpark. (This book is mostly limited to the mental links, conscious and unconscious.)

If I think my frustration is "bad," how am I to get over it?

In two words, rethink it.

☞   A sponsor may ask "How important is it?" The question encourages me to rethink priority and perspective. With a resentment, sponsors ask what the Big Book asks, "What was your part in it." This is a rethinking question that is almost as irritating as it is healing. The AA slogans are handy mental tools to paste on my own "stinking thinking" as it occurs. The steps? If a "spiritual awakening" doesn't change how you think, you have not had one.

☞   Cognitive therapy has built an entire therapeutic system around identifying beliefs that cause pain and/or painful behavior. All the cognitive tools are designed to replace "distortions" with "rational responses." Rethinking! As a system, the shortcoming of cognitive therapy of addiction seems to be that of making belief the *only* "cause" of behavior or emotion. The author makes considerable use of cognitive therapy tools. But if there is one point this book is dogmatic about, it is this: the idea "One won't hurt" is frequently caused by craving, physical or emotional. Wishful thinking is

☞   caused by the wish!

Traditional psychotherapies focus more on childhood experience, but what do they do back there? Among other things, bring mistaken notions to the surface where they can be corrected. We cannot change our childhood. But we can change how we think about it and how it impacts our adult thinking.

To increase understanding of the above section, complete Recovery Exercises #13, #14, and #15 at the end the of chapter.

"O" Is for "One Day At a Time"

Why does this particular slogan get to take up a whole letter when all the others are buried in submenus under "Rethink?" Because it is so important and so useful, and because it applies to such a broad range of situations. Besides which, we really need an "O" for "SPARROW".

What is "One day at a time" as a tool? It is the tool by which most recovering folks first learn to abstain from alcohol or drugs. It is a slogan that puts the lie to the projections of endless misery created by craving and imagination. This slogan becomes a realistic way to deal with any problem in life that will not resolve immediately. It is second only to the Serenity Prayer as the ultimate "rational response." It is the foundation for the principle of living in the here-and-now. And presence of mind, in the most literal sense of the words, is the hallmark of spirituality.

So how do you do it?

☞ First, you recognize feeling overwhelmed by the seemingly endless course of some problem or another. Your self can't see how to endure for so long. So you explain: "Self, this does seem like way too much to handle and way too long to handle it. Tell you what. Let's forget about all that and just deal with the part that is here today." We really can't do anything about the rest of it anyway. The essence of the tool is realistic self-talk under duress.

☞ Another way to do it is by time management. Writing out a detailed, hour-by-hour schedule for the day, I reduce the stress of multiple decisions by deciding in advance. In this way, I get my "head" into the activities of this day, letting go of the rest, one planned day at a time.

Maybe I can't get over this heartache in one day, but I can live with it for this one day. And I can use all the other toolboxes in SPARROW today to help me grow toward acceptance. If by chance I am thinking "One won't hurt," I can at least consider putting it off until tomorrow. If "F--- it" is on my mind, I can probably cope with "it" for one more day, today.

To increase understanding of the above section, complete Recovery Exercises #16, #17, #18, and #19 at the end of the chapter.

"W" Is for "Writing"

☞ Writing is a toolbox with two main compartments. One is for the kind of writing that is expressive and exploratory. I get things off my chest and then read them to find out what they were. If my writing was spontaneous, there will be surprises. And there are six other toolboxes with which to process my surprise. Seven, counting the other compartment in this one.

☞ The second compartment contains structured written protocols to help me see more clearly. The grandaddy of structured writing processes is the written "searching and fearless moral inventory" found in the Big Book. Columns and lists that would make Aaron Beck, the father of Cognitive Behavioral Therapy, proud, plus two key processing questions that some sponsors and counselors turn into further columns. The little recognized "Recovery, Inc." [8] created a language and a four-step process, written or spoken, for coping with the "trivialities of everyday life." It is a clear forerunner of the cognitive therapy worksheets for dealing with upset. These, in turn, are quite helpful for helping an alcoholic "in emotional disturbance" [9]. In effect, they provide what Bill W. called a "spot check inventory." Interestingly enough, the Recovery, Inc. method is called "spotting."

The number of written exercises is potentially unlimited. This book adds the "Dr. Jekyll and Mr. Hyde" exercise, as well as the problem-solving format described in Chapter 14. The "Addiction Conviction" scale can be used separately or as part of the "Learning From Relapse" questionnaire, which is also included. Each chapter has a set of questions for the recovering reader. Likewise an appendix addresses the student of chemical dependency counseling to engage the ideas and tools of each chapter. The exercises work best if written out and then discussed. But feel free to use any other tool at any step of the way.

"SPARROW" shows us one positive fact about all the problems we may run into in life. There are always a lot of things to do about the things I cannot change. In other words, acceptance is an active process, something we can work at and for.

To increase understanding of the above section, complete Recovery Exercises #20, #21, #22, #23, #24, and #25 at the end of the chapter.

Tools for the Courage to Change

But what if I *can* change something? – there is something I can *do* that might actually bring about what I want. Only I'm scared or don't feel adequate or even worthy? Maybe I know I could change something, but don't see why I should have to do the work. What tools will help me get unstuck, get me working "to change the things I can?"

     Answer: SPARROW! The exact same set of tools, and here is the secret. If I work to change myself from frustration to acceptance the object of the exercise is me. If I work to change myself from "stuck" to unstuck, the target is still me, my ideas, feelings, and behavior. Heck, frustration itself is just a kind of being stuck. And being stuck is usually the frustration of my appetite to have my cake and eat it, too. No wonder I use the same set of tools to change the same self that is often both stuck *and* frustrated.

Conclusion

The Serenity Prayer defines the process of all human coping. Whatever it is and whoever I am, I must first face what bothers me. Having done this, I must continue to sort out what I must accept from what I may change. I then proceed accordingly, using tools the author has organized under "SPARROW." How long must I do this? Until the problem does not bother me any more. In Chapter 14 we will look at an example of actually doing this. But first, we will look at a common barrier to constructive problem-solving, and how to punch holes in it.

References

[1] Black, Claudia. *It Will Never Happen to Me.* Denver: M.A.C., 1981.

[2] Anonymous. *Alcoholics Anonymous.* New York: Alcoholics Anonymous World Services, Inc., 1955.

[3] Milam, James R., Ketchum, Katherine. *Under the Influence, A Guide to the Myths and Realities of Alcoholism.* New York, London: Bantam Books, 1983.

[4] Inaba, Darryl S., Cohen,William, E. and Holstein, Michael. *Uppers, Downers, All Arounders, Physical and Mental Effects of Psychoactive Drugs, (Third Edition).* Ashland, Oregon: CNS Publications, 1997.

[5] Mehl, Duane. *The High Road.* Center City, Minnesota: Hazeldon, 1988.

[6] Westberg, Granger. *Good Grief.* Minneapolis: Fortress Press, 1962.

[7] Kuchner, Harold S.. *When Bad Things Happen to Good People.* New York: Avon, 1983.

[8] Low, Abraham. *Mental Health through Will Training, A System of Self-Help in Psychotherapy as Practiced by Recovery.* Incorporated. Boston: The Christopher Publishing House, 1950.

[9] Anonymous. *Twelve Steps and Twelve Traditions.* New York: Alcoholics Anonymous World Services, Inc., 1952, 1981.

Recovery Exercises

1. If you can, think of something that really bothered you before the age of six. Then see if you can think of any time you tried to share it. What happened? If you were not sharing, see if your "inner child," the part of you that lived through this time can say why you did not share. Then ask if s/he still feels the same way about the risk of sharing with others today. Does

this connect with any of your adult reactions? Try the same questions with age 6—10 and 12—18.

2. Rate yourself on a scale from "1" (No way!) to "10" (comfortable, willing, even eager) on your comfort/ability to share the things that really eat at you. Rate yourself from "1" (little chance) to "10"(almost 100%) on the likelihood you will remain clean and sober at you current level of sharing.

3. Think of three problems you have drunk/drugged over. Who were you sharing with about each (before using?)

4. For each relapse you may have had, indicate whether you said "F--- it" or "One won't hurt." Indicate one healthy person you might have shared with at the time, before picking up the first drink/drug. What difference do you think it might have made?

5. Ask three different people, a member of the clergy, someone in recovery who is not a counselor, and a treatment professional who is not (to your knowledge) in recovery, for their favorite books on prayer and/or meditation. The list is arbitrary — ask anyone you want.

6. Wait until something happens that bothers you. While upset, try saying the Serenity Prayer at least three times, slowly and deliberately. While saying it, think about how what you are saying relates to the situation that has you upset. Notice whether this seems to have any effect. Write, share, discuss!

7. Whether you believe in God or not, try saying the Third Step Prayer (p. 63, Big Book), on your knees, thinking about what it means. Do this first thing in the morning, repeating the prayer at least three times, and last thing at night, for a week. Then

stop doing it for a week. Keep a journal and notice any difference. If you cannot make yourself try this experiment, write down all the reasons that stop you, including feelings about it. Write, share, discuss!

8. Individually or as a group, create a real list of things that have been hard to accept. Then try to spell out how the person's behavior will change if they really do accept each particular thing that cannot be "fixed."

9. Pick something that bothers you now, one of your current living problems. Identify one thing that is hard for you to accept about it. Rate your level of acceptance from "1" (minimal) to "10" (serenity!). Now, identify one action that would be different if you were a "10," had completely accepted this one thing. Try doing that one thing for a week. Rate your serenity about this issue each day. Report back to group and/ or counselor.

10. Do the reading assignments your counselor or sponsor has given you!

11. Ask a clergy person, a person in long-term recovery, and a helping professional what *they* read when the chips are down. (If they get huffy or give you a blank look, delete them from your list.) Again, the list is arbitrary — ask anyone the good Lord puts in your path.

12. Write a list of reasons you don't read about your problems. Ask your group/counselor to help you counter each one.

13. Have you ever said "One won't hurt" and picked up the first drink/drug? If so, what ideas about yourself will have to change for you to stop doing this?

14. Have you ever said "F--- it" and picked up the first drink/ drug? If so, what ideas about yourself and about life will have to change if you are to stop doing this?

15. Write down something that was bothering you the day of relapse. What might you have done about it that day, instead of relapsing? (Hint: look in the other toolboxes.) Did you do it? How can you use this information and understanding *today* to deal with one of the problems you have today?

16. Think of one of the worst living problems you have today. If you knew the world was ending tomorrow, and you only had to do whatever you could about the living problem for today, how hard would it be?

17. Picture the part of yourself that is worried about some problem sitting in a chair. Now read this section ("One Day at a Time") out loud to that part of yourself. Do it with feeling and conviction. Absolutely no laughter is permitted. In group, you could try having someone else be your worried self, or let someone else be the reader. Or both. Whatever you do, follow "Rule 62."

18. Ask someone in a meeting of AA what "Rule 62" is. Keep asking until you find out.

19. Every day for a week, write out a daily plan for all of your activities of the following day. Break it down, hour by hour, including rest, meals, recreation and recovery activities. The following week, do not do this. Track your stress and craving levels. (If you are taking to the daily planning, it's okay not to stop.)

20. Pick a resentment you have currently. Take it through the process described for "Step Four" in the Big Book. Once you have completed each of the columns, write out how the other person is ill. Then write down everything you did to contribute to the situation. Share and process with group and/or counselor.

21. Pick one or more Twelve Step slogans. For each one think of a situation where it might apply. Spell out the thought that the slogan replaces.

22. Select a negative or self-defeating attitude you have or that others say you have. Ask others to help you select a healthier attitude to replace it. Try to spell out how this would change your reaction to some real situations and how this would change your life.

23. Try reacting with the new attitude for some specific period of time. Notice and share what happens. What other tools would help you make the healthier attitude last?

24. If you can, identify a false belief from your dysfunctional childhood. Imagine that your inner child is sitting in a chair. In a loving way, explain your understanding of how s/he came to believe this, how the belief has continued to cause pain, and what the truth is. If you do this alone, write down how it feels and what you learn. In group, ask for feedback.

25. Look at a relapse process you lived. Try to identify as many false or dysfunctional beliefs as you can. Counter each one with the truth. Use other toolboxes to help you do this.

13

Direct Treatment of the Minimization Links

In Chapter 11 we explored the problem of acceptance, defining it in practical terms. In Chapter 12, we mapped out the "SPARROW" system for doing the actual work of acceptance. In the next chapter, we will build on this material to spell out and illustrate "How to Cope With a Problem, Any Problem." First, this chapter addresses a "link" that stymies the need to cope, much less to learn how. This link is closely related to denial. Where the voice of denial says "what is, isn't," this one says, "what is, is so small I really don't have to deal with it." It does not deny the problem exists, just that it is big enough for me to have to deal with it. It assures me there is no reason to bring such a small problem up in counseling or group. It is like looking at my own problem from the wrong end of a pair of binoculars. This voice is usually called "minimization."

 If I am going to share real problems (frustrations) in counseling or in self-help meetings, I can't keep telling myself they are too small to be worth mentioning. It is my counselor's job to help me with this. What follows are two tools for my counselor and I to get started.

I. How to Help a Minimizer Get Started

The minimizer is a person who shrinks a real mountain down to an imaginary molehill, shrivels the molehill down to an anthill, and then steps on it.

"I'm fine."

"No big problem at all this week."

"Nothing really bothered me all week."

"Frustrations? Nah. Nothing important enough to talk about."

This person is hiding, aware of it or not.

> *As long as I hide my frustration we are not going to be able to treat it. Minimization blocks healthy problem solving – I convince myself the problem is too "petty" to be worthy of my attention or effort. Unattended, suppressed, it builds in force and tension. This allows emotional pressure to build to the point where I can only say "F--- it" or "One won't hurt."*

If we are going to interrupt the relapse process, we are going to have to help the person recognize and alter this minimization. One simple way to make it safe for the minimizer goes like this:

"Mizer, think for a minute of all the things that happened this week (or today). Of all those things, however big or small, which one was the best?"

"Well, nothing really great happened."

"I know, but something would be on the top of the list."

"Oh, I guess the raise my boss gave me and I didn't even ask."

"Felt pretty good, huh?"

"Yeah."

"The money is nice. But to give it to you without being asked means that he appreciates your work and wants you to know it."

"Yeah." (Blushing.) "And I was worried he might fire me!"

"Sounds like you're relieved."

All the therapist does is try to show understanding by active listening or paraphrasing.

"I'll say. I don't know why I can never convince myself I do a good job and don't have to worry. One of these days I'll learn to trust myself and not worry."

Ignoring this spontaneous but not uncommon self-disclosure, and noting a major issue for future clinical reference, the fictitious therapist proceeds. "Sounds like a plan. Now, Mizer, picture that list of all the things that happened this week again, with the surprise raise on top."

"Okay."

"Look down to the bottom of the list. What was the worst thing that happened, no matter how small. If you don't want to talk about that, just go up the list to the next worst, until you see one you feel okay telling us about."

"Oh, that's not so hard. Car broke down on the freeway and I caused a jam that got on the radio."

"Wow!" says the therapist, "sounds like a pressure cooker."

"Yeah, and I just had the car serviced. I just wasn't expecting a problem."

"Pressure and surprise," therapist surmises. "You must have been pretty torqued at the mechanics," pun intended.

"I wasn't trying to figure out what to get them for Christmas," he says. It makes sense, when you stop and think about it, that a minimizer would have a knack for understatement.

"What were you thinking and feeling as your car died and traffic piled up?"

"Well, at first I was scared shitless that I would get creamed."

"How did you handle that?"

"I tried to get out and see if I could get my car started and the guy behind me helped by stopping a ways back with his flashers on."

"Did you try to say anything to calm yourself down?"

"Like what?"

"Oh, any of the tools from the program. That sort of thing."

"Hell, no, I was just trying to hold onto my ass."

"Did you do anything with your anger?"

"Yeah, I pounded the hood too hard. I left a slight dent."

"Feel better?"

"Hurt my hand so bad I didn't feel as scared and angry," he grins.

"What was the worst part of this?"

"Waiting. Being stuck there and helpless while all those people who are trying to get home have to wait."

"You felt guilty?"

"Sort of. And like they all thought I'm some kind of jerk who doesn't take care of his car and ran out of gas or something stupid like that."

"You felt they were judging you?"

"Yeah, looking at me and judging."

"Sounds embarrassing."

If we add a fictitious group, the therapist can ask if others have been stuck behind a breakdown, what they thought of the driver whose car broke down. These answers will generally be supportive and some will share when they broke down in traffic. The last step in this exercise, unless we are going on to full-scale problem-solving, is to ask the client, "How do you feel now?"

A common answer is, "I feel better, that knot in my belly is gone. Funny, I didn't even know this was still bothering me."

"What do you think made you feel better?"

"I guess just talking. You [and the group, if there was one] seemed to understand. It looks different when you share."

The counselor may also go after a behavioral connection. "This knot you weren't so aware of, ever do anything about it in the past?"

"Sure, when it got tight enough I knew just what to do. Drink!"

"You realize what you've learned today?"

"Well, I guess I can talk and feel better and not drink."

"Not a bad day's work."

Fictionalized counseling always goes smoothly, of course. But this simple approach consistently produces both sharing of real problems and relief of real tension. It has given relief to people frustrated by everything from "worthless" stepsons to hard yolks in a cafeteria. Many of these sessions have gone on to the problem-solving process described in the next chapter on how to cope.

Generally, this tool works better with an individual. There is risk of making a client feel shown up in a group, or the group may see the technique as manipulative. However, much depends on the real attitude of the therapist. Behavior modification researchers may not be able to see an "attitude," but group members will. *If* you are persistent but don't push, and are prepared to be rebuffed, *if* you can spot and accept the kind of shame or self-will that won't yield, you will help your minimizer overcome this block a healthy percentage of the time. And the minimizer will get real relief. Do nothing more than invite the sharing and listen empathicly to the feelings. You will be surprised how often the person will experience relief from a tension they did not know was still there.

The recovering reader may squirm at this example of a therapist so consciously trying to remove blinders. Hopefully, the reasons make sense to you. Perhaps, you have seen yourself or someone else relapse from minimizing instead of coping. The author has a fantasy of a group in which members themselves understand minimizing. No, not all group members will be minimizers. Yet group members might actually facilitate or invite this procedure for each other. They can then follow it with sincere sharing of their own experience of admitting how much some "little things" bothered them. One thing a newly recovering reader can do even now: identify a seemingly small but real problem. Then take that specific frustration to group or to an open discussion meeting to share. Alternatively, make a phone call and share that way. Create your own experience and test whether the tool works!

To increase understanding of the above section, complete Recovery Exercises #1 and #2 at the end of the chapter.

☞ Recipe for Counter-Minimizing

One minimizer.

One high-minded helpful, slightly frustrated therapist.

Invite minimizer to review events of past day, week, longer.

Pause.

Invite minimizer to assemble events into mental list, best event at top, no matter how small.

Invite minimizer to share best event.

When s/he does, demonstrate concrete and emotional understanding. (Actively listen, invite group to share if appropriate.)

Diffuse further client response.

Invite client to look at list again, picking worst event, no matter how small.

Pause.

Invite minimizer to share the worst event s/he is willing to share, not necessarily the bottom of the list. It doesn't have to even be "bad" or "that bad" or "really bad" or major, or to have upset the person. You may have to reassure him/her of this.

Pause.

If s/he shares (about 80 percent will) just try to demonstrate understanding, connect with feelings by active listening, etc.

Person will probably share more.

Actively listen more.

(Don't try to problem-solve yet, unless you make it explicit and you can see some obvious work to be done. Ask person if they want to work.)

Ask if person notices any difference in feelings since before sharing.

If the response is "no difference," accept this.

If they feel better in any way, see if they can spell out what made them feel better.

If the person can say something about the process that gave

relief, see if they can look back and identify what they did to get relief in the past.

If they identify drinking or other unhealthy self-comforting, reinforce this experience of a new alternative. Emphasize it is something they can do, that they have control over.

Note: Very rarely, a person feels worse after sharing. They may have gotten in touch with some buried upset. You and group may have to concentrate longer on giving understanding and you may ☞ have to go into problem-solving. Even if the person feels worse, you can spell out the advantage of knowing what the "bother" is. Namely, that they have a choice (now) of what to do about it.

☞ II. Frustration Tag — Getting a Group to Talk

This tool can be used to bring out a problem for the group to work on. It can also be used as a warm-up, an ice-breaker. Generally, the therapist explains the above facts about daily frustration: that all of us want something all day long, that no one gets everything they want, not even for one day. Then ask one group member to share a frustration they had this week. It doesn't matter how small it is, only that it is real. This person then picks the next person to share, and so on, like a "tag" meeting of Alcoholics Anonymous. Almost every group has members who will generate humor in sharing their frustrations. The therapist may comment supportively ☞ or ask for a hand count, a quick "me-too" from others. Emphasize how the person felt at the moment of frustration, not just the objective gap between "want" and "got."

Many addicts/alcoholics have never consciously connected feeling and frustration, frustration and drinking/drugging. In any group, you may have one or two die-hards who just "can't" think of ☞ anything. There is no need to make an issue of it, as they will feel some of the group energy in spite of themselves. Once the sharing is complete, the only question is whether anyone wants to focus on their particular frustration and take it through the problem-solving process described in the next chapter.

Recipe for Frustration Tag

Explain a problem as something not the way you want it, that everyone wants something at all times, that no one gets all they want for even one day.

Ask members to think of one frustration they had in the last week, day, etc., no matter how small.

Pause.

Ask group if they have been able to think of at least one thing (show of hands).

Tell group you need one person to volunteer, or you will pick someone, that the first person will "tag" the next to share, and so on.

Pause.

Get one or pick one.

Try to get person sharing to spell out feelings about frustration. Actively listen.

Encourage and utilize humor as appropriate.

Seek brief, concrete sharing, even hand-counts for same experience. "How many other people have erased a hard day's work on their PC?"

As group finishes up, ask them to check how they feel. Increased energy and relaxation will generally be visible. Explore/explain what this can mean as with the minimizer, or go on to problem-solving or other group process.

A delightful variation: Have each volunteer share one small frustration. *Then* have this person spell out what they must accept versus what they may change. In settings where it is appropriate, follow this by having the group say the Serenity Prayer, *using the*

name of the person who has just shared. (Always ask the person's
permission!) It is delightful to watch the expression of someone
newly sober as they hear their peers say the Serenity Prayer for
them. The author has used this variation at the end of a long, drain-
ing day any number of times. He can always count on it to re-
charge his own batteries. This exercise is an effective teaching
process in itself. It also prepares the group for the problem-solving described in the next chapter, and for actual use of one of the
primary tools of Twelve Step recovery.

> The recovering reader might also consider whether this
> could not be a perfectly acceptable format for an AA meeting.
> No cross-talk — I just share my problem and how it breaks down
> according to the Serenity Prayer. The group then says the Prayer
> with my name, as it does for each person who shares in this
> way.

*To increase understanding of the above section, complete Recov-
ery Exercise #3 at the end of the chapter.*

Recovery Exercises

1. If you have had the experience of letting a problem build up
    to the point where you relapsed over it, try writing down a list
    of reasons you gave yourself, or would have given if asked,
    for not doing more about it. Do any of your reasons sound
    like they make the problem smaller than it was? Share with
    group or counselor and ask for feedback.

2. On paper, try doing the exercise described: write down the
    best things that happened all week and the worst. Write down
    your feelings at the time. Then write down what you actually
    did to cope with the worst things. Could you have done more?
    If so, do not beat yourself up. Try to understand your reasons

for doing less, as you would try to understand a friend. Share with group/counselor and ask for feedback.

3.   Pick three (5, 10, etc.) real frustrations you have had recently, or keep a log as the week goes on. For each frustration, write down what you must accept versus what you must change. What do you notice about how you think and feel as you do this? What difference might it make to do it consistently. Share/discuss with group and or counselor. Get feedback.

14

How to Solve a Problem, Any Problem

The system illustrated in this chapter can solve any living problem that a human being may encounter.

For some readers, such a claim will seem more audacious than Columbus declaring he could find the Far East by sailing west. You deserve an explanation: the author making this bold statement attended fourth grade at East Buffalo Township Elementary School in Lewisburg, PA. It was there he learned about Christopher Columbus and how he discovered America. But first, we were told how he solved the problem of getting money for the *Nina, Pinta,* and *Santa Maria.*

Chris did not have his own ships and men to test his idea that the world was round, that he could find China by sailing West! Apparently, there was some reluctance on the part of the Finance Minister to finance something so preposterous. So Chris supposedly staked it all on an equally outrageous wager.

"I can make an egg stand on its end," he bet. "If I do, will you give me my ships and men."

The Queen's advisors, no candidates for Gamblers Anonymous, took what they thought was a sure thing.

"You're on, Chris!"

So Christopher Columbus took out an egg and proceeded to smush it on its end. It cracked and it oozed and it stood up. Thus, the ministers wound up with egg on their *faces and the tab for an expedition to the "New World" in their budget.*

☞   Remember, a problem is anything that bothers you.

And things bother you and me and everyone else because they are not how we ***want*** them to be.

The "Serenity Prayer" elegantly formulates the only two *healthy* ways to stop being bothered or frustrated. Chapter 11 went into some depth on one of them, why we need acceptance and what it is. The essence of it is to stop wanting what you cannot have. If this,

☞   in fact, brings an end to your bother, your problem is "solved." Not fixed, or changed, just solved. Your assumption that you have to get what you want to be at peace may have to be *smushed*. Your preconception may have to get stood on its end and develop a few cracks.

Chapter 12 also spelled out the "SPARROW" system for doing the work of acceptance. As the Serenity Prayer lays out, the other healthy way to stop being frustrated is to take action under your control to get what you want. And the same "SPARROW" system can help you do the work to "change the things I can."

Accept versus change. Change versus accept. This is the constant question in all human coping. But some people know only how to do one of the two. They are like boxers entering the ring of daily life with but one glove. It falls on the helper to string on the missing glove and show how both are to be used. The below example spells out one way to do this. Worksheets are provided at the end of the chapter, with exercise instructions to follow the illustration, or to create one of your own.

What Joe Wants

Joseph D. Niles, Jr., has a problem in his very first group at the inpatient treatment program.

"My doc says I have a biochemical insufficiency that makes me drink addictively. He says I have to quit altogether or I die a drunk and I say he is a crock. My dad was a drunk and I'm nothing like him."

"Well, Joe, maybe the group here can help you come up with some way of dealing with this that makes sense to you. Will you give it a try?"

"Sure," says Joe.

☞ "Great." Moving to the whiteboard, counselor Yubi Wiseman draws the first column. He marks it "Want." "What do you want, Joe?"

"I want that doc to take his biochemical insufficiency and put it where the sun doesn't shine!"

"A retraction?"

"Sounds good to me!"

"What is it you want that makes you want him to not say that?"

"Hey, I want to be like anybody else. And I sure ain't like my dad."

"So, you want to be "normal" and you think he's saying you are not. And it sounds like you swore you would never wind up like dad."

"You bet."

Yubi puts these wants on the board, in the order in which they appear.

"Group, do you hear any other wants."

"Yeah, he wants to keep drinking!"

"He wants to be a social drinker."

"He wants to be in control of himself."

"He wants a choice whether to drink."

One by one, Joseph agrees to these things.

Yubi adds one more, "If you don't want to have the doctor say this, would it be fair to say you want him to be wrong?"

"Yeah, of course."

Getting a little inspired, Yubi clarifies, "Would you like the doc to tell you you have an underlying emotional problem that makes you drink compulsively and you need treatment for that?"

"Hell, no. I'm not crazy!"

"Any other wants here, Joe? Group?"

"If not, we seem to have a complete list." (Yubi is omitting an exploration of what Joe wants alcohol for, what it does for him. This might be a useful clinical approach but is not necessary for this particular illustration.) "But remember," says Yubi, "we can always add to the "Wants" column as we work with the others. Sometimes, when you look at the rest of the problem, other wants become clear."

What Joe Got (Objective and Subjective)

Labeling the second column, "Got," Yubi writes "objective" at its top and "subjective" about half way down. He asks Joe, "What would you list here?"

"A quack MD!"

"Any specifics?"

"Yeah. You know. He says I'm a biochemical fuck-up."

Yubi writes under "objective:" MD diagnosis — biochemical insufficiency. Treatment recommendation — abstain from alcohol. Prognosis given — extremely poor without abstinence, treatment, probably AA.

"Yeah," Joe agrees. "That's pretty much what he told me."

"Anything else? Group?"

One of the experienced group members is eager to start on feelings. "He's pissed off."

Beginning under "subjective" with "P.O.'d," Yubi asks for more.

"He seems threatened by the idea of the doctor being right," the group begins.

"Like he might lose something?" Yubi leads.

"What do you mean?" asks Joe.

"Can someone explain?"

"Well," says a member, "if your doctor is right, you are going to lose a very good friend."

"How so?"

"You don't want to say good-bye to drinking, to whatever it does for you, maybe some of the people you drink with."

"Ah, that's no big deal."

"Anything else he might lose?" Yubi asks.

"Well," says one group member, "you sound like you might lose some pride if you feel you are anything like your dad. I read a book ..."

☞ In the interest of structure, Yubi cuts in, "Thanks, but can you save your book suggestion for when we look at what Joe might do. It sounds like you're getting into a solution and that's in the next columns. But whatever it is, there does seem to be a feeling of threat."

"Right," says the group member. "And shame."

"Along those lines," says Yubi, "it seems Joe had a big frustration growing up — he got something he doesn't want to this day."

"My dad!" says Joe.

Yubi asks Joe what he wanted to be different about his dad.

"Everything," Joe responds with conviction.

"For now, would you agree you wanted a sober, functioning dad instead of an alcoholic, abusive (this is a guess) dad?"

"That would have taken care of most of it."

Yubi enters "alcoholic, abusive dad" under "objective" in the "Got" column.

"I don't know where this fits," says the Book Reader, "but it sounds like he made a vow not to be like his dad."

"You bet your ass."

"No, Joe, you are betting your ass, and we hope to get you to look at your payoff and your odds."

Pausing to let Joe give that some thought, Yubi writes under "Want"— "to be totally different from dad." Under "Got" he writes "MD opinion."

"I don't think I like where this is going," says Joe.

"Can you describe how you feel now?" asks Yubi.

"Like you really agree with the doctor and you are going to prove he is right."

Yubi writes under "Got," below "subjective," — "beginning to feel railroaded, ganged up on, victim of company line."

Joseph D. Niles, Jr., chuckles and relaxes a little.

Yubi says, "Joe, can you look at what we've got up there, one by one?"

"Sure."

He does so, taking his time.

"Is there anything up there that shouldn't be, doesn't fit?"

After a further pause, Joe concedes, "No, you've about got it."

"I hope we have got it," says Yubi gently.

After another pause, Yubi proceeds.

"Are you ready to look at solutions?"

"Sure, let's go."

What Joe Must Accept Versus What He Might Change

Yubi now adds two more columns, "Accept" and "Change."

"What we could do now," Yubi reminds the group, "is to take each of the "gots," one-by-one, and see which ones Joe may be stuck with and which ones he may be able to do something about. However, it seems to work better if Joe picks a focus.

"Joe, what I would like you to do is pick one thing from the objective list and one from the subjective list. It might be the thing that bothers you the most or it might be the thing you feel most ready to work on. By the time we take your two choices through SPARROW, we will probably have covered most of the related issues. At the very least, we will have given you plenty to do.

Joe sticks with the concrete fact of what the MD said as the objective, external fact that troubles him the most. For his second choice, he has trouble putting into words the subjective "bother" that troubles him the most.

"It's just the idea of being told that," is all he can come up with.

"Horrified," says one member of the group.

"Sounds like the shame and threat feelings to me," says another.

"I like 'horrified,'" says Joe.

☞ "Then that's what we go with," says Yubi, highlighting it on the board under "Got." "Now what about control — this is the critical question we have to ask about everything that bothers us. Is there anything we can do that even potentially might change our frustration and give us what we want? Joe, is this feeling something over which you have no control? In other words, where does 'horrified' go, under the "Accept" column or under "Change?""

Joseph comments, "I don't know how to not be horrified when someone like that, a doctor, I mean, tells you something so horrible."

Yubi agrees. "If you're determined it's untrue, and you think it's bad and you think it hurts you, you are going to be appalled. Shall I write "horrified" under "accept"?"

"Yeah," says Joseph, somewhat reluctantly.

☞ Yubi picks up on the hesitation and asks him about it.

"Well," Joseph says slowly, "I hate to admit it, but I'm not nearly as upset as when we started."

"How about this?" says Yubi, putting ("initial reaction") in front of "horrified" under the "Accept" column. Under "change" he ☞ writes "(over time), horror." Then he writes the acronym SPARROW in a vertical column under both "Accept" and "Change." Next to the "S" (for "Share,") of the "Change" column, he writes, "talk in this group."

"Yeah," Joe says, "that's about what we did, plus the whiteboard."

"What does the whiteboard do?"

"Well, this all looks more clear up there, even what I don't like."

☞   Yubi writes "Use SPARROW/whiteboard" next to the "W" for "Writing," again under the column for "change." "We're doing it right now," he observes. "You can step back from the trees and see some of the forest?"

"Yeah," says Joseph, "even if it is on fire!"

☞   The group laughs with him again. Yubi writes, "objectivity, humor," next to "R" for "rethink," still under "change."

"What about the Dr.'s words?" Yubi asks.

As he does so, he draws another column for "accept" and one more for "change". He enters "SPARROW" vertically in each. Above the two new columns he writes "what MD said."

"Well, if he's saying I'm just like my dad, no way I'm going to accept that!"

"Right now, we're just dealing with the fact he said it and you don't control what he said. Not whether it's true."

"Can you think of anything you can do about it?"

"Get a second opinion!"

"By all means," says Yubi, writing it on the board next to the A (Action) under the second "change" column. "Who would you ask?"

"Well, I might go to my family doc, but he would probably refer me to the quack again. Just because he's written a bunch of books and makes videos about it."

"Your family doctor referred you to Doctor Quack?"

"Yeah."

"How come?" asks the group.

"Well, actually, my wife called him."

"How come?"

"I just been working hard lately and she says I had a couple blackouts and I'm getting to be a Jekyll-and-Hyde."

Yubi asks, "You want to stay married?"

Joseph says, "Of course."

Yubi adds that to the board, back under "want."

"Look," Yubi says. "We've got a second opinion here as an

option that we would offer anyone else diagnosed with a chronic, lethal disease. Is there anything you want to say to Doctor Quack?"

"Well, I'm not as ticked as I was, but I'd still like to give him a piece of my mind."

"Anyone here want to be a doctor?" Still working in the "change" column, Yubi writes "express/role-play" next to "A" (for "action"), under the feeling of "horrified."

"Just-a-Drunk" speaks up, "I used to tell women in bars I was a brain surgeon."

"Great," says Yubi, "why don't you sit here and be 'Doctor Quack', facing Joseph."

"Just-a-Drunk" takes the seat and sits rigidly opposite Joseph, eyebrows arched and arms folded across chest.

"Joseph, you can tell Doctor Quack here what you really think of him."

Joseph pauses a moment and begins, "You think you're some kind of God, judging me like a bug under a microscope! I'm not just some lab rat with biochemicals for brains. I'm a man! I know the score! I made up my mind to never be alcoholic and I'm not. No way you can put me in the same box with my old man."

Gently, Yubi prompts, "Can you say how he hurt you, what it feels like?"

"I just did."

"What about the threat, what he's taking away from you?"

"You're taking away my choice! My confidence! My self-control. How can I believe in myself if I think I'm controlled by loose chemicals?! I can do anything I set my mind to."

"Anything else?"

"I don't think so," says Joseph.

"Anyone in the group want to be Joe and express feelings he may not be saying?"

"Read-a-Book" says, "I'm scared, doc. I'm terrified and ashamed I could be like my dad and I feel like I'm losing control of my life. I'm wounded by my wife and it feels like you're kicking me when I'm down. But most of all, I'm scared you could be right."

Joseph's eyes moisten and he can't speak for a moment. Then he says quietly, sheepishly, "Shit. You people are f----ing mind readers."

The group laughs.

☞ Others debrief and share. They offer their feelings about their own addictions now and in the past, about the first time someone in authority told them they had a problem. And they share the complaints of spouses past and present, how they heard those concerns then and now.

☞ Yubi notes that a role-play interview of Mrs. J. D. Niles might be useful. It could still be used later, as can extensive work with "dad." Role-playing "I-statements" to the MD would be yet another possibility, whether to help Joseph accept or change the doctor's opinion. There is often some form of assertion or communication to be made on the "change" side of the board. Role-play can be very useful in preparing for this kind of action. Additionally, such experiential work often surfaces whatever blocked assertivenes in the first place. Other tools can then go to work on the blocks.

☞ Meanwhile, Yubi proceeds, "Let's continue to work with the words the doctor said, as a fact that has happened in your life. Can you change the fact he said them?"

"No," says Joe.

"So if you can't change that fact, where does it go?"

"Under 'Accept,'" says Joe, who is getting the idea.

Yubi enters "MD words already said" under the second "Accept" column.

What about the feelings about dad – they seem to be a lot of why you are so horrified?"

"No way that changes!" says Joseph.

"Even if dad had a physical disease he didn't know about?"

"Oh great, I'm an asshole and he gets off the hook," says Joseph.

"Why don't you want him off the hook?"

"Because he enjoyed what he did to us, the insults, the sarcasm, even the physical stuff."

"You see him as sadistic?"

"The Marquis de Dad," I call him.

The group likes this.

"Sounds like he needs to do something about his feelings about his dad," Positive Thinker proposes.

"What about my book idea?" asks you-know-who.

Yubi encourages this "solution" now, to read Claudia Black's *It Will Never Happen to Me* [2]. He lists the book next to the other "R" for "read," under the "Accept" column for "what MD said". (The location is somewhat arbitrary, as it turns out.)

"You will identify," Yubi cautions Joseph, "but don't look for a lot of discussion about the sadism of some drinkers. And don't feel you have to forgive anybody yet. The idea is to begin looking at how your dad's behavior affects the way you see yourself today. A lot of people have said what Claudia's title quotes, "it will never happen to me." You certainly have. Anything else he can do about what the MD said?"

One group member pipes up, "Psychodrama!" Another says somewhat sheepishly, "What about psychotherapy?"

"Aren't we missing the main point?" asks Just-a-Drunk. "Is he or isn't he?"

"The main point of today's problem is how much it bothers Joe to be told he has this disease, not whether he does or not."

"Yeah, but I gotta wonder," says Joe.

"Were you wondering forty-five minutes ago when you were enraged at the MD?"

"No," says Joe, sheepishly.

"But you are wondering now?"

"Yeah, I mean, something got me here."

"Can anybody give him some constructive ways to wonder?"

The group tells him about the AA Twenty Questions. They talk about doing a drinking inventory, about how they felt when they were at this point in denial/acceptance, about just being willing to be open. A previously quiet member indicates the "Accept" side of the board. She shares "I got a lot from reading Dr. Milam's *Under the Influence* [4]. He tells just about all they know about what goes on in the body and how some bodies really are different. It helped me see I won't be able to take a drink even if I can get over some of my hang-ups. That might help Joe with accepting what the doctor said."

☞   The suggestions go in their various toolboxes under SPARROW.

Yubi offers one further thought. "The doctor poured salt in old wounds and told you you have failed to keep your sacred vow to not be like dad, right?"

"Yeah."

"Did your dad ever come to a group like this?"

"Mr. Perfect? You gotta be kidding!"

"That's where you can still keep your vow. Nothing could be more different from dad than for you to admit having the problem. To face it, and commit yourself to recovery from it, as he never did."

"I never thought of that," says Joe D. Niles, Jr.

☞   Yubi puts "list ways to be different from Dad if MD right" under "W" with the SPARROW for "what MD said." This could also go under "rethink" and under "share with group."

He has one last thought.

"Joe, do have any kind of spirituality that leads you to pray?"

"If there was a God, he sure wouldn't have given me an old man like that and let him get away with all that stuff."

☞   Yubi leaves "P" for prayer blank on Joe's list and adds it to his own mental list.

Joe has not solved all of his problems. If anything, he started with one immediate irritation and ended up with a list that includes unresolved lifelong issues. He has not accepted his alcoholism. Yet, he feels more clear and calm. He is prepared to do some footwork to accept and some footwork to change. Loose ends abound, as they always will in life. But specific tasks have been developed that fit the problem as Joe is living it.

☞   Yubi has other options, depending on context. Most in- and outpatient programs offer ways for the person to step back and look at drinking behavior. Feedback from the spouse and others might help, an "intervention" after entering treatment. Feedback to the treatment team, if one exists, is important. Scheduling one-on-one visits sounds essential, if Yubi is the team. Clearly, Joseph needs help to separate feelings about dad in the past from realities of his own current drinking/drugging behavior. Sending/taking Joseph to AA may be possible, if his initial outrage has sufficiently calmed and his openness proves more than temporary.

It should be obvious that this is an allegorical sample of problem-solving. It has been built out of the Serenity Prayer and well-known tools for doing the actual work of acceptance and of changing. A couple of editorial points were slipped in that have little to do with the technique itself. Few clients will come in wearing "it will never happen to me" on their sleeve as Joseph does. Yet 50 percent or more of our clients are adult children of alcoholics and much of their denial may be fueled by that omnipotent and subconscious childhood vow. We may not have the luxury of waiting
☞ a year to deal with this aspect of the childhood psyche.

This technique has developed considerably in the years since the first edition of this book. The author has enough confidence in it that he will walk into a room full of people and announce, "I'm looking for trouble. Anybody got some?" The method has held up under the fire of newly served divorce papers, loss of custody, all sorts of medical problems, endless variations of relationship battles. It has even gotten surprising results in individual sessions with people not being treated for addiction. "SPARROW" seems to remind people of all the ways they already know how to cope. It gives a focus to the confused and concrete tools to the overwhelmed.
☞ The reader may use it for your own living problems, both because it

works and because it is the best way to master any tool. Whether using it for your own benefit or someone else's, you will undoubtedly develop your own ways of using it.

SPARROW and the Moment of Relapse

The SPARROW system provides the tools to cope with virtually anything, including the diagnosis of "addiction." That is the good news. The bad news is that it is all work. "F--- it" can mean "It ain't worth it to do the work." And "One won't hurt" clearly implies "I don't need do any other work, since I'm not alcoholic to start with." To sustain the effort for learning to cope while you are actually doing it, especially when your brain has not yet physically healed, requires energy. Most people seem to find that sort of on-going energy from a support group. This means some sort of community practicing the "S" in SPARROW by sharing the struggle to meet "life on life's terms."

Spiritual note: The Serenity Prayer is a prayer. Those who use it successfully will tell you that it works best when it is said as such. They will also tell you "It works when you work it." Whether you use prayer or not, "SPARROW" offers a common sense way for people of all backgrounds and stages of recovery, normies included, to do just that.

References

[1] DuWors, G. New Use For an Old Tool. Alcoholism, the National Magazine, Oct., 1983.

[2] Black, Claudia. *It Will Never Happen To Me*. Denver: M.A.C. 1981.

[3] Milam, J. R., and Ketchum, K. *Under the Influence*. New York: Bantam, 1983.

Recovery Exercise

1. Use the table on the next page to set up Joseph's problem as it is put on the whiteboard by Yubi. Once you have entered the two items to "Accept" or "Change," the two that Joseph chooses, use the form on the following page to complete "SPARROW" for each. You will need 4 "SPARROW Worksheets."

    If you would rather do the whole thing for a problem of your own, feel free. If you do work with your own problem, try using the "SPARROW" worksheet, which asks you to choose specific tasks for just one thing you are trying to "Accept" or "Change." You will need to use one of these sheets for each part of the problem you are going to work on. Either way, it will probably be less frustrating if you learn to use these worksheets the first time with a group and/or counselor. Remember, they are just taking the Serenity Prayer down off the wall and putting it to work.

Problem/Solution Worksheet

WHAT I WANTED	WHAT I GOT	MUST ACCEPT/ STOP WANTING (NO CONTROL)	MIGHT CHANGE/ GET WANT (MAY CONTROL)
	OBJECTIVE (facts, situation)		
	Subjective (thoughts, feelings, impulses)		

SPARROW WORKSHEET: COPING PLAN

I NEED TO ACCEPT/ CHANGE:	_____
	(PART OF MY PROBLEM)
I WILL USE THE FOLLOWING:	
SHARE:	What _____
	With Whom _____
	Daily__Weekly__Monthly _____
	Other _____
PRAY/MEDITATE:	Time _____
	Place _____
	Form or subject _____
ACTION	What _____
	When _____
	How I will prepare _____
	_____
	Report Progress to: _____
READ	Title _____
	By _____
	Discuss with _____
RETHINK	Method (i.e., Step 5, RET) _____
	_____
	Reality Check with_____
	By _____
ONE DAY AT A TIME	Specific self-talk _____
	_____
	_____
	How often (mimimum) _____
	Any time I experience _____
WRITE	Method (12 Step, RET, Cognitive _____
	Therapy, Journal) _____
	Share with _____
	Frequency (Minimum) _____
	Any time I experience _____

15

When Those Relapse Thoughts Come Back

"One won't hurt" and "F--- it" are two thoughts that do what a good AA member does – they keep coming back! How could we finish a book about this "dynamic duo" without discussing at least one way to battle them? A tool that strikes directly at the links involved and shows them the door? No, it is not the only one. But it is the one on which Twelve Step Programs are based, and which all of the other relapse prevention systems seem to incorporate. It is the tool of "one drunk talking to another."

This is the tool Bill W. used the first time he called eventual co-founder "Dr. Bob." Bill W. wanted to drink that day, badly. The wishful idea that he could go in the bar for company was teaming up with the wishful idea that maybe he could have "just three"[1]. By his own account, he was under enough stress that many would have simply said "F--- it." Five-and-a half months sober, Bill was poised to have exactly the same kind of relapse he had had four times since "waking up" [2] to the fact he could not take "so much as one." But what he had been doing during *this* five-and-a-half months was different – constantly trying to help other alcoholics. How? By *talking* to them about his own experience. And what he did this particular day was also different than what he had done on each previous occasion. He picked up the phone and started looking for "another drunk to talk to." Bill Wilson died thirty-six years later without yet having picked up that first drink.

What follows may sound like heresy to some: the important thing is the talking. Sober alcoholics make good audiences for this, mostly because they have personal experience. Those in self-help groups recognize how much it helps their own recovery to receive such calls, making them more available and receptive. And they are a lot less likely to add to the shame about having an urge in the first place. But anyone who understands the principle can be enormously helpful. There are many non-recovering therapists who learn to routinely ask for drinking thoughts and/or impulses. It is like taking the blood pressure of a hypertensive, measuring the blood sugar of a diabetic. One objective of this chapter is just this. To increase the frequency and confidence with which therapists of every background seek out and treat this particular kind of "stinking thinking." Another goal runs parallel. To increase the frequency with which the recovering reader may pick up the phone and/or talk about these thoughts when they pay a visit.

Chapter 10 in the AA book *Living Sober* [3] describes "telephone therapy." A tool in itself ("R" is for "read"), that brief chapter describes the tool of picking up the phone instead of a drink. It addresses some common reasons we give ourselves to *not* pick it up. And it spells out concretely how such calls lead to a much more lasting foundation for recovery. They lead directly to the establishment of a support network. What that powerful chapter in a powerful little book does not spell out is:

How Willpower Gets You Drunk

Picture this.

A "dry" alcoholic who wants to stay sober starts to feel an urge to drink. Like any other impulse or feeling, this one tries to be expressed. Impulses and feelings are like burps, they want to come out.

The white-knuckler "pushes it out of mind." (Sometimes we know we are doing this and sometimes we don't.)

☞   You can demonstrate this to yourself or anyone else isometrically. Put the book down for a minute and turn one hand open, palm upwards. Place the other hand on top, palm downwards. Using enough strength to make it hard work, press up with the bottom hand (craving) and down with the top hand (willpower).

What is the net result, physically and mentally?

Tension.

What happens to the urge to drink as tension increases?

It goes up.

"Willpower" pours gas on the fire!

Now it pours on more, suppressing the increased urge.

More tension.

More urge.

More blocking.

More tension.

Blocking.

Urge ... where does it end? ... "F--- it!" and the isometric hands cease their futile struggle, as the white-knuckler throws them in the air. When they come down, they will not be empty. Of course, by the time "One won't hurt" comes whispering around, we don't even need to fight. If there was a fight, it took place at the unconscious level, and the bottom hand won.

How Talking Keeps You Sober

How does mere talking about it prevent this?

> *First, when I talk, I don't fight to bury the impulse by pretending I don't have it. My will is not banging its head against the stone wall of my craving. So I don't pour gas on the fire by creating tension.*

Second, talking about how I feel and think expresses the feeling and the impulse. The pressure is relieved by verbal expression rather than by physical acting out. The relief may not be as complete, but it will generally be enough that I can control what is left. I can choose not to drink.

Third, I get the support and help of as many allies as I talk to. They can fight the urge with sharing, reminders, practical tools. And their fighting my craving from without does not create tension within.

Fourth, I am no longer alone with my problem. I have affirmed my own commitment to sobriety and to my sober-minded family. Together, we have demonstrated an alternative to drinking, even when I want to drink. I am not alone with my overwhelming self-will or "Ego." And my "inner child" gets much of the comfort s/he really wanted and needed.

Fifth, if this is not purely a biochemical urge, the door is now wide open to facing whatever problem I wanted to escape from in the first place. And if the craving is physiological, cognitive, social, spiritual, and physical tools can all be brought to bear. A trained counselor can offer all the tools of "craving management."

One thing is both assumed and necessary in order for the person to talk instead of drinking when the urge returns — they have to be aware of it. You can't call your AA sponsor to talk about feeling like a drink if you are so emotionally disconnected you don't know you want one. One of the great secrets of AA may be that daily meetings can counteract the urge in people who may not know they have it. This may borrow time, even a year or two. But, sooner or later, the person needs to need to know not just *how* to pick up this tool, but *when*. The development of such here-and-now self-awareness may be one of the primary contributions of professional treatment. The foundation for Gorski's [4] system of relapse prevention seems to rest on being aware when you are heading for trouble. Any thera-

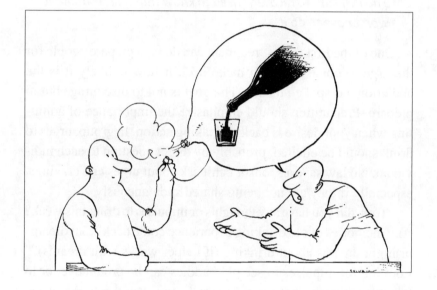

py that increases the ability to connect with feelings that call for drinking is going to be a step in the right direction. However, the addictions treatment professional must be most immediately concerned about awareness of the urge to drink/drug itself. Many people are both terrified and ashamed of their urges.

A whole lifetime of experience says that the urge is the beginning of the end: if I do let myself feel it, I am going to have to do it. If I am to recover, I need to know that if I talk about it, I won't have to do it.

☞ One of the first things treatment can do is to prepare people for the urge to come back. To make it clear how unlikely it is the addiction has spoken its last. The goal is not to discourage but to prepare. Preparation should emphasize the importance of admitting when your desire is back and taking action. In group, urges to drink should be elicited, probably by direct question to each individual. No law says a sponsor can't ask about urges and cravings, especially if they are not being shared spontaneously.

"Tom, did you have any thoughts or impulses to drink this week? Any memories of old drinking experience come back? Daydreams or night dreams about drinking (if helper works with dreams)?"

☞ Looking for impulses to see old buddies can be productive, or to take up activities that seem to strive for substitute highs or escapes. Beware the sober alcoholic who becomes obsessed with hang-gliding!

The helper has to assume the person's defenses are all up and running. Specific questions are much more likely to yield accurate answers. Why? Because I won't "think about it" until asked.

Tom's Urge

What if a fictitious group member named Tom admits he did have an urge to drink this week?

☞ First, reinforcing the disclosure, however reluctant, is vital. "You have just taken a big step, Tom, being able to admit it."

Second, see if he is willing to work with it.

"Do you want to see if we can learn something from it?"

"Okay," says Tom, as patients generally will.

"Will you give us a picture of what was going on around you and what you thought and felt at the time you felt the urge?"

"Yeah. It was last Thursday, and I was just sitting there watching TV and started wanting a beer."

"What were you watching?"

"Thursday night football."

"How many beer commercials?"

"Oh shit," he grins. "I didn't even think of that."

"Professional psychologists, writers, actors, musicians, make millions of dollars, Tom, because of their ability to get you salivating for a drink."

"I love the mountains," he admits sheepishly. "There were a couple of those cool mountain scenes."

"Why don't you go to the mountains?" an experienced group member says.

"No car. No money."

"How about the Sierra Club?" another offers. "They have bus trips real cheap, even if you had to save for a while. You had money to drink ..."

☞ The leader might check with "Tom", "How do you feel about your urge and your sharing so far?"

"Well, I just never thought about how those commercials get to me. I feel like I know something now. And I feel a little more relaxed. It really scared me to be wanting it that soon after I just quit."

"Anyone else here willing to share some of your urges?"

No group has ever failed to support each other in this way. The group might get into the pros and cons of watching football at all. They might discuss watching it alone. Using recovery tools and other techniques to cope with the suspense as well as the advertising might also provide fruitful sharing.

This is just one example of one approach. Sometimes having the person express the way they felt, at the time they felt it, can give much relief. One question we always go back to — what feeling did you want to change by taking the drug alcohol (or by gambling, eating, snorting, fixing)? This particular example develops another important question — was there an external trigger?

Our second fictitious example explores an urge that seemed to come "out of the blue."

Ida's Urge

Ida had been sober two years when she first complained of a sudden recurrence of the obsession that "One won't hurt." Very ashamed to be thinking this after so much time sober, she had shared it only after direct prompting.

The therapist's practical question is "Why is this happening now?" S/he begins to explore, "When did this start, the very first time?"

"About three weeks ago," says Ida, who had apparently been to group two times without sharing it.

"Let's go back to three weeks ago," says the therapist. "Anything going on in your life — something upset you?"

"I don't know. I have problems, but I've had problems for two years, that's life, isn't it?"

"Sure is," says the therapist, "but maybe there is one bugging you, one you don't feel able to deal with."

"Well," says Ida, "I've been working some overtime lately."

"How much?"

"Oh, I do about sixty hours a week, and I haven't had a weekend for a month."

"That goes back to about when your urges started, huh?"

"Yeah," says Ida. "I didn't think about that."

"Can you tell your boss you need to cut back?"

Ida hesitates. "Well ..."

The therapist waits.

"Well," she continues finally, "I could, but I'm afraid he will close the shop if I do." She begins to cry.

What comes out now is that the other staffer in the small business walked out a month ago, after yet another NSF paycheck. While Ida also has had to clear her checks more than once, she feels sorry for her disorganized boss. She has apparently taken on responsibility to keep him going. At this point the group goes into both problem-solving and support. By the end of the group Ida says, "I haven't felt so clear in weeks. I don't know why I wasn't even looking at how this was affecting my sobriety."

The next week she reports, "I had one thought of a drink this week, before I went in to tell my boss I could not work this weekend. But I knew where it was coming from this time. And he took it okay. I even told him I had my resume out and I'm looking for another job like the group told me to." (Actually, we merely suggested it, to have a back-up plan.)

The heart of this example is the connection made between drinking urge and the feeling/situation that appears to have triggered it. Often, the problem is painfully obvious and we marvel at how the person failed to see it. But the very fact the urge has appeared suggests the person has shied away from facing something. This also means s/he may have suppressed it enough to sever the conscious connection between pain avoided and relief sought. Other times, the person will see the connection but won't have been able to actively engage in dealing with the problem. Sharing the urge in group is virtually a plea for help. Just telling the person "Don't take that first one today," is, quite literally, the least we can do.

☞ Every helper will have times when the emotional detective work is unproductive. No problem can be found to be solved. Maybe the urge was purely physical and maybe the defenses are too strong. Fortunately, there are tools for dealing with any urge, whether we know what triggered it or not. Talking about it is just one of them.

Preparation For "Telephone Therapy"

This chapter is meant to prepare both helper and recovering reader to make more effective use of this tool. The main idea has already been presented and may be used or shared as such.

Yet explanations by themselves are seldom enough to change behavior. Especially if I am going to change from reaching for a drink or drug to reaching for the phone. Two other tools seem to get results.

The first is to identify and diminish mental or emotional "barriers" to picking up the phone or finding someone to talk to. Just asking people whether they thought of calling someone when tempted can get you started. If the person did think of it, you can ask for any reasons to not do it. A group can do a collective exercise of generating a list of all their reasons for not calling. Either way, we can then begin to disassemble these blocks intellectually. Another way to get at both mental and emotional barriers is by the use of "Sentence Completions":

"When I think of picking up the phone to talk about my urge, I feel _____ ."

Or, "When I think about calling someone, my biggest reason not to is _____ ."

Yet another way to identify my barriers is to have me relive the urge as was described in Chapter 2. Don't be afraid to try these tools more than once. "One won't hurt" and "F--- it" will give you ample opportunity!

The second level of preparation is behavioral. The author has seen nice results with "the phone call not made," described below, but any actual or potential situation of craving will do.

A Tool — Role-Playing the Phone Call that Was Not Made

☞ This tool prepares alcoholics/addicts for using the telephone next time by role-playing what it might have been like if they had used it last time. Just set up two chairs back to back — one chair for the person with the urge, the other, for the "sponsor," or "counselor," or whoever the caller wants to call, anyone except the "dope man!" The author likes to be the telephone — after he "rings" a few times, the support person picks up. The caller's job is to be him/herself the day of the relapse, to say what they would have *if* they had called.

Emotional triggers often come out unsolicited in this way. Strangely enough, the "caller" will often experience relief even now from whatever stress contributed to the relapse. Apparently the real problem never did get dealt with — it was still festering! "That would have worked," is common feedback from someone who participates in this process. Variations of it include letting different members respond to the call in their own ways. Or have the caller switch chairs to respond to his/her own call. Even though the relapse has already occurred, the group is working through inhibitions about use of the phone and about being called. Obviously, they are being trained to make more effective use of AA and of each other.

☞ A note of caution. This tool works best with cravings triggered by an upset or by "subliminal craving" (see Chapter 3) It can sometimes be effective with powerful drug cravings triggered by some sort of reminder in the environment, things like the sight of a dealer or of the drug itself. This sort of craving may also be prevented and reduced by tools that are far beyond the scope of this book. The two sorts of craving least responsive to telephone therapy are those of physical withdrawal (detox) and those triggered by taking the drug itself. This is one reason self-help groups emphasize calling *before* the first drink/drug. "Social model detox" has shown that people can help each other get through this kind of craving. But some of the other tools may have to wait for blood and brain to clear.

☞   With an inexperienced group, preparation of the person receiving the call may make the whole process more effective. It turns out that one reason we don't call someone else when craving is the fear someone will call us. And we don't think we know what to do. There are three simple principles.

One, "be there." You do not have to be Sigmund Freud or even Bill Wilson to help an addict/alcoholic who feels like drinking or drugging. You do have to be there, emotionally and, when possible, physically. To "be there" emotionally is mostly a matter of staying as calm as possible and listening deeply. Not trying to fix anything, letting them talk. Arranging to meet for coffee provides the person craving with an action, a distraction, and with the assurance they are not alone to fight the battle they have so often lost. If they are too shaky, going directly to their location may be necessary. It may also be necessary to get them on the phone with someone else until you can get there.

☞   Two, see if you can get a feel for whether this is more of a wishful ("One won't hurt") kind of craving. If it is, focus on having them use the old AA/counseling tool of "thinking it through." Get them to draw you a graphic and concrete picture of what happens for them when they take "just one." Most will readily recognize there will be a second and a third and so on. Have them picture themselves the next morning when they wake up. How would that be and feel? What you are doing is helping them reconnect to their own experience and judgment in a way that is mysteriously blocked by a powerful wish of any kind. If this does not reduce or eliminate the impulse to drink/drug, use the next principle.

☞   Three, if "thinking it through" was not enough, or if they are clearly upset about something, get them talking about it. If I feel like saying "F--- it" and drinking or drugging, *something* is bothering me. If my heart is breaking because s/he doesn't love me anymore, telling me to not take the first drink may be a start, but it falls far short of what I need. Ignoring the feelings I crave to medicate will be as ineffective as it is insensitive. Again, you don't have to be Sigmund Freud – listening and sharing between two relative newcomers can be quite powerful. A sponsor or therapist, on the other hand, has a number of tools for dealing with the issues ("links") that show up. Chapter 14 was devoted to a systematic way of working through a problem, when the person is ready. Either way, recognizing which sort of relapse (white-knuckle or wishful) is drawing the person, may tell us which rope will pull them back.

References

[1] Anonymous, *'Pass It On' (Bill Wilson and the AA Message)*. New York, N.Y.: Alcoholics Anonymous World Services, Inc., 1984.
[2] Anonymous. *Alcoholics Anonymous*. New York: Alcoholics Anonymous World Services, 1955.
[3] Anonymous. *Living Sober.* New York: Alcoholics Anonymous World Services, 1975.
[4] Gorski, Terrence T., Miller, Merlene. *Counseling for Relapse Prevention*. Independence, MO: Independence Press, 1982.

Recovery Exercises

1. If you have had a relapse without calling someone to tell them you were thinking of drinking/drugging, ask your group/counselor to role play "telephone therapy" as described in this chapter.

2. Read Chapter 10, "Telephone Therapy" in *Living Sober.* High-
    light and share the parts you identify with personally. High-
    light and share the parts you find hardest to believe. Try-
    rereading the chapter every day for a week, slowly and
    thoughtfully, like a meditation. Write down how your reac-
    tions or understanding change, if they do.

16

Linking The Links: Character And Craving

Two things "link" the various parts of this book. First, the chapter-by-chapter exploration of various *reaction* links culminating in "One won't hurt" and/or "F--- it." Second, the persistent attempt to spell out how each link contributes to the saying of those words at the moment of relapse. Every chapter has tried to connect relapse links to recovery tools or concepts that reduce, contain, or replace them. One lesser theme addresses how physical and mental links may interact. Another proposes that the unconscious mind and its defenses are inseparable from both. And yet another important theme affirms that Twelve Step Recovery was meant to be a system of "relapse prevention" from the start. The more you understand the moment of relapse, the more you will see this, and the more effectively you can present it to anyone you would help. In fact, the more you understand these links of both relapse and recovery, the more effectively you will use *any* tool or system of treatment, including systems of relapse prevention which offer effective tools that AA does not.

Readers both recovering and helping may have noticed most of this material is descriptive. To be sure, the author uses concepts and logic that pre-select one thing over another, which seems inescapable in human thought and language. The very act of labeling something puts it in one conceptual box and excludes it from others. The most pure "objectivity" turns out to be spiritual, precisely because it is only possible through direct, wordless contact with "reality." And the minute you talk, think, or write about it, you lose it! This, of course, makes it scientifically useless.

Still, the author has tried to leave the reader's vision free to see whatever "links" may be there, unobstructed by a theoretical position. It is hoped you will simply see whatever link may appear, physical or mental, conscious or not, "cause" or "effect," yours or mine. It appears to be true that no link ever happens by itself — this would be a strange "chain" indeed! It also seems to this observer that the most purely mental or spiritual links of human reaction cannot occur in the absence of a living brain. At least, not the links we can see or work with in treatment. At the same time, the rawest physical reaction "means" something to the person having it. And this meaning immediately modifies the person's reaction chain! Just to complicate things further, physical reactions seem to be subject to mental defenses in some way that is very hard to pin down. I can deny my chest pain just as surely as I can deny my lust for my best friend's spouse, or for my best friend, for that matter.

In Chapter 3, the author did offer one speculative concept involving the subtle changes that accumulate as the "wishful relapse" develops. He called it "subliminal craving." As a concept, it allows that the "wish" in wishful thinking draws its power from a "desire" that is powerful but unrecognized. The fact I do not feel my craving as it twists my thinking around backwards gives it much of its control. The concept is a crude, low-order inference to make sense of "seemingly irrelevant decisions" [1]. It would label the inner flame that draws me back to my drug of "choice" like the proverbial moth. It also accounts for much of what is "cunning, powerful, and baffling" [2] about the experience of relapse. And it leaves the theoretical door wide open for seeing the craving as physical, mental, or varying combinations of both. The fact that anti-craving drugs work at all supports a physiological "cause." The fact that "talking to another drunk" works suggests a more psychological one. The fact that no one thing works all the time suggests we need more than one gun for more than one kind of target.

As a concept, "subliminal craving" also creates a conceptual and intuitive link to the "F--- it" relapse. It may help to first clarify what a craving is.

Dr. Alex Stalcup [3] puts it in terms of "instinctual drive." In drug addiction, the brain comes to respond to the drug as if it were a "need." Something the body cannot live without, like food, air, or water. The compulsivity, desperation, self-destructiveness and amorality of addictive behavior make much more sense in this light. An alcoholic in withdrawal may die from the brain's reaction to a too-sudden abstinence. If I need a drink to not die, I *need* a drink.

But withdrawal craving is precisely *not* the subject of this book. Rather, we have here contemplated the already abstinent alcoholic/addict in the act of the first drink/drug of relapse. We have tried to understand the person apparently free of life-threatening withdrawal. In fact, we are as interested in the person with one, two, five and ten or more years of abstinence, every bit as much as the person who may still be subject to "post-acute" cravings – those biological aftershocks of withdrawal that may rumble the psyche as the brain adjusts to abstinence.

So how does craving connect with the "F--- it" relapse, especially long after the subacute phase?

To increase understanding of the above section, complete Recovery Exercises #1, #2, and #3 at the end of the chapter.

Fear of Abandonment As Craving

Well, most people saying "F--- it" and reaching for a drink or drug are frustrated. Levin [4], speaking with the authority of a seasoned clinician and addictions educator, observes that most "slips" of those trying to recover are "rage responses." Sounds to this observer like they would be saying "F--- it!" As we saw earlier, a frustration can only happen if I want something and I am not getting it. Surely, it is possible to want something without "craving" it. Yet, just as surely, it is possible to experience any desire as something you *must* have. A "need!" Worse still, it is possible for others to see my behavior as driven and compulsive when I do not. I am not even conscious of the "need" that may be transparent to any objective observer. It is obvious to them, "subliminal" to me.

If *any* want feels or acts like a need, something that seems like it will torture and gnaw until it is satisfied, why not call it a "craving?" What else would you call something that will cause restlessness, irritability, compulsivity — not to mention use despite perceived negative consequences, *and* repeated decisions to quit followed by periods of temporary abstinence?

For example?

For example, an "attachment" as described briefly in Chapter 11. This is what Anthony deMello is talking about in his book *Awareness* [5]. If I believe I must have something to be happy, I perceive it as a "need." I will remain frustrated until it is fulfilled. If I believe my very life depends upon it, I will be not only frustrated, I will be anxious, driven, and utterly ruthless. I will be blinded to other realities, beginning with anyone else's needs or feelings. True, my belief may be a "cognitive" link. But anyone who has observed or lived this condition will recognize that it grips the physical being. Can there be any doubt that the neurotransmitters are having a field day? *They* certainly do not care whether they are the chicken or the egg or the salamander! It is in this context that DeMello concludes, "Craving is the root of all sorrow."

Evidently, we are not talking exclusively about the common attachments of a materialistic culture. Money, cars, houses, sex, status, power, as much suffering as they continue to cause.

What else are we talking about?

Let's start with "fear of abandonment." In fear of abandonment, I subconsciously perceive my existence coming to an end if you leave me. Should you threaten or try to leave me, I will experience a host of physiological symptoms — racing heart and thoughts, shortness of breath, difficulty concentrating, energy loss. These may well trigger rage and ruthless, demanding behavior. An objective observer might say my reactions are a bit excessive, that my behavior is not rational. Lay person and clinician alike might describe my outbursts and demands as "childish."

The clinician might recognize childhood links are indeed operating in this reaction, and very early childhood at that. Early enough that my brain was still forming. This is a time when "touch" and "attention" are still biological (developmental) needs, in the same sense that alcoholic withdrawal is a need – if it is not met, I may die. Should I live to adulthood, the experience that started as lack of "nurture" may be permanently engraved in my developing brain as "nature." Have you ever tried to explain to a three-year-old the difference between a "want" and a "need?" How did it go? Have you ever tried to tell a room full of sober alcoholics they could no longer smoke in that room? More to the point, have you ever been confronted by a sober alcoholic/addict who decided you were not meeting their "needs?"

As we saw in Chapter 3, Harry Tiebout [6] made sense out of "self-will run riot" as "Ego." "The persistence in the adult psyche of the psychological traits of the child," he called it. And he spelled out its core traits — egocentricity, low frustration tolerance, and haste. Many years later, "Self-psychologist" David Levin [7] writes of the emptiness within the "narcissistic personality," an emptiness remaining from childhood and/or brought back by years of addiction. He sees addictive behavior as the futile, compulsive attempt to fill this bottomless pit. Levin writes more fluently than anyone this author has read of the interaction between brain chemistry and developmental scars. Both Levin and Tiebout are talking about developmental gaps as links in self-destructive adult reactions.

What we are interested in here is that self-destructive reaction in which I say "F--- it" and pick up the first drink/drug. Is there any doubt that many an "F--- it" relapse occurs in response to "abandonment," feared or actual; and the fear is often unconscious? Further, one characteristic of this reaction is a feeling of intolerable (infantile) helplessness. And how do children restore their sense of power and control. Imaginary omnipotence! Pretending! The sort of I-can-do-anything fantasy routinely reported by alcoholics of their drinking — when I drink, I'm "Superman," "King Kong," a "real know-it-all."

"F---" what?

"F---" feeling helpless in a Reality that stubbornly defies my will and denies my "needs." Gimme some juice!

Yes, "stress" may trigger physiological craving. But how often is stress the accumulating pressure of a want that seems like a need, the psychological links triggering the physical ones. To say the same thing another way, frustration of mental or emotional cravings may trigger the physical ones.

Always? No.

Sometimes? Certainly.

☞ So how do you know?

By looking. By setting aside theoretical blinders and opening yourself to the experience of the person. By understanding the emotional reaction of the person at the point of saying "F--- it." Whether that person is yourself or someone else, it often takes two people to do this. One relives and one observes, but neither may condemn, or it won't work.

> _What was I upset about? What did I want? How often have I had this reaction before? And just how badly did I think I "needed" whatever I was not getting when I said "F--- it." What was my deepest feeling when I did not get it? If I said "one won't hurt," do there appear to be issues I was escaping? Even if my craving was "subliminal," does a "Relapse PostMortem" reveal frustrations as triggers to the process? Again, what did I want? How badly? How often have I done this before?_

What we have done so far in this chapter is link both the wishful relapse and the white-knuckle variety to the concept of "craving." We have pictured one psychological reaction as a form of craving. What we can do now is link "craving" to other concepts or experiences with which the reader may be familiar.

To increase understanding of the above section, complete Recovery Exercises #4, #5, #6, and #7 at the end of the chapter.

Character Defects As Cravings

The recovering reader is probably acquainted with the concept of "character defects" as used in the Twelve Steps. Just what is a "character defect?" The Big Book makes it clear that they are "blocks," things that "caused our failure"(to remain sober.) Chapter 5 of the AA bible emphasizes resentment, fear, and sexual misbehavior, all in the context of "self-will run riot." Over a decade later, in *Twelve Steps and Twelve Traditions* [8], Bill Wilson described them as "instincts run wild." He spelled out the excessive demand for love, money, recognition, etc., again emphasizing the excess of wanting. In fact, at one point in the same book, Bill writes that all character defects are activated by fear "... primarily fear that we would lose something we already possessed or would fail to get something we demanded" (p. 76). Another decade later still in his recovery, Bill [9] struggled with depression yet again. And he "broke" it when he realized he still had an excessive dependency on "people, places and things." After all those years, he realized that when he got what he wanted he was ecstatic and when he didn't he crashed. Bill's concept for what he was seeing in himself after all those years was "absolute emotional dependencies." The author has no doubt Bill would recognize his own experience in the DeMello/Buddhist concept of "attachment." The author cannot be so sure the founder of AA would have accepted the use of the term "craving" for the power of his non-chemical desires. That term is reserved in the Big Book exclusively for what happens after one takes the first drink. But there seems little doubt that Bill would agree that such "absolute emotional dependencies" are at the heart of "character defects." And that they play a major role in relapse.

> *To sum it up, "character defects" are the attachments I crave. They are what blind me, make me both selfish and self-defeating. Both Bill W. and DeMello repeatedly refer to the attitudes involved as "demands," as "expectations." If they are not reduced to the level of "requests" (Bill's word) or "preferences" (deMello's word), my frustration will mount. It will reach the point where I cannot live within my own skin. I will "need" relief as much as I "needed" the object of my attachment. If I be addictive, we all know where I will seek that relief.*

☞ *Still more briefly: frustration of craving for objects of attachment often triggers craving for drugs of relief.*

☞ To understand this is to understand much of both the relapse and the recovery processes. Yes, we must first get "the plug in the jug" or "the stash in the trash." But then we must systematically reduce the demands, expectations, and frustrations that result from our other cravings, and we must keep them reduced. If they originate in the same part of the brain as the drug addiction, this may be a lifelong task. And spirituality in every culture has addressed this task in a way that modern psychology never has. The Buddhists call it "the problem of desire." Interesting, — Dr. Stalcup [10] calls addiction "the disease of desire."

However, there is one particular form of craving that "modern" (20th century) psychology has shed considerable light on. And it drives the number one "trigger" for relapse in long-term recovery. *Relationships.*

To increase understanding of the above section, complete Recovery Exercises #8 and #9 at the end of the chapter.

Transference As Craving

We looked above at the "fear of abandonment" as a craving. Whatever else the psychoanalytic tradition came up with, the phenomenon of "transference" appears to be alive and well. What is it? Nothing more than my unconscious tendency to see all people as I experienced my early caretakers, to assume that I will always get what I got while trying to get what I did not. And, especially in an intimate relationship, to interact as I did with my parents, to follow my family "rules" and to play my family role. This includes trying to get you (mon amour) to meet the very needs they did not. It also includes the reason I picked you in the first place — you remind me of them! When we fall in love, I feel like I have known you forever because, at the level of your similarity/my transference, I *have.*

Harville Hendrix, in *Getting the Love You Want,* [11] refers to this "transference" in my head as my "Imago." He spells out, elegantly and poignantly, how we pick each other to finish what Mom and/or Dad started. And the pathos is that we pick too well. You <u>are</u> like my Mom/Dad. And for that very reason, you will frustrate the "needs" I (unconsciously) picked you to fill. Hendrix builds a good case that this is the point at which we can butt heads or grow. If we butt heads, sooner or later, one of us is likely to say "F--- it" to the relationship. If we grow, we may actually meet some of those childhood needs for each other. Others, we will grow out of.

So why clutter up the concept of "transference" with the concept of "craving?" What's in it for the helper? What's in it for the relapse victim? For the person already in recovery and trying to stay there?

The main advantage to the helper who routinely works with transference may be the window it gives for communicating with the addictive person. A cocaine addict has experienced the craving triggered by the sight of the drug, of cash, of a dealer or of a using buddy. Most alcoholics have experienced something similar, if not always so dramatic. Yet rare is the alcoholic/addict who understands that their romantic fantasy is triggered in just about the same way. Not to mention their self-defeating demands and expectations, which are merely the flip side of the romantic/transference coin. The biggest difference is the memories and wishes triggered by romance may be unconscious. I feel like I have known my new love forever, (just like I did with the last one.) I have! Because what I am in love with is the image I created in childhood. "You" just activated it, mon amour! The helper who can get this across is making sense of relationship reactions in the language of addiction. You can help the person connect drug addiction to relationship addiction (and probably to relapse.) The person will then be able to train a whole battery of recovery tools on the problem. Relationships will get better and relapse will decrease.

This is not to say the helper may not benefit from simply understanding transference as a form of craving. Those trained in transference may be more willing to share treatment of the person they would help with groups that address craving. You may also become more modest in your treatment goals, looking to "arrest" the process rather than "cure" it.

What about the person in recovery and/or the relapse victim? What's in it for you to see all these other "character defects," especially those triggered by relationship, as so many different kinds of craving?

Let's talk about some resistance found in those committed to a black-and-white view of "disease." These are the folks enamored of the latest brain research. They argue it is already *proven* that the "physical" disease is always there first, that all alcoholics have this biological predisposition. They are supremely confident that personality factors play no part in the development of addiction — they are only a result of the physical disease. This may relieve a sense of shame, reduce stigma, and satisfy the hunger to have a single cause for every single case of addiction.

It is only dangerous if it keeps me from facing a part of my problem that just might get me drunk again. If I admit my emotional or worldly cravings were there before my first sip, I may have to admit they played a part in my developing the disease. Even if I did have a genetic predisposition, even if my cravings for love or power had taken on the nature of "instinctual drives" in their own right.

So what's in it for me? What do I gain by admitting my addictive behavior is not controlled exclusively by my reptilian brain? That my "inner lizard" gets a boost from the cravings of my "inner child?"

Well, we could start with the obvious: lizards don't have language. They neither need nor use alibis. Little kids learn language, and one of the first uses to which they put it is excuse-making. You won't hear a lizard saying "One won't hurt" nor is there a single recorded instance of a lizard saying "F--- it." Far more important, there is no recorded instance of a lizard having a "spiritual experience." Not even the alcohol-loving lab rats have done that!

If Harry Tiebout (or AA, or Jesus or Buddha) [12] is anywhere in the ballpark, it is not the animal brain that "surrenders."

What we have is the image of a small child banging its head against the wall until that little person "gets it."
Gee, this hurts!
And look at this, will you — I'm the one doing it!
Aha!

This description is consistent with the experience of millions of recovering alcoholic/addicts. It is also consistent with the experience of thousands of therapists and counselors. Those who do not see the emotional links in addictive reactions (both recovery and relapse reactions) are those who refuse to look.

What happens the minute you increase your understanding of the disease of addiction to include emotional craving?

First, it enlarges the first of the Twelve Steps. We are not solely "powerless" over cravings for drugs. In fact, it may be easier to abstain from a drug for one day than it is to abstain from "people pleasing." The craving for approval is too strong and too easily triggered, more powerful and enduring than craving for cocaine triggered by the sight of drug or cash. Seeing character defects as craving can be a source of both humility and of motivation. The motivation arises from suddenly seeing a path to "emotional sobriety" [12], as Bill W. apparently did, using the same Twelve Steps and other tools of recovery that brought about physical sobriety. As with physical sobriety, professional help also may be needed, especially to develop an awareness of self-defeating reactions and their origins. Transference! Defenses! Cognitive distortions! This heightened awareness may then be submitted to the Higher Power and all the other tools of recovery. Ideally, a clinical helper who understands transference reactions teams up with a person who already knows what to do about cravings.

To increase understanding of the above section, complete Recovery Exercises #10, #11, and #12 at the end the of chapter.

How to Use This Book

The beginning and end points for this book are experience, author's and reader's. Hopefully, everything you have read so far has been screened against your own experience, personal and/or professional. There is a sense in which all experience is personal, because it happens only to the person having it and to no one else at that point in time and space. Each reader brings your own prior experience to the reading, and each will experience reading the book in a way that is personal.

Some will find ways to use the book that never occurred to the author — door jams, kindling, weapons, perhaps. Or maybe someone will make it an object lesson for creative writing 101 on how

not to use humor or a dual point of view. A few humble suggestions are offered for those as interested in recovery as in literary
criticism.. The author would relish hearing what happens when
other people try them out.

☞   The most obvious use of this material is to connect it with issues plaguing you or someone you are trying to help, on the spot,
when they come up. Don't tell my publisher the author said this,
but you might even xerox specific topics that come up repeatedly.
Working in detox, the author had many occasions to hand out the
material on "beating yourself up" (Chapter 8). The material on
"perfectionism" (Chapter 4) can work very well, especially with
men or women who like baseball. "Dr. Jekyll and Mr. Hyde" became a topic and an exercise because it kept coming up in group.
It still does, and it will in *your* groups — it is mentioned even in the
Big Book. Whether you use the chapter on the "wishful relapse,"
the "white-knuckle relapse," "how to cope with a problem," you
will be reading or assigning material that tries to make sense out
of experience the alcoholic/addict has had.

☞   Many readers may have already done what the author would
suggest next, underlining the parts that trigger a personal reaction. Write about them and share with others. Generate your own
list of personal examples, including those that seem to contradict
☞   what you have read. Feel utterly free to disagree. But do so in the
spirit of trying to pin down the truth better than the author has, not
to defend yourself or a theory. You might be surprised how much
of the first edition of this book went in the trash. If this material
keeps growing, if the author keeps growing, that will probably
happen again in five or six years.

☞   This book is itself meant to be a toolbox. The ideas, exercises,
questionnaires and examples are there for any reader to use, for
your own recovery or to help others, clients or students. Some will
work for sponsors, others only for counselors or psychotherapists.
(The author has no objection to working counselors incorporating
all or part of various chapters in to treatment lectures for your agen-

cy. Just don't publish them or go around doing workshops!) Still
others will be most useful to drug and alcohol educators and their
students. Every effort has been made to connect these tools to those
of Twelve Step Recovery and of other therapies. Cognitive therapists, psychodynamic therapists, and pastoral counselors — you
will also find linkages to your customary tools.

☞   One thing the author has never personally tried is to use the
book for discussion group, whether for warm-up or as the primary activity. He has never heard a group read passages together and
then share their reactions. Such discussion groups could be lay or
☞ professionally led. A group of counselors could also go through
the book together. Alternatively, read it alone and meet for discus-
sion(s). Hey, it would be cheaper than attending the workshop!

*To increase understanding of the above section, complete Recov-
ery Exercise #13 at the end of the chapter.*

The Bottom Line

The bottom line is that there is no bottom line.

This is not a book advancing a bold new theory of addiction or
relapse. It is not even creating a new system of "relapse prevention." At most, it gives the reader a way of understanding the moment and process of relapse based on experience. This experience
includes recovery tools and what happens when they are used, as
well as when they are not. The author regards it as a legitimate
quest to seek alternative tools that help those who have not (yet)
responded to Twelve Step Recovery. However, the direction of
this work has been the opposite. Its thrust has been to understand
the relapse experience in such a way that it more effectively connects the alcoholic/addict to their own recovery process. It has
striven to increase the number of people who are able to make
effective use of a recovery system that, quite literally, "works when
you work it."

In following this course, *White Knuckles and Wishful Thinking* has followed one guideline of *Alcoholics Anonymous,* the "Big Book" itself. To be sure to talk to the "new man" about that "strange mental twist" that precedes the first drink. We have talked, not only to the new-comer, but to the old-timer, the sponsor, counselor, family member, psychiatrist. Anyone, in fact, who takes the time to read these pages. That "twist" has been the entire, even obsessive, focus of this book. It begins and ends with the empirical fact that we all say one of those two things as we relapse, "One won't hurt" or "F--- it." These two stereotyped thoughts do not explain relapse, nor can they be considered as "causes." They are simply links in a chain reaction that "fires" at that moment. And they are clues as to what "links" have been increasing or diminishing during the *process* of relapse that builds up to them. This in turn leads to the necessary tasks of recovery. In effect, our two clues help us look back to understand the process of relapse. In so doing, they help us look forward to the process of recovery and what it will require.

No bottom line.

Just a summary:

> *In order not to relapse to any addiction, I have to do two things. I must accept the physical reality of my addiction, that one will hurt, always. And I must learn to cope with the frustrations of life without my "fix" of choice, instead of saying "F--- it." The only relapse prevention system designed to help me with the first task for the rest of my life is Twelve Step Recovery. The only one directly challenging my problem of excessive desire, offering lifelong containment, is Twelve Step Recovery. Understood in this context, various other therapies and relapse prevention techniques can be enormously helpful and vitally necessary — I may die without them..*

That's it.

Stick a fork in us.

We're done.

To increase understanding of the above section, complete Recovery Exercise #14 at the end of the chapter.

References

[1] Anonymous. *Alcoholics Anonymous.* New York: Alcoholics Anonymous World Services, Inc., 1955.

[2] Kim, Eleanor, Marlatt, G. Alan, and Dimeff, Linda A. "The Road to Relapse," in Professional Counselor, June, 1996.

[3] Stalcup, Alex, MD. "Contemporary Approaches to Treatment for Substance Abuse" Workshop. Seattle, 1996.

[4] Levin, Jerome David. *Introduction to Alcoholism Counseling, A Bio-Psycho-Social Approach.* Washington, DC and London: Taylor and Francis, 1995.

[5] deMello, Anthony, S.J. (Edited by Stroud, Francis J.). *Awareness, The Perils and Opportunities of Reality.* New York, London, etc.: Image Doubleday, 1992.

[6] Tiebout, Harry. "The Ego Factors In Surrender In Alcoholism", Quarterly Journal of Studies on Alcohol, Volume 15, pp. 610-621, 1954.

[7] Levin, as above in [4].

[8] Anonymous. *Twelve Steps and Twelve Traditions.* New York: Alcoholics Anonymous World Services, Inc., 1952, 1981.

[9] Bill W. "The Next Frontier: Emotional Sobriety." found in *The Language of the Heart: Bill W's Grapevine Writings.* New York: The AA Grapevine, Inc., 1988.

[10] Stalcup, Alex, as above in [3].

[11] Hendrix, Harville. *Getting the Love You Want, A Guide for Couples.* New York: Harper Perennial, 1990.

[12] Tiebout, Harry, as above in [6].
[13] Bill W., as above in [9].

Recovery Exercises

1. Read the first 164 pages of the AA big Book and highlight every reference to relapse or starting to drink again. If it is a group, you can divide it up by chapters and share. Alternatively, you can make it a competition to see who finds the most. The winner gets to enforce "Rule 62" for a week.

2. Review the Table of Contents of this book and your personal highlighting and or notes. For each chapter, try to spell out any links that played a part in your last period of abstinence and relapse. Be sure to include the positives, things that kept you sober.

3. Using your notes from other exercises, and talking to group, professional helper, and/or sponsor, try to spell out the biggest frustrations in your most recent relapse. With this help and support, can you see yourself treating any wants as needs, especially at any point of saying "F--- it?" It is as important to be gentle with yourself as it is to be honest. Develop a plan to address this "need," including both your spirituality, and professional therapy, if they are part of your recovery.

4. Do you identify with "fear of abandonment" as a relapse trigger? This is a clinical term and it would be wise to describe your experience to someone clinically trained and see if they think that is what you experience. If so, develop a plan, one that includes all aspects of your recovery program, for dealing with this powerful reaction instead of relapsing. Try to be

specific and concrete about how each area (AA, professional help, religion, secular relapse prevention, even diet, exercise, and work, as well as your current relationships) will work together toward this goal.

5. Do you identify with drinking to feel "bigger," like Superman or King Kong. If so, look at your moment(s) of relapse. Did you feel helplessness at the time? Even if you did not, is it reasonable to say that helplessness was part of your frustration before you drank? If so, develop a plan, with your helper(s) for dealing with this reaction instead of relapsing. Again, try to be as specific and concrete as possible.

6. Do you resent anyone saying you have an "inner child?" If so, take this resentment through all five steps of the process (Step 4) in Chapter 5 of the Big Book for dealing with resentment, and then do Steps 5 through 9 about it. Alternatively, make a list of ten times you drank/drugged over a problem. How mature was this reaction? If your "inner child" was not in control of you, who was?

7. How does Alcoholics Anonymous or any other form of therapy help the "inner child" grow up?

8. Read what Bill W. says about "character defects" in the Twelve Steps and Twelve Traditions. Then read his article on "Emotional Sobriety" in the book cited. Has the author twisted what Bill W. said, taken it out of context? If so, how? If not, how does this apply to any "excessive demands" you make of life, especially at the moment of relapse? Write, share, discuss with helper, and/or group.

9. If your helper thinks you are ready, read deMello's *Awareness*. Write down how what he says fits you. Try to spell out

how the various kinds of help in which you are participating cultivate this kind of awareness. Are there any ways in which they resist it, AA included?

10. Has relationship failure and/or frustration played a significant part in your drinking and/or relapse? If so, does your helper and/or group think you are ready to start addressing this issue, as part of your plan for long-term recovery? If not, what specific priorities do they think are more important to your recovery and survival at this time? If you are already in a troubled relationship, how do they suggest you deal with it for now? And what will tell them and you when it is time to focus on your unhealthy patterns in relationships? If they think you are ready, develop a plan together.

11. Are you a "people-pleaser?" If so track your cravings for approval and/or attention for a week. How frequent and strong are they? How long can you abstain? What are the slippery places? Is there any realistic way to avoid them?

12. Make a list of the three (5, 10) worst characteristics of whoever raised you, the things that hurt you the most. Make a similar list for your "significant others in adulthood," past and present. Any similarities and/or patterns? Write, share, discuss.

13. Make a list of the three most useful things you have found in this book. Try to spell out what you found so useful and how it will support your recovery. If possible, spell out what you will do differently or more. Write, share, discuss.

14. In no more than two sentences, summarize what this book says is required for recovery from addiction. Evaluate yourself from "1" to "10" on how completely you meet those

requirements. Ask your group and or helper to evaluate you, too. If they see a vulnerable area, ask them for specific feedback on what they see, and how to work for improvement. If you are willing to ask for honest feedback and to listen to it, your chances improve significantly.

Appendix

Appendix for Chemical Dependency Students

Chapter 1

Review Questions

The Case of the Broken Shoelace:
1. Name two mental links that are part of a reaction.
2. Name two physical links that affect how we react.
3. Name two links in a reaction of which the person may not be conscious.

A Model, Not a Theory
1. According to the author, what is the difference between a "theory" and a "model" of human behavior?
2. What are the two thoughts that seem to always accompany the moment of relapse?
3. How can a question be a "tool?"

Schools of Thought
1. Name three theories of human behavior and the "links" they emphasize.
2. How do "links" of "Ego" and "rice bowl" affect the behavior of those who subscribe to various theories?
3. What sort of links does this book emphasize?

Distillation of Purely Biochemical Theory
1. According to the purest form of biochemical theory, how is an alcoholic different from a non-alcoholic?

Putting Biochemistry in Perspective — *Without* Getting Rid of It
1. List three aspects of addiction that do not seem adequately explained by an exclusively biochemical account.
2. Name two things the human brain can do which the laboratory animal cannot. How do they (potentially) affect development of the disease and/or recovery?

What Is a Hang-up?
1. List three characteristics of a "hang-up."
2. What word has come to represent a comprehensive view of addiction as arising from multiple factors?

How to Permanently Alter an "Automatic" Reaction
1. What is required for those reactions which cannot be permanently altered? List three such reactions affecting recovery from addiction.
2. List three levels at which an automatic or self-defeating behavior may be altered.
3. Which therapy specificly addresses links that are missing?
4. Which therapy builds on links already present?

Links Over Time and the Process of Relapse
1. What AA acronym is, in fact, a relapse prevention tool?
2. Describe the relapse process in terms of what is happening with the "links."

The Tool: Reliving the Recent Past
1. List three things that make it so hard to change an ingrained reaction.
2. If the mind carries a tape of experience as it happens, what does "reliving" do with that tape? How does this begin to offset the things you listed in question one?"

Exercises

1. Do recovery exercise #1. Discuss with peer and/or class. Ask someone who knows you what they would say about how your reactions change. If you don't like what they tell you, identify the links in your negative reaction.

2. Do recovery exercise #4.

3. What is the basic premise of this chapter and (apparently) of the book?

4. Compare two schools of thought about human behavior, chosen by yourself or your professor. Spell out what links each emphasizes as the causes of human behavior. Where do they overlap? What do they seem to leave out? When do they actually use different words for the same links of reaction? Do a comparison of how each would explain the alcoholic/addict saying "F--- it" or "One won't hurt" at the moment of relapse. Pick any other reactions and compare how each would describe/explain it, link by link.

5. Pick a character from movies, TV, books, etc. who appears to change by the end of the story. How have his/her reactions changed? What links are different than they were in the beginning? Does the plot seem to be an adequate and realistic cause for the changes?

6. Pick a reaction you have had, not too personal, that changed. See if you can identify the links that changed and what made that happen.

Chapter 2

Review Questions

The Moment of Relapse — Using the "Lost Keys" Approach

1. What does the tool of "reliving" do with the "links" of a reaction?

Into the Moment

1. If "reliving" works in looking at a moment of relapse, what two thought/links will we hear?
2. What will the facilitator likely have to remind the volunteer of during the exercise?
3. What are the other group members to use to measure the validity of the exercise and of the "fact" asserted?
4. List five things (at least) to ask a relapse victim when they wake up the day of relapse.
5. If the client "reliving" a relapse connects other feelings and desires to the mental/action link "F--- it," how can you and your client use that?
6. What is a paper-and-pencil alternative to doing the role-play exercise?

Predictable Resistance

1. List five different ways a person may initially resist this exercise.

Different Tools, Same Job

1. Describe two other ways to bring out the thoughts, "One won't hurt" or "F--- it" at the moment of relapse.
2. What makes it possible to do this exercise with "normies?"

Exercises

1. Do recovery exercise #2.

2. Do the exercise described in the last paragraph of the chapter. Try it with a group of "normies." If you have access and supervision, try it with a group of clients who have relapsed. Write up your experience and/or report back to class. Be sure to spell out where the instructions were inadequate and/or could have been improved.

3. Write a two-page paper on why it makes no significant difference *what* people say at the moment of relapse. Alternatively, have a debate in class where two groups take opposite sides of this opinion. Be sure to use references from this class and others that show you are integrating what you have learned about chemical dependency.

Chapter 3

Review Questions

Why Look?

1. List four variations of "One won't hurt."
2. What do all of these variations assume or assert?
3. What two groups in the chemical dependency field have taken explicit interest in the thinking at the moment of relapse?
4. How does AA's Big Book suggest this thinking be used during a Twelve Step call?
5. List two reasons the field does not take more interest in this thinking.

One Won't Hurt — Moment of Decision

1. What is the "Thomas theorem?"
2. What has it got to do with what an alcoholic/addict may be thinking at the moment of relapse?
3. Picture a person who has already been through treatment with recovering and professionally trained counselors. What does it tell us if this person says "One won't hurt" at the moment of relapse?
4. What are the most important links to identify in the person's reaction at the moment of relapse?

Break With Reality

1. What is the most obvious thing about the belief "One won't hurt" in the mind of an addict/alcoholic?
2. What is there about this that makes addiction a "mental illness?"
3. List three exercises to bring home the fact of being drug-free at the moment of being controlled by the thought "One won't hurt."
4. List at least six other things we may know about an addict/alcoholic who is relapsing with the thought "One won't hurt."
5. If a person recognizes this thought as a mental symptom of the disease, what emotion will they experience if they hear it in their own head. In general, what are they more likely to do?

Denial of Denial

1. Give three different ways to paraphrase "One won't hurt" which shed light on its meaning.
2. How does a "wishful" relapse contradict a person's claim to have "known for years that I am alcoholic?"

Experience, a Missing Link

1. How do we come to know we have a "chronic problem?"
2. What is it that AA says "We are unable, at certain times, to bring into our consciousness with sufficient force...?"
3. Name three defenses operating when a person is having "euphoric recall."

4. How are "buried memories" of a relapsing alcoholic/addict like a photo album?

Desire, Another "Missing Link"
1. Name two possible reasons for the person's unawareness of how much the drug is desired.
2. What do we call a craving of which the person is not aware?

A Decision in the Dark
1. Give two different ways to describe a decision "made under the control of something other than reason or reality."
2. What kind of self-awareness must treatment try to develop?

The Affirmation
1. What is affirmed by the words "One won't hurt?"
2. What makes the human mind affirm what is not true?

One Drink of What?
1. What is an "emotional problem?"
2. Even if a person had no "diagnosable emotional problem before drinking/drugging," how could alcohol/drugs create one?
3. How can "One won't hurt" (or "F--- it") become "an 'open sesame' to the world of feelings?

The Wish for Wishes
1. What is AA's "theory of the emotional/psychological problem of addiction?"
2. What psychological state or experience, enhanced by alcohol, gratifies the craving for omnipotence?
3. Describe (sketch) the approach to this psychological state when counseling a still-abstinent alcoholic.
4. How is this experience radically different from "spiritual experience?"

Euphoria
1. Which "Step" of AA has the person in euphoria lost at an emotional level?
2. What makes the person in euphoria rebuff "reality?"
3. List four things you may hear from a person who relapsed in a state of euphoria.
4. List four possible treatment responses to euphoria.
5. How are people who feel inadequate vulnerable to euphoria?

Boredom
1. In general, from what does boredom result?
2. What makes "one drink" so appealing to the bored alcoholic?
3. List three ways to deal with boredom in AA/NA/CA.
4. What is the "antidote" for complacency?

The Hidden Guilt
1. How does saying "One won't hurt" reveal that the relapsing alcoholic/addict has some guilt about taking that first drink/drug?

A Living Problem

1. Describe how to rule out (or in) a triggering event for the thought "One won't hurt" when it appears to come "out of the blue."
2. List two indicators that seem to confirm the trigger was emotional.
3. List three "connections" that may be developed from looking at a "One won't hurt" relapse.

Psychological Core Links

1. Summarize Tiebout's account of "self-will run riot."
2. How does an alcoholic/addict validate this theory (and AA's) every time s/he relapses with "One won't hurt?"
3. How did Tiebout define the two objectives of his interventions with alcoholics/addicts?

Instant Regression and the "Adult Child" Connection

1. List five characteristics of regression.
2. What do some alcoholic/addicts experience at the moment of relapse that confirms they have "regressed?"

Links Over Time

1. Roughly what percentage of people will score themselves "Start high/End low" on the Addiction Conviction Scale?
2. For those who scored themselves "Start high/End low," what recovery task have they spelled out (and even graphed)?
3. What "Step" have they graphed?
4. What kind of "craving?"

Exercises

1. Interview 5 (10, 20, etc.) relapsed alcoholics/addicts with the list of variations of the wishful relapse in hand. Get their exact thoughts at the moment of relapse. How many said one of the exact phrases at the beginning of this chapter? How many said some variation of "I can control my drug use" that is not listed?

2. Read Beck's *Cognitive Therapy of Substance Abuse* and describe how it goes about "corrupting the alibi system" of alcoholics/addicts.

3. Read and summarize everything you can find in the first three chapters of the AA Big Book about the wishful relapse.

4. Interview 3 (5, 10) chemical dependency professionals about the moment of relapse. Find out what they think are the two most common thoughts at the moment of relapse. Then ask how they try to help a patient to never again say "One won't hurt." Being sure to be respectful, see if they seem uninterested in the question and why, using the three reasons given in this chapter. Write up responses and analysis as your instructor requires.

5. Give 3 (5, 10, etc.) illustrations of the "Thomas Theorem" which do not involve addiction. Illustrations from literature and media are acceptable. For each example, spell out the "definition of the situation" and the real consequences.

6. Summarize in one or two sentences what the author is trying to say in the entire section on "Two Obvious Facts and an Exercise," after you have done the exercise. Be sure to include his apparent emotion about the subject.

7. Create a list of questions you could ask to determine whether a relapser has faced the fact there was no drug in his or her brain when he or she decided to take "just one." What responses, verbal and non-verbal, would suggest the person has or has not faced this?

8. If you have access and supervision, ask 3 (5, 10) relapsers how long they have known they were alcoholics/addicts. Then find out how many were saying "One won't hurt" on the last relapse. Gently point out the contradiction in this. Give them a chance to share their reactions and to talk about what it means to them. For an assignment, have them read Chapters 2 and 3 of the Big Book, highlighting what they find about relapse thinking.

9. With supervision, xerox the section on "Experience, a Missing Link" and have 3 (5, 10, etc.) wishful relapsers read it. Ask them to share their emotional and intellectual reactions. Write up and analyze their responses for your instructor and/or class. (If they are troubled, encourage them to read the first three chapters of the Big Book.)

10. Ask 3 (5,10) wishful relapsers to revisit their moment of relapse. Ask them to describe their exact feelings at the time. If they report craving, ask them to rate it from "1" to "10." If they report no craving, ask them if there was anything in their feelings that said "just one" would not satisfy the desire of the moment.

11. Ask 3 (5,10) wishful relapsers to rate themselves from "1" to "10" at the moment of their relapses on their:
    - belief they would, in fact, get hurt
    - memory of the suffering that got them to quit in the first place
    - acceptance, awareness, realization of being alcoholics/addict
    - awareness of emotional pain from current living problems that might be relieved by the drug.

12. Generate a list of 3 (5, 10) examples of denial. Spell out the positive beliefs each tries to protect.

13. Critique the author's claim that all alcoholics/addicts have an "emotional problem." Summarize his argument and try to punch at least three holes in it.

14. Interview 3 (5, 10) wishful relapsers for fantasies they may have had while drinking/drugging. Look especially for recurring ones. On your own or with instructor and class, try to spell out what "wish" the fantasy is fulfilling. Look at both the story content of the fantasy and the inner experience it creates.

15. Using the section on "Euphoria," create a list of questions and/or indicators to determine whether euphoria played a part in your client's relapse.

16. Do a mini-paper comparing this section on "Euphoria" and Chapter 17 of *Living Sober.* What does each say that is similar and how are they different?

17. Use this section on boredom to create a set of questions you could use to evaluate whether boredom was an issue in a client's relapse. Then use it to create a list of possible homework assignments for someone who is struggling with boredom. Let your instructor determine how many of each, depending on what is in the chapter, your experience level, and how many are doing the exercise together.

18. Complete the hypothetical example of "Jane Doe" in this section two different ways. In one, answer the questions as if their is a living problem which is contributing to her urge, but she has not connected it. In the second, have her answer in a way that pretty much rules out any living problem as a trigger. You might also role-play each scenario for the class, possibly with "Jane Doe" knowing how she will be answering but the interviewer having to find out as he or she goes along.

19. Using the list of characteristics of (instant) regression and the observations of that section and of the section on "core issues," generate a list of questions and/or indicators to assess whether a client was in a state of regression at the moment of relapse.

20. Do the "Addiction Conviction Scale" as a class, using other "bad habits" or compulsions, or even other addictions if you are not in recovery. Share with each other what the process is like for you and what you learn from it, about yourself, and about relapse in general.

21. Give the "Addiction Conviction Scale" to at least ten relapsers. Do you get the results the author describes, a "backwards Z" with about two-thirds in the "Start high/End low" group?

Chapter 4

Review Questions

From Questions to Observations and Back
1. If questions are "interventions," what are they designed to do?
2. When would a cardiac or diabetic patient be likely to say "One won't hurt" or "F--- it?"
3. Looking for the meaning of "F--- it," what is the immediate puzzle?
4. Why is this important?

"I Quit"
1. What is one possible connection between quitting and emotional maturity?
2. How do Twelve Step programs help members to not say "F--- it" and give up?
3. How do some alcoholics/addicts achieve long-term goals (before recovery)?

4. List four questions that can be asked of someone whose "F--- it" meant "I quit."
5. How do counselors help people apply general principles to specific problems?
6. What "nerve" is usually hit when a relevant question triggers irritation and defensiveness?
7. What two "precious qualities" are required to help an addict/alcoholic face these questions?
8. What is the first healthy choice of an addict/alcoholic whose frustration is building toward "F--- it?"
9. What makes talking to someone else so unappealing to the person about to say "F---you" by drinking/drugging?
10. What is "self-consciousness" really an excessive consciousness of?
11. Of what attitude is getting drunk "at you" a perfectly logical expression?
12. When is the experience of shame healing?
13. List three kinds of therapy and how they help people deal with the shame of facing addiction.

I've Had It! (With a Feeling of Snapping)

1. What is it that builds up to the "snapping" point?
2. What is the most direct way to reduce this before it is too late (and relapse is unavoidable)?
3. How can the professional helper contribute to preventing this kind of relapse?

Futility ("What's the Use!")

1. List three questions for the person who relapsed with this feeling.

Futility and Serenity

1. What is the difference between the person who says "F--- it" and relapses and the one who says "F--- it" and relaxes?
2. What is there about "DuWors' Law" that makes it neither hopeless nor helpless?
3. What is the connection between hope and responsibility?
4. How is AA "the bane" of the "hopeless" alcoholic?
5. What is the key to understanding a particular "F--- it" relapse?
6. How is the word "just" an obstacle to this?

Perfectionism and Futility (The Koufax Principle)

1. List five questions for the relapsing perfectionist.
2. How does perfectionism cause us to do less than our best?
3. What is "The Koufax Principle"?

"Who Cares?"

1. Why does someone who denies caring still need a "painkiller?"
2. What are two alternatives for the person who is hurt as a result of caring?
3. Describe one way in which the "wishful" and "white-knuckle" relapse overlap.

Author's Translation: "I Can't Cope"

1. In what way is this translation (or summary) a handle for preventing the next relapse?
2. What is the Catch-22 of early abstinence?

3. What aspect of being "powerless" is often subtly denied by those who admit loss of control with one drink?
4. Describe the difference between someone who has faced this and someone who has not.
5. At what two levels may we address "the problem of coping?"

The Three P's: Partialization, Perspective, and Prevention
1. What relapse feeling results from the inability to partialize?
2. What must the helper try to do for one who has lost perspective?
3. What role do "others" play in the "F--- it" relapse?
4. What related emotional attitude is said by AA to "....destroy(s) more alcoholics than anything else"?
5. What am I no longer able to do after passing "the point of no return" in an "F--- it" relapse process?

Awareness, a Specific Role for Psychotherapy in Relapse Prevention
1. What can the trained psychotherapist help the addict/alcoholic "uncover" in early recovery?
2. Describe the tool of "silence."
3. What Step of the Twelve Steps does the tool of silence resemble?

"My Way or the Highway:" The Spiritual Significance of "F--- it"
1. What is the significance of the fact the person has no drug in the brain when saying "F--- it?"
2. List five names for a profound change in a human personality.
3. How is the attitude in "One won't hurt" similar to the attitude in "F--- it?"
4. If these attitudes do not change, what is likely to happen?

Exercises

1. Think of 3 (5, 10) times you were trying to do something or get somewhere and had to quit in frustration. What did you say to yourself at the moment of quitting? How is this similar to the alcoholic quitting and relapsing? How is it different? If you do this as a class, try to generate a list of real situations in which you said "F--- it" to something you were trying. If you happen to be in recovery, do *not* use examples involving drinking or drugging.

2. Reading the section on "F--- it" as "I quit," develop a list of 5 to 10 questions to ask a client to assess if this was the main emotion involved in saying "F--- it." Then develop 5 to 10 questions to assess what sort of quitting was involved. Finally, develop a list of questions to assess the relapser's difficulty talking about frustration when it is occurring.

3. How do you tell if someone is staying clean and sober for themselves or someone else? Develop a list of five questions you might ask and a list of five indicators, verbal or otherwise.

4. Look at your list of things you have quit from #1. For each situation, list anything you did that made things worse. Then list at least one thing you felt like doing or could have done that *would* have made it worse, if you had. What coping reaction or tool stopped you from doing the thing that would have made it worse?

5. Use the text to develop a set of questions to tell whether a relapse involved the "I've had it" of emotional build-up. Create questions to assess what was building up and what blocked the person from sharing. Practice using the questions through role-play or (under supervision) with clients.

6. Referring to the text, create a list of 10 questions, 1) to assess the extent to which perfectionism was involved in a relapse and, 2) to assess the "standard" for which the person was striving, both what it was and where it came from.

7. Using a group of students who have not read this chapter, or a group of clients for whom you have supervision to do so, tell the Koufax story and ask them what *they* think it has to do with addiction and/or relapse. (Do not tell them the Koufax principle — just give the Koufax anecdote itself, as he might have told it.)

8. As a class, try to develop three examples in which a person was emotionally hurt without caring about whatever the hurt was? Discuss your process and what you think it means.

9. Make a list of 3 (5, 10, etc.) times you suffered emotional pain. For each, identify what you cared about that made the pain possible. Describe the difference it would have made if you had *not*.

10. How do you tell that an addict/alcoholic has not accepted the part of the disease that requires a strenuous commitment to learning better coping skills? How might you use their relapse experience to try to bring this home?

11. Develop a set of questions to evaluate the relapser's degree of awareness leading up to the moment of relapse and another set to help them *see* it.

12. In five brief points, summarize the logic by which the author connects the "F--- it" relapse and the need for spiritual experience.

13. Critique the above argument. Develop an alternative explanation and an alternative solution.

Chapter 5

Review Questions

Acceptance Reaction

1. Explain how "One won't hurt" and "F--- it" both represent lack of acceptance.
2. How does a person's level of distress or disturbance change with genuine acceptance?

The Myth of the Overnight Cure

1. How does the belief in a single moment of "surrender" lead to counselor burnout?
2. What is the primary issue in a typical intervention?
3. In focusing on acceptance of the disease, with which step of AA does treatment overlap?

The First Pill — Connecting Alcohol to Problems

1. What is the pattern recognized in swallowing the "first pill" of acceptance?
2. How does this milestone of acceptance lead to "the great obsession of every alcoholic?"
3. Why is inpatient treatment "mutually unacceptable" for the alcoholic/addict who has swallowed only the first "pill?"
4. Describe an approach to working with an alcoholic in outpatient counseling who denies "it's the first drink."

The Second Pill — "It's the First Drink"

1. What is the most crucial single event in the process of accepting addiction?
2. What is the death-grip of what people in recovery call "white-knuckle sobriety?"
3. What is the person who swallows the "second pill" (only) still denying?
4. List three questions you might ask such a person to engage them in treatment and/or recovery.

The Third Pill — "Power of Alcohol Equals Need for Help"

1. List two common ways people in recovery describe the experience of swallowing the "third pill."
2. What percentage of people who live through this experience use the above formula to describe it?
3. After a person "realizes" something, what has changed?
4. List three indicators a person has swallowed the third pill.
5. What is the difference between being "tough" and being "strong?"

Something to Say Instead of "F--- it"

1. What do recovering addicts/alcoholics "say," by word or deed or attitude, instead of "One won't hurt" or "F--- it?"
2. Name three ways to help increase a person's realization of the power of the addiction.
3. Describe "involuntary treatment."

4. List four ways to respond to a counterdependent other than confrontation or coercion.

5. If you cannot get an alcoholic addict to join a partnership with you to deal with the problem, what are your two remaining options?

Exercises

1. Read this chapter and create a list of ten questions to ask an alcoholic/addict to assess which "pills" they have or have not swallowed. Include questions to identify where the person might be stuck and need help.

2. Pick 3 (5, 10) real patients who have been in treatment at least twice before and interview them for their acceptance, using your ten questions for an outline.

3. Pick 3 (5, 10) real patients who have never been in treatment or tried to quit drinking before and interview them for their acceptance. Again, use your ten questions for an outline.

4. Compare and contrast the answers of the two groups above.

   Note: instructors and students feel free to vary number of questions, patients, etc. Use role-play instead of real patients as appropriate. Do not interview real patients without supervision.

5. Make "asking for help" a discussion topic or wait for it to present as an issue in counseling. Elicit reasons people resist asking for help until the issue of "weak versus strong" appears. At that point, present the question about "who is stronger" from the last section of this chapter. Try to get each person to look at and share their reaction to this way of thinking about it. If it is true, how does this change things for them and for their willingness to ask for help?

6. Start as above, but present the "tough versus strong" analogy instead of the "who is stronger" question. Again, try to get each person looking at and sharing what this means personally.

   Note: Variations of #5 and #6 might include having clients write about their reaction to these distinctions as assignments, sharing what they wrote later. The exercise can also be done through role-play and/or in 1:1 counseling.

Chapter 7

Review Questions

When Does Denial Exist?
1. When does denial exist?
2. List four reasons to "not admit" something.

The Wall Between Alcoholic Self and Others
1. What is the person behind the "wall" of denial unable to do? (What does the wall "keep out"?)

Some Painful Reasons to Stay Out of the Other's Moccasins
1. List three painful consequences of beginning to empathize with the suffering I cause others.
2. What is the last barrier of denial to fall?
3. How does "the wall" set me up to say "One won't hurt" or "F--- it?"

The Wall between Alcoholic/Addict and Self
1. What must an addict/alcoholic realize in order for "voluntary treatment" to have a chance?
2. What specific denial is the seed of most "F--- it" relapses?
3. How are treatment and self-help like two drugs?

The Will Behind the Wall
1. How is the mental blindness of denial different from physical blindness?
2. What is a mind "in denial" determined not to do or experience?
3. Using James' definition, how does denial itself function like a "will?"
4. List three cravings motivating denial.

Exercises

1. If you have access to clients and supervision, do 10 Relapse PostMortems as described in the last chapter. Try to spell out the gaps in acceptance that appeared in each. This could be a term project. The number may vary and more than one person may share in it.

2. Read this chapter critically. Try to make "bullets" — brief statements for each insight or understanding about denial that you find. For each one, try to identify a way that this understanding would help you help an alcoholic/addict.

3. Generate a list of 3 (5, 10) examples of someone denying something that can be seen by an objective observer. Make examples concrete, even if you fictionalize or borrow from fiction. This can be done as a group, with discussion as to whether the definition of denial holds up.

3. For each of the examples in #2, spell out how the person in denial fears the others will react if s/he admits to the denied condition or problem. Is the fear realistic?

4. For each of the examples done in #2 and #3 above, identify how you would help the person deal with the fear.

5. Have you ever felt helpless, like you were "talking to a wall," when you tried to help someone see a problem they refused to see? How does your example compare to the one in this chapter — the man who lies to a wife who has caught him in the act? How is your example different? Can you see anything in this chapter that might give you a way to try to help such a person?

6. In a class which has not yet read this chapter, create two role-plays, one in which the wife sees her husband acting as described (reverse gender at will) and he denies it to her face. Have group discuss this, what it means and how they might help. In the second, role-play the counseling session as described. Discuss again. Experiment with different counselor responses as you see fit.

7. For a class that has not yet read this chapter, read or give the example of the man for whom other people were becoming real. Lead a discussion of what, if anything, this says about the nature of addiction. See if they can connect ways to help people recover from this, using both treatment and Twelve Step tools.

8. Generate a list of 3 (5, 10) examples of alcoholics/addicts defending themselves against the truth in counseling sessions. For each one, spell out the pain they are protecting themselves from. Then try to describe a counselor response that might be both empathic and effective. Experiment by role-play, if you have a class with the time.

Chapter 8

Review Questions

Relapse Prevention as Denial Reduction
1. What is denied by "One won't hurt?"
2. What is denied by "F--- it?"
3. What do all defenses do?

A Patient's Definition
1. Give two descriptive definitions of denial.

Denial as Prejudice
1. Who is the object of my "prejudice" in denial?
2. How is "One won't hurt" an expression of "prejudice?"
3. How is "F--- it" an expression of prejudice?

Denial as "Not-Thinking-About-It"

1. List three things the person saying "One won't hurt" is "not-thinking-about."
2. List three things the person saying "F--- it" is not thinking about.

Denial as "Isolation-of-the-Connected"

1. What are the two necessary conditions for the human mind to form a pattern?
2. How can this sort of "isolation" create a gap between assessor and addictive client?
3. How do assessment interviews sometimes reduce this defense?
4. How does "One won't hurt" block a pattern?
5. How does "F--- it" block a pattern?
6. What is the pattern of experience that unites all human frustration?
7. What is the three-letter exclamation often heard in those for whom a pattern has just emerged?

Pseudo-Responsibility: "Beating Myself Up" as Denial

1. What is the primary fact of addiction denied by "beating myself up?"
2. What is the second, deeper level of denial?
3. List three things the person may do instead of "beating myself up" after drinking/drugging.

Exercises

1. As group or individual, generate a list of prejudices, with concrete examples. See if you can describe how the person avoids or rejects facts which contradict the belief. Again, be as concrete as possible, even if your example is fictitious.

2. Generate a list of beliefs about self you have seen protected by denial in others. What does the person think they would lose if the denied reality were faced? Try to develop possible counselor responses that would take into account what the person is protecting. Again, try to work with concrete examples, even if some are fictitious.

3. Using this book and your own experience or common sense, generate a list of things for someone who has said "F--- it" and relapsed to think about. Do the same for someone who has relapsed saying "One won't hurt."

4. As group or individual, generate examples from personal experience, literature, films, etc. of people experiencing an "aha." See if you can use hindsight to spell out "dots" that were present but unconnected until that moment. Another way to put it, look for trees that existed before the person finally saw the forest. It may be enough for the class to process one example provided by the instructor. Another possibility, do an individual assignment of studying one story or case, such as Chapter 1 of the "Big Book," identifying both dots that were not connected at the time and distinct "aha's" that occurred over time.

5. For instructors, try to create an inclass experience in which students are provided with some sort of "dots" that consistently produce an "aha." Have them notice and

share this artificial experience and connect it to personal experience and clinical observation. If the author can create such an exercise, he will put it on his web site. If you find or create a good one, he will be happy to put it there and give you credit.

6. Study the section of this chapter on "pseudo-responsibility." Role play counseling someone who is beating him/herself up. Find different ways to explain about the two levels of denial and get them interested in understanding rather than beating themselves. Process as a group and be sure to listen to the feedback of the "client" about what seemed to work and what didn't.

7. If you are working with clients and have your supervisor's permission, try using the material on pseudo-responsibility to help those who beat themselves up. In group, you might make it a topic, having them read and discuss the section (permission granted to copy!). Then have them try Recovery Exercise #8 for this chapter. Alternatively, have one person with this issue read the section, do the exercise, report back to group.

Chapter 9

Review Questions

Dr. Jekyll, Meet Mr. Hyde — An Exercise
1. Name two different forms of deception generated by alcoholism (and most other addictions.)
2. List four ways "Dr. Jekyll" changes after drinking.
3. List three reasons "Dr. Jekyll" might take the first drink anyway.
4. What is the "powerful illusion of power?"
5. List two ways this exercise in looking at the problem can lead right back to solutions.
6. What is the most consistent reaction to this exercise?

The Devil of Disownership
1. Define "disownership."
2. Give three examples in which language creates or expresses disownership.
3. How can the disease concept be used for disownership?
4. What kind of pain is said by Father Martin to be "the greatest gift God can give an alcoholic?"

Two Cultural Supports for This Dualism

I. The Spirit Versus the Flesh
1. How is an epileptic who stops taking medication that prevents seizures similar to an alcoholic addict who stops working at recovery?
2. How are they different?
3. How did Ted Bundy "disown" his behavior?
4. What realization do those who recover seem to have in common?

Pavement for the Road to Hell

1. Why is knowing I have a "disease" not enough by itself?

Dr. Jekyll and the Wishful Relapse?

1. List three ways the wishful relapse disowns personal reality.

Dr. Jekyll and the White-Knuckle Relapse

1. List three ways the white-knuckle relapse disowns personal reality.

Exercises

1. Do any of the recovery exercises that may apply. Be sure to share with appropriate support — sponsor, course instructor, counselor, etc. Be sure to journal about your reactions and to save for future reference when you use "Dr. Jekyll and Mr. Hyde" with clients.

2. Try doing "Dr. Jekyll and Mr. Hyde" with a group of real clients. Give them a chance to process about their reactions afterwards (as this chapter does not). Do you get the responses the author got? What do your clients find most valuable and enlightening in the exercise? Is your population different; are they in an earlier stage of the disease, cultural differences, etc.? (You may wish to practice by doing the exercise with one individual first, perhaps with several, until you are comfortable enough to do it with a group.)

3. Read or play "Silver-tongued Devil" for a group. Ask them to share their reactions to the song and what it says about how alcoholic thinking works. Make sure they bring in their own experience. Document and bring back to class.

4. As a class or individually, brainstorm examples of disownership from all areas of life, including fiction. Politicians and bureaucrats are good sources. One of the author's favorites is the Watergate classic — caught in an out-and-out lie, the White House responded, "That statement is no longer operational." If the class watches TV and/or reads the paper for a week, you should have some live ones. If you have some of your own, you can throw them in the pot without admitting they are yours!

5. A variation of #4, if you are seeing real clients and/or attending AA, collect examples of disownership that you hear over a one or two-week period. To make it a bigger, more clinical project, write them down, along with possible and actual clinical responses. Try to spell out what the person is ashamed of, or otherwise blocked from accepting. What does the disownership tell you about where the client is at that moment? What does it imply about prognosis?

6. Class exercise: Take real examples of alcoholics involved in drunk-driving fatalities. Have a class debate on what their responsibility is and how society ought to respond. Alternatively, just divide the board in half. Generate a "Pros and Cons" list for treatment/punishment.

7. Interview three people who have had a "wishful relapse." Try to get enough of their thinking at the time to identify specific things they were disowning. Note any language they used to do this. (If possible, use the "lost keys" technique of Chapter 2.)

8. Do #7 with three people who have had a "white-knuckle relapse."

Chapter 10

Review Questions

1. In what two ways is "ownership" the opposite of "disownership?"
2. If ownership is what gets us to work on problems, what gets the "codependent" to do all that work on someone else's problem?
3. For recovery to occur, what is the most important fact about an addiction?

The Iron Law of Ownership

1. What is the "iron law of ownership?"
2. Why is no deed required for the one piece of property with which we are all born?

"So What" Number One — Ignorance is No Excuse

1. Give three examples in which "Ignorance is no excuse."
2. In what sense is it "fair" that you get cancer of the stomach and I get acid indigestion?
3. In what sense does a chronic alcoholic lack experience?
4. Explain how we "own" our behavior as we "own" our livers!
5. What makes intention irrelevant under the "Iron Law?"
6. What must you suspect, the instant an alcoholic/addict says he or she was not thinking about something important to them?
7. How can you tell that ignorance is "willful?"
8. What positive pain does denial protect me from?
9. How does "One won't hurt" demonstrate that "Ignorance is no excuse?"
10. How does ignorance itself contribute to the white-knuckle relapse?

"So What" Number Two — Ownership is a Fact, Not a Should

1. What makes a "should" from others such a weak motivation?
2. If shoulds don't motivate us to change, what does?
3. What is the real authority of a doctor telling any patient what they "should" do about a medical condition?

"So What" Number Three — Two Things Only the "Owner" Can Provide

1. What are the two things only the owner of a problem can provide for its solution?
2. What can "involuntary treatment" realistically provide toward the solution?
3. Describe how a person's reactions will change after accepting a problem they had previously disowned.
4. What is owned by the person who owns a wishful relapse?

5. What is owned by a person who owns a white-knuckle relapse?

Ownership Versus Blame: a Parable
1. What is the difference between the responsibility of blame and the responsibility of ownership?
2. Why is this important in addictions treatment?
3. How do people avoid ownership by taking *too much* blame?
4. How can shame be healing for an alcoholic/addict?
5. How is ownership itself healing, even when painful?

Exercises

1. If you are in recovery, do the recovery exercises, taking care to note your inner reactions to the process and any "aha's." Would you change any of the questions? Can you see some that need to be asked? If you are not in recovery, try answering the parts of #3 that apply. If you share this with a class, feel free to reveal only your conclusions, not your personal experience.

2. Read or describe the "Everyman" parable to a group of recovery patients, if you are in a position to do so. Ask them to share their reactions, how it relates to recovery and their own experience. If you can, try reading it in a different group when someone is clearly speaking of woundedness and showing resistance to taking active responsibility for their own healing. Try to note both emotional and cognitive reactions of the patients. (The most important one is, "I never thought of it that way before".)

3. This chapter was and continues to be a treatment lecture. Try giving it yourself, if you are in a system that allows this. You might prepare by thinking of your own examples for each of the three "so what's." Be sure and allow time for questions and reactions. Take note of these. (An instructor might give this assignment ahead of time to one member of the class, to give the lecture to the class, before they have read the chapter.)

4. Individually or as a class, generate a list of examples of people "owning" something about themselves. Feel free to use fiction, movies, etc. Take as much or as little time as the class permits.

Chapter 11

Review Questions

The Moment of Relapse as a Moment of Rejection

1. What does the wishful relapse reject?
2. What does the white-knuckle relapse reject?
3. What is bothering any alcoholic or addict who says "One won't hurt" and relapses?
4. What is bothering the alcoholic/addict who relapses with "F--- it?"
5. What makes it so important where the "bother" is?
6. What is the one thing that all bothers have in common and what difference does this make?
7. What is a frustration?

Powerless — The Problem of Where Wanting Comes From

1. Name three ways in which all humans are "powerless" over their wanting.

Powerless — The Problem of Turning Off Unwanted Wanting

1. Explain how "the psychology of temptation is the tasting of possibility."
2. Explain "relative impossibility," with examples.
3. What kind of want stops us from knowing some of our other wants?

Spiritual Note

1. How does spirituality help with unwanted wanting?
2. Where is a recovering alcoholic/addict taught to look for "God's Will?"
3. Give five descriptive definitions of "Acceptance."
4. Explain how each definition relates to both the wishful- and the white-knuckle relapse.

Exercises

1. Why is the physical location of emotional pain so important in treatment of addiction? How would you explain this to clients?

2. Try to generate an example of something that bothered you [or anyone] that was not a frustration. Note your process as you go through this, individually or as a group.

3. List ten major negative feelings you or someone you know has felt about real-life situations. Spell out the wanting in each reaction.

4. List ten trivial frustrations you experience over a day or two. Spell out what you wanted in each case. What do you learn about who you are? What do others see, when you share this?

5. Spell out how "the simple fact we do not control the wants that come to us" is what keeps psychotherapists, clergy, marketing and sales people, cops, judges, lawyers,

prison guards in business. Give specific examples for how each occupation addresses or uses this fact. Hypotheticals are okay!

6. Individually or as a group, generate a list of examples of people denying something. For each example, what "should" blocked the person from facing and/or admitting the truth?

7. Explain your understanding of "relative impossibility." Give personal and/or concrete examples.

8. Assume there really is no such thing as a "Higher Power." Explain from the theoretical perspective of your choice how "surrender" works when it works.

Chapter 12

Review Questions

1. Which of the coping tools given here are new?

"S" Is for "Share"

1. How does the verb, "to share" imply the actions of someone other than the one doing it?
2. Which set of tools in the "Share" toolbox are the most important?

"P" Is for Prayer (and Meditation)

1. What do prayer and meditation do that science does not?
2. Why might it be helpful for a secular therapist to be able to talk about prayer and meditation, even to have appropriate references?
3. How can a therapist who works with resistance help someone who is trying to pray and/or meditate?
4. Name three prayers from Twelve Step Recovery.
5. If humans in prayer are like horse whisperers, what is the "horse?"
6. If a human being is like a fish, what is the "water"?

"A" Is for Action

1. Why does real acceptance usually require behavior change?
2. How does appropriate action help us heal from loss?
3. If I can identify actions that might help me accept something painful, but I can't get myself to do them, what other toolboxes might help?

"R" Is for "Read"

1. Describe three different kinds of reading that can help us accept.
2. If no one else has written about my suffering and how to cope with it, what might I do?
3. If I can't find information or encouragement in a book, where else might I look?

The Other "R" Is for "Rethinking"

1. Name four "menus" for rethinking.
2. What did Shakespeare say about the relationship between thinking and "problems."
3. On what critical point does the author differ with cognitive therapists?
4. Give three ways that AA helps with "stinking thinking."
5. What aspect of thinking does traditional therapy try to access and change?

"O" Is for "One Day At a Time"

1. Describe two ways to actually "do" this tool.

"W" is for "Writing"

1. Describe two different ways to use writing as a tool.
2. What AA Step is found in this toolbox?
3. Name three written exercises this book adds to the toolbox.

Tools for the Courage to Change

1. Which of the seven toolboxes may be used to "change," rather than "accept" something?

Exercises

1. As individuals, think of the silliest thing you or anyone else has ever been upset about. Treating as if it were a matter of life and death for the planet, develop a plan to cope with this problem using each of the seven toolboxes in "SPARROW", at least twice. Identify at least one thing that must be accepted and one that must be changed, so that you can use "SPARROW" twice.

2. As a class, share your problems and your plans from #1. Rate each on a scale of "1" to "10," for absurdity and completeness and apparent understanding of SPARROW. Buy the winner a copy of this book, if he or she does not already have one.

3. Go through the list of recovery exercises for this chapter. Identify and do the ones that do not refer to having an addiction and/or a relapse.

Chapter 13

Review Questions

1. How is minimization like denial and how is it different?

I. How to Help a Minimizer Get Started

1. How does minimizing lead up to saying "One won't hurt" or "F--- it?"

2. What are the risks of doing the counter-minimizing exercise in front of a group? What may eliminate that risk?

3. Once the minimizer has shared, what are the two connections you hope to have them make about the experience

4. What might you do if the minimizer feels worse after your technique got them to share?

II. Frustration Tag — Getting a Group to Talk

1. What are the two functions or uses for "Frustration Tag?"

2. What has any of this got to do with staying clean and sober?

3. What additional tool of recovery does the addict/alcoholic learn by using the variation described in the text?

Exercises

1. Use fellow students to role-play the two exercises in the chapter, in group and/or dyads. Notice and discuss the effects on self and others. If appropriate and supervised, try the exercises with real clients.

2. Do the recovery exercises for this chapter, especially #2 and #3. Share and discuss what you learn about coping and/or counseling from this.

3. Look at David Burns' (Feeling Good, the New Mood Therapy) list of "cognitive distortions." Is minimizing on the list? Why do you suppose not? What does this suggest about the difference between addiction and depression, even in the same person?

4. Develop a visual way to explain minimization to clients. Present to class.

5. Generate a list of "automatic thoughts" alcoholics/addicts use to minimize their problems. For each one, create a counselor response.

Chapter 14

Review Questions

1. What must be "smushed" if we are to understand that all living problems can be solved?

2. What are the two not entirely gratuitous puns included in the illustration of problem-solving? What makes them not entirely gratuitous? What does "gratuitous" mean?

3. What does "SPARROW" stand for?

4. What determines whether an item goes under "Accept" or under "Change?"

5. If a person is not going to say "F--- it" and drink/drug over a problem, what is the only healthy alternative? Where can the addict/alcoholic get the energy for this?

Exercises

1. Do recovery exercise #1 for this chapter, either way. Share and process with class.

2. Do the SPARROW process for one real but not too personal problem in your life. Log how you do with each toolbox, each day, and log your progress over at least two weeks. Share and discuss with class, or turn in as written assignment.

Chapter 15

Review Questions

When Those Relapse Thoughts Come Back

1. What primary AA tool for coping with craving has been incorporated into virtually every other system of relapse prevention?
2. What routine procedure in the treatment of addiction is like taking high blood pressure in a hypertensive?
3. Besides relief of craving, what is another direct benefit of one alcoholic calling another?

How Talking Keeps You Sober

4. Describe how willpower gets you drunk.
5. Describe three of the five ways that talking keeps you sober.
6. Why should we prepare patients for cravings to come back?
7. Describe two ways to do this.

Tom's Urge

1. What did Tom learn by sharing his urge?

Ida's Urge

1. What is there about the thought "One won't hurt" that suggests the person is already shying away from facing something?
2. What is the heart of this example?

Preparation For "Telephone Therapy"

1. Name two tools for reducing the barriers to picking up the telephone.

A Tool — Role-Playing the Phone Call That Was Not Made

1. For which types of craving is "telephone therapy" least effective?
2. Describe three principles for responding to a call from someone who is craving.

Exercises

1. Individually or as a group, generate a list of examples of craving/urges to drink/use. Try to rapidly assess which ones sounded more like "One won't hurt" and which more like "F--- it."

2. Role play "telephone therapy with" your fellow students, practicing both "thinking it through" with those who seem more "wishful" and supportive listening with those who seem stressed. Use both approaches when appropriate. Debrief what was most useful to the role play caller, how the support person made decisions, what it looked like to observers.

3. As a variation, role play responding to clients who have had urges in individual or group sessions. Be sure to practice asking for urges when they have not been volunteered.

Chapter 16

Review Questions

1. What two things "link" all the chapters of the book?
2. What is a "craving"?

Fear of Abandonment As Craving
1. Give three criteria for saying a "want" is, in fact, a "craving."
2. What indicators qualify fear of abandonment as a "craving?"
3. Give two psychological viewpoints on the sources of emotional craving.
4. How does alcohol "solve" the problem of abandonment helplessness?
5. How do you know if any given relapse was triggered by emotional craving?

Character Defects As Cravings
1. Name two other concepts for "character defects" that came from Bill W. and seem to support the idea of character defects as "craving."
2. Summarize the relationship between non-chemical cravings and relapse.
3. What is the number one trigger for relapse in long-term recovery?

Transference As Craving
1. What is "transference?"
2. How is falling in love like being triggered for your drug of choice?
3. What is the danger in an alcoholic believing in a strictly physical cause for his or her disease?
4. How does it help the therapist to think of transference as craving?

5. How does it help the alcoholic/addict to think of their relationship problems as "emotional craving?"
6. What is "emotional sobriety?"

How to Use This Book

1. List three parts of the book that might be handed to a client for help with a specific issue.

The Bottom Line

1. How has this book tried to address the problem of large numbers of clients who do not appear to respond to AA? What other response is valid?
2. What is the empirical fact with which everything in this book begins and ends?
3. If these two phenomena are not causes of relapse, what are they?
4. Based directly on these two facts, what are the two requirements for recovering from any addiction?
5. Even if many alcoholic/addicts need other things, and some stay sober without it, what are the two things that are provided only by Twelve Step recovery as a system of relapse prevention?

Exercises

1. Based on Chapter 1 of the AA Big Book, and on the various biographies (if you have time), write a formulation of Bill W's "case" at the point in time where he was visited by Ebby. Develop a treatment/relapse prevention plan that accurately describes what he did to stay sober up to the point at which the Big Book was written, about three years. This could be a class project or a term paper.

2. If you have the background and/or the time to develop it, describe Bill's progress and self-help in terms of cognitive-behavioral therapy. Again, this could be a class project or term paper.

3. Do the same thing as in #2 for the theoretical school of your choice, or your instructor's.

4. With supervision, interview three (5, 10) relapsers and see if you can identify any upset at the time of relapse. If so, can you identify specific frustrations that appear to have become intolerable "needs," when they were, in fact, wants.

5. How many of the examples in #4 involved an excessive need for another person, depression and/or fear and/or rage at (even the possibility of) losing them?

6. With supervision, interview three (5, 10) alcoholics about what alcohol did for them when it worked the best. If they do not volunteer, ask if they ever had fantasies while drinking, and if they experienced them any differently than while sober. Take notes, compare and discuss in class.

7. With supervision, make "what alcohol did for me" the topic of a group. See how often fantasy and power come up.

8. Using this book and any other sources you and/or your instructor see fit, develop a list

of questions for evaluating whether abandonment and or transference were involved in a relapse. This could be a term project or a class discussion/project.

9. Compare and contrast the concepts of "character defect" (AA), "cognitive distortion" (Beck, Burns), "transference" (Freud, psychoanalytic therapy), and "attachment" (DeMello, Buddhists). Use concrete examples of real human reactions, hopefully involving addiction and relapse, to develop how each concept would explain or attempt to help. Spell out similarities as well as differences. Any two of the concepts may be used for a less ambitious comparison. The task may also be done as a group, in class or out.

10. Summarize this book in two sentences or less. Then create a ten-question check-list for each of the two kinds of relapse. The questions are to determine how much the individual now meets the necessary conditions for recovery from addiction.

Acknowledgements for First Edition

This book could not have come together without the gifts of many people, including some I have never met. I break it down this way.

Family

Richard E. DuWors Sr, the father who taught me to read with my dictionary open and to write with it closed. Just as important, he taught me (and a lot of people) that there is more than one way to skin the cat of human behavior. Sometimes a wave; sometimes a particle.

Luella Maude (Manter) DuWors, the mother who wanted us all to be good people, and we are.

My brothers and sisters, Edna, Dick, Helen and Robert, who may have had more to do with who I am and how I see than our parents did.

Writers

Novelist Jack Cady *(The Jonah Watch, Singleton, McDowell's Ghost),* who shared his passion for storied truth and the red pencil that makes it shine.

Songwriter Buddy Kaye (Sinatra's "Full Moon and Empty Arms"), who showed us the whole story could be told in three verses, if only you persist. Being a poor student and something of a quitter, I had to write a whole book.

Jim Defoe, PhD, writer, sociologist, healer, who gave me as much spiritually as I was ready to receive, guiding me from fiction to nonfiction into the bargain. Even in this work, he handed me the tools to sharpen my focus, to draw out the connections. If the reader feels he is reading a single work with a consistent line of thought, he can thank Jim. If not, blame me — I didn't get it!

Editor Cliff Creager, CADC, while at *Professional Counselor Magazine,* in-the-trenches counselor, activist, and friend.

Mark Worden MS, former editor, *Alcoholism, the National Magazine. Co-author, Of Course You're Angry, and Here Comes The Sun.*

Frank O'Connor, both for his stories and for his ideas about the human story in *The Lonely Voice* (New York: Bantam Books, 1968).

Academic/Scholarly

The University of Washington at Seattle, which gave me Jack Cady, and the University of Washington School of Social Work, which gave me Lorie Dwinell and Bill Satoran and gave all of us Claudia Black.

Sociology and the School of Symbolic Interaction: Cooley, Mead, Thomas, and Blumer. The significance of the "significant other," the "definition of the situation," and the "self-as-object," is ground into the lenses with which I see.

Grudging debt to the "behaviorists," who so often chain the rest of us to real behavior while abandoning it themselves for laboratory and dogma. If only more of them would accept alcohol as an unconditioned reinforcer for some people, not for others.

Clinical/Experiential

Brendon B., who attracted me to his program of recovery and to the field for which I appear to have been born. Bren, are you out there somewhere? Connie?

Carol Bley, MSW, BCD, the first clinician who told me to "start where the person is."

Alcoholics Anonymous and all the Twelve Step Programs. I have taken your strength and hope for myself. Your experience I pass along in forms you may not recognize or even agree with. Take what you can use, as I have.

Abraham Low, MD, founder of Recovery, Inc., who understood and made use of the role of thought, language, and muscle in mental health, at a time AA was just being born and "cognitive behavioral therapy" was not even a gleam in psychology's eye.

The profession of social work, which has clung so stubbornly and effectively to the reality of the Person-in-Situation. No wonder Carl Rogers hung out with social workers! No wonder Kohut pled guilty to the accusation that he was "doing social work!"

Jules Meisler, MSW, BCD (and his late mentor Dr. Louis Booth), author of *Effective Psychotherapy for Patient and Therapist* (Praeger, 1991). Without Jules and "the method" that Dr. Booth developed and Jules described, this book does not happen.

Harry Tiebout, MD, who described his experience with early Alcoholics Anonymous and started a tradition of making clinical sense of what AA does and does not do.

Lorie Dwinell, MSW, ACSW, teacher, therapist, author and keen-eyed fellow pilgrim.

Jim Conway, MS, therapist, bibliophile, fellow teacher, who saw my tools and picked them up and proved their teachability.

Reading and feedback on the manuscript: Bill Satoran, MSW, Lorie Dwinell, MSW, Jim Conway, MS, Joe Ruzek, PhD, Jim Defoe, PhD, Al Pierce, PhD, Richard DuWors Jr, PhD, Luella DuWors, BA (Bates '39!)

Terence T. Gorski (author of *Counseling for Relapse Prevention*).

Special acknowledgement to Florence Goldy, MSW and Marve West, MSW, BCD, two people who are no longer with us. Two people who believed in our profession and who believed in me. May their spirits visit these pages whenever they are in town.

And, where would this book be without all the clients and pilgrims who passed my way and marked my being? Alcoholics, co-alcoholics, bingers and misers of all types, from high school to college, to the Navy to the Veterans Administration, to Pacific Missile Test Center, to Alcohol Information School, to private practice, to this book.

My comrades-in-arms at the Alcoholism Treatment Program of the Veterans Administration Medical Center West Los Angeles (which will always be "Brentwood" to me). Ilse Lowenstam MD, David Pearson PhD, Bill Wells, PhD, Bob Taylor, MS, Sara Lane, Zoe Sinclair, George Heaton, Don Wissusik, MS, Joe Raymond, Sam Williamson.

Also to John Fulton, MSW, retired Chief of Social Service for the Veterans Administration, who gave me my first job as a helper. The Social Work Unit in Substance Abuse — Quita McBride, MSW, Curt Bramble, MSW, Jim Dwyer, MSW, Jacqueline Randich, MS, Charles Dabbs, MSW, Bill Hard, MSW and John Smith, MSW. And I cannot leave out Peggy Cullinane, who always suspected I was writing a book.

My shipmates on "USS Drug and Alcohol Program," Pacific Missile Test Center/Naval Air Station Point Mugu, CA. Larry Pakkenham, Mary States, Dave Talley, Del Sinclair, Jose Valenzuela, Kathleen Stevens, CADC, and "the Exec," Commander John Shutt.

California Society for Clinical Social Work. I hope this book supports our effort in some small way.

National Association of Social Workers, "NASW," especially the Ventura County NASW Referral Service, which has twice provided forum and feedback for these ideas.

Employee Assistance Professionals Association ("EAPA," formerly "ALMACA,") especially the Central Coast Chapter, which gave me a chance to be President, and the Western Regional Conferences, which are nearly as down-to-earth, practical, and inspiring as a Twelve Step Meeting.

Finally, Margaret Yun and Caryn Spencer, for typing and retyping and coping with my absent-minded perfectionism. And Christine Foster, correspondence and research department par excellence.

Acknowledgements for Second Edition

Editorial Help
Toni Wilkinson, RN, MS, practitioner and bibliophile, who read and did more than anyone to improve the manuscript.

The Reverend Amanda Aikman, who shook me out of complacency and got me to go through the MS one more time.

Jim Defoe, PhD, who has nurtured this work since before it started.

Bill Satoran, MSW, Mike Wagner, MA, Larry Lombard, NCACII, Dana Ryder, CDC, all reviewed the manuscript.

Clinical/Experimental
The second edition is the fruit of a three and one-half year growth spurt that occured while working at Providence Recovery Center Everett, WA, with the following co-worker/teachers: Barbara Allen,

Larry Burns, Doug Wharton, Joe Parsons, Dana Ryder, Jan Long, Penny Thomas, Patricia Sekelsky, Dannis Sakowski, Deb Lujan, Ceal Anderson, Bill Dickenson, Cheryl Sackrider, Tom Robbie, Judy Woods, Angela Potts, Betty Moser, Emily Carter, Lynne Price, Angie Gonzales, Debby Vessey.

Index

Bill W. 230
Biochemistry (Biochemical, neuro-
    chemistry, neurochemical) 6, 35,
    40, 41, 46, 131, 187, 188, 241,
    304
  and artificial acceptance 117
  and behavioral reactions that are set
      up by a genetic 80, 88
  and fantasy 50
  and inherited "temperament" 47
  and last drink 8
  and no emotional problem 129
  and pain 211
  and part of brain that cares 84
  and power to alcoholics 46
  and research money 195
  and surrender 191
  and Ted Bundy 229
  as excuse 227
  as necessary condition 61
  black-and-white view of "disease"
      342
  controlling behavior 230
  distillation of theory 6
  insufficiency 305
  putting in perspective 7
Buddha 343
Bundy, Ted 229
Burton, Richard 250

Cancer 239, 246
Cassandra 84
Cognitive therapy 86, 144, 196
  as at least half right 278
  shortcoming of 279
Columbus, Christopher 301
Compulsivity 80
Constructivism 192
Coping 102
  "link" that stymies need to 289
  necessity to learn to cope 155
  two levels of intervention 102
Counterdependency 138
Craving 7, 10, 28, 35, 42, 251, 259,
    263
  and "attachment" as 336
  and buried grief 276
  and feeling 327
  and rational punishment 228
  and theoretical door 334

and transference as 341
as "instinctual drive" 335
as something "good" or "bad" for
    survival 278
as the root of all sorrow 336
character and 333
character defects as 339
fear of abandonment as 335
for approval 344
intensity of 60
least responsive to telephone therapy
    329
non-chemical 339
oblivious to 186
"post-acute" 335
reason we don't call when 330
struggle with 101
subliminal craving 42, 70
types of 42
underestimation of 191
"wish" of "wishful thinking" 40

Denial 40, 45, 63, 77, 91, 96, 101,
    156
  and AA speaker 178
  and biblical admonition 190
  and craving 181
  and delay of surrender 187
  and links of disownership 217
  and pain 190
  and plea of Jesus 186
  and power of the unconscious 187
  and test for willful ignorance 244
  and that strange mental twist 207
  and transferring helplessness 180
  as a philosophy 191
  as a will of iron vigor 191
  as "beating myself up" 208
  as Groucho Marx syndrome 180
  as help by field 129
  as "isolation-of-the-connected" 203
  as lack of empathy 182
  as making it impossible to learn 40
  as mental posture of blocking all
      questions 82
  as mind/body separation 227
  as "not-thinking-about-it" 199
  as playing ostrich 243
  as separation of purpose from
      behavior 229

as an assertion of fact 247
as an ignorant statement 245
as caused by craving 279
as childlike wishful thinking 244
as emotional problem 46
as infantile logic 63
as instant regression 64
as isolating that particular drink 206
as making a decision 42
as "open sesame" 46
as rejecting idea anything hazardous
257
as "self-will run riot" 109
as "subliminal craving" 334
as voice of denial 37

complete translation of 36
exploring links of 27
need for healthy fear of 57
neurochemistry 70
places to be protected from 35
process of 67
protective action against 36
psychological core links of 62
reality an intruder in 52
sharing of 272
two observations about 32
where physiology fits 66

Yubi Wiseman 304

Revised & expanded 10ᵀᴴ edition of this widely used guide to psychotropic medications

Clinical Handbook of
Psychotropic Drugs

Editors   Kalyna Z. Bezchlibnyk-Butler, BScPhm
J. Joel Jeffries, MB, FRCPC
Clarke Institute of Psychiatry site
Centre for Addiction and Mental Health
Toronto, Canada

Hogrefe & Huber Publishers
Seattle • Toronto • Göttingen • Bern

10ᵗʰ revised edition

This book has become a classic, due to its ease of use, reasonable cost, high productivity, and broad appeal to thousands of psychiatrists, physicians, psychologists, nurses...

New psychotropic drugs are now being released and marketed with an ever-increasing speed, making it even more vital to keep pace with changes, whether this be newly released drugs, new or revised approved indications, recently reported drug interactions, or changed recommendations about use in pregnancy.

If you ever feel the need for an up-to-date, easy-to-use, and accurate summary of all the most relevant information about psychotropic drugs, then this is the book for you.

Over the past 9 editions, the *Clinical Handbook of Psychotropic Drugs* has acquired an unrivalled reputation for presenting its readers and users with reliable, easy-to-find, state-of-the-art information. With its spiralbound horizontal page format, its succinct, bulleted outline information, its clearly laid out comparison charts and tables, and its comprehensive index of generic and trade names, the latest scientific data, clinical guidelines, and patient instructions are uniquely accessible in the *Handbook* — almost literally, everything you need to know about psychotropic drugs is at your fingertips in a single, inexpensive book.

For more information — www.hhpub.com

2000, 266 pages, hardcover, ISBN 0-88937-233-0   US $49.00 (plus p&h)

To order: **Hogrefe & Huber Publishers,** Customer Service Dept.
PO Box 388, Ashland, OH 44805, Tel. **(800) 228-3749**, Fax (419) 281-6883.